Giovanni Boccaccio

Twayne's World Authors Series

Carlo L. Golino, Editor
University of Massachusetts

TWAS 644

Fresco photograph by Alinari

Giovanni Boccaccio

By Judith Powers Serafini-Sauli

Sarah Lawrence College

Twayne Publishers • *Boston*

Giovanni Boccaccio

Judith Powers Serafini-Sauli

Copyright © 1982 by G. K. Hall & Company
Published by Twayne Publishers
A Division of G. K. Hall & Company
70 Lincoln Street
Boston, Massachusetts 02111

Book Production by Marne B. Sultz

Book Design by Barbara Anderson

Printed on permanent/durable acid-free
paper and bound in the United States of
America.

**Library of Congress Cataloging in
Publication Data**

Serafini-Sauli, Judith Powers.
  Giovanni Boccaccio.

  (Twayne's world authors series : TWAS
644)
  Bibliography: p. 151
  Includes index.
  1. Boccaccio, Giovanni, 1313–1375
—Criticism and interpretation.
I. Title. II. Series.
PQ4277.S4   858'.109   81-23776
ISBN 0-8057-6487-9   AACR2

*To the memory of
my father*

Contents

About the Author
Preface
Chronology

Chapter One
An Age of Upheaval   1

Chapter Two
Naples   7

Chapter Three
Florence   40

Chapter Four
The *Decameron*   58

Chapter Five
The Later Years   95

Chapter Six
Boccaccio and Posterity   127

Notes and References   133
Selected Bibliography   151
Index   157

About the Author

Judith Powers Serafini-Sauli has a B.A. from Sarah Lawrence College and a Ph.D. in Romance Languages from Johns Hopkins University. She has lived in Florence, Italy, for the past fifteen years, where she has been assistant professor of Italian language and literature, and for two years resident director, at the Florida State University Study Center in Florence. At present, she teaches Italian at Sarah Lawrence College.

Preface

The works of few authors have been as controversial as those of Boccaccio. In his own time he was hailed as a great scholar and humanist, yet his fame has ultimately rested on his unscholarly collection of stories, the *Decameron*. The *Decameron* in turn has aroused its own controversies and has been dealt with in a variety of ways. During the Counter-Reformation it was expurgated of all its abundant anti-clericalism by simply changing all the clergymen in the stories into laymen. In the nineteenth century its licentiousness was dealt with by omitting notes for certain passages, or, in some English translations, by neglecting to translate the more ribald sections. And in our own day the *Decameron* is being studied by some scholars for patterns of moral allegory.

It is clear that the vicissitudes of Boccaccio's works in six centuries of criticism would themselves constitute a fascinating history of criticism and of taste. It is equally important that these six centuries have provided much fine scholarship on the works of Boccaccio: an abundance of important information and tools, and many illuminating insights, particularly during the recent rebirth of interest in Boccaccio studies. Thanks to the fine efforts of numerous scholars in the past few decades, we have a wealth of historical and biographical information and a good number of vital critical editions.

It would be folly to hope to pay all one's debts within the covers of one brief volume. The purpose of this book is to introduce the reader to the range and scope of Boccaccio's works and to offer what I consider some of the most valid and compelling interpretations, be they other scholars' or my own. The notes refer the reader to some more specific and more general works on the subject. Since Boccaccio was a man of broad culture and had a significant influence on letters in his own and subsequent eras, an effort has been made to place him and his works in an historical frame, but here again, much is left unsaid and much remains to be done.

I have organized my treatment of the works chronologically, following the chronology that has gained consensus among the largest number of critics. The introductory chapter briefly familiarizes the reader with Europe and Italy in Boccaccio's time. The following two chapters treat his early works, first those written in Naples and then those that followed his return to Florence. Chapter 4 is devoted entirely to the *Decameron,* and is all too brief for such an extraordinary work. Chapter 5 presents Boccaccio's Latin and scholarly works, mostly written in the latter part of his life, and the final chapter is a short survey of critical evaluations of Boccaccio's works through the centuries and his influence on Italian culture and abroad.

This book was written amidst the turmoil of daily life. I therefore feel even deeper gratitude to mentors and friends who taught and inspired me. To Professor Charles S. Singleton, "primus studiorum dux et prima fax" (as Boccacio said of Dante), I owe more than I can ever acknowledge. My indebtedness to Professor Fred Licht, an endless source of inspiration, knowledge, and friendship, is also beyond recounting; as is true of Professor Lawrence S. Cunningham, at whose suggestion I began the book. I must also thank Professor Victoria Kirkham for a precious amount of stimulation and information and for her generous help with the manuscript; and Dr. Susan Scott, who was always ready to lend an ear and give incisive advice. I am also grateful to Professor Stephen A. McKnight and Professor Jerome Stern for their help and suggestions, and special thanks go to Daniela Boschi for her patient assistance in preparing the manuscript.

Judith Powers Serafini-Sauli

Sarah Lawrence College

Chronology

1313   Born between June and July, in Tuscany. Death of Henry IV of Luxembourg.

1314   Death of Philip IV of France.

1316   John XXII elected Pope.

1319   Begins studies with Mazzuoli da Strada.

ca. 1320   Father marries Margherita de' Mardoli. Birth of half-brother Francesco.

1321   Death of Dante in Ravenna.

1324   *Defensor Pacis* of Marsilius of Padua.

ca. 1327   Moves with father to Naples.

1330   Studies with Cino da Pistoia at Studio in Naples. Frequents court library.

1332   Father leaves Naples for Paris.

1334   Benedict IV becomes Pope. Boccaccio probably writes *Caccia di Diana*.

1336   Probably writes *Filocolo*.

1337   Beginning of Hundred Years War. Death of Giotto. Probably writes *Filostrato*.

1339   Probably writes *Teseida* and first *Epistole*.

1340   Birth of Chaucer. Boccaccio leaves Naples and returns to Florence.

1341   Petrarch crowned Poet Laureate on Capitoline in Rome. Boccaccio writes *Comedia delle ninfe fiorentine* (*Ameto*) and perhaps *De vita et moribus domini Francisci Petracchi* [Life of Petrarch].

1342   Clement IV becomes Pope. Acciaiuoli founds the Certosa. Walter of Brienne, Duke of Athens, rules Florence for one year. Boccaccio writes *Amorosa Visione*.

1343   Death of King Robert of Naples, January 20. Boccaccio writes *Fiammetta*. Failure of Peruzzi Company.

1345   Boccaccio probably in Ravenna at court of Ostasio da Polenta. Translates *Decades* of Livy. Durazzo and Taranto struggle for throne in Naples.

1346   Failure of Bardi banking house. Boccaccio writes *Ninfale fiesolano*.

1347   In Forlì at court of Ordelaffi. Birth of S. Caterina da Siena.

1348   Black Plague. Boccaccio begins *Decameron*.

1350   Jubilee in Rome; Petrarch passes through Florence. Boccaccio on mission to Romagna; goes to Ravenna to give florins to Dante's daughter on behalf of Florentine government. Probably begins *Genealogie deorum gentilium*.

1351   Expansion of Visconti. Boccaccio visits Petrarch in Padua to offer position at *Studio* in Florence. Mission to Tyrol to Ludwig of Bavaria.

1352   Innocent VI becomes Pope.

1354   Final fall of Cola di Rienzo. Boccaccio sent on mission to Innocent VI.

1355   Charles IV crowned Emperor in Rome. Zanobi da Strada crowned Poet Laureate in Pisa. Acciaiuoli visits Florence. Boccaccio is officer in Florentine government from May to August, visits Naples, writes *De montibus*. Perhaps writes first version of *Trattatello in laude di Dante* and probably writes *Corbaccio*.

1356   Begins *De casibus virorum illustrium*.

1357   Makes trip to Ravenna.

1359   Visits Petrarch in Milan.

1360   Conspiracy against Florentine government involving Boccaccio's friend Pino de' Rossi. Boccaccio receives papal dispensation regarding his illegitimate birth and probably had received minor orders. Revises the *Amorosa Visione* and the *Trattatello*. Receives Leontius Pilatus and begins to work on Greek translation.

1361   Writes *De mulieribus claris* and *Letter to Pino de' Rossi*. Moves to Certaldo.

1362   Urban VI made Pope. Langland writes *Piers Plowman*. Boccaccio revises *De mulieribus,* probably works on *Genealogie*; receives visit of monk representing Pietro Petroni.

1365   Sent on mission to Avignon to offer support of Florence to Pope.

1367   Sent on mission to Rome.

1368   Visits Petrarch in Padua.

1370   Gregory XI becomes Pope. Boccaccio makes last trip to Naples.

1371   Revises *Genealogie.*

1373   Revises *De casibus.* Asked to comment on Dante's *Commedia* by Florentine government; begins *Esposizioni.*

1374   Death of Petrarch at Arquà, July 18.

1375   Death of Boccaccio in Certaldo, December 21.

Chapter One
An Age of Upheaval

We know relatively little about Giovanni Boccaccio from his contemporaries. His earliest biographer, Filippo Villani (fl. 1364–1405), describes him as ". . . large and portly; round of face with large but attractive lips, a dimple in his chin that was lovely when he laughed; merry and jocund in aspect, pleasing and human in speech, and one who took great pleasure in conversation."[1] For us of the twentieth century, familiar with Boccaccio as the author of the delightful stories of the *Decameron,* this portrait meets our expectations, for it depicts a jolly storyteller. Apparently he was also humble and modest. The humanist Coluccio Salutati, a younger contemporary of Boccaccio, remarked upon this and, indeed, found his modesty so exaggerated, that he saw fit to rewrite the epitaph Boccaccio had prepared for himself. As we can still see today on his tomb in the church of Saints Michele and Jacopo in his hometown of Certaldo, Boccaccio had written simply: "Here lie the ashes and bones of Giovanni; his mind sits before God adorned with the works of his mortal life; Boccacius was his father, Certaldo his homeland, poetry his calling." Boccaccio speaks broadly of poetry as his calling. Coluccio, in noting his modesty, takes the trouble of specifying his works, but certain ones. He mentions only the scholarly Latin works Boccaccio wrote later in life. ". . . Why do you speak of yourself so humbly, bard? You have listed mountains and rivers, fortunes of men and women and ancient gods. Famous in a thousand things, no age will not speak of you."[2]

The portrait of a pleasant, humane storyteller hailed by his contemporaries for erudite works in Latin creates a certain confusion. Is Boccaccio to be characterized as the bemused, unbridled narrator of the *Decameron,* first author of the Renaissance, or is he really more medieval, the stern moralist of his later, and even his earlier works? The question is confounding. If we look beyond the caprices of taste from age to age—Boccaccio was hailed throughout the fifteenth century for his scholarly works, whereas subsequently the *Decameron* has generally been considered his masterpiece—we find that this confusion is hardly dispelled by Boccaccio himself. In a moment of religious crisis he threatened to break up his library which was rich in classical works (Petrarch, *Sen.* I,5,1362). A few years later he may have commissioned an altarpiece for the church of Certaldo;[3] and in one of his last letters (*Epist.* XXI,1373) we find him exhorting his friend Mainardo Cavalcanti not to let the ladies of his house read the *Decameron* or his "domestic trifles," as he called them.[4] It would seem, then, that if some of his works were indeed secular and pagan, he had repented. But as we contemplate the life and works of Boccaccio, the conflict between the sacred and the profane, the didactic and the delightful, is never quite resolved, for as recent scholarship has shown, at the end of his life this supposedly repentant Christian undertook the enormous task of recopying his least sacred work, the *Decameron.*[5]

Any scheme applied to a personality or to the entire course of a lifetime is ultimately inconclusive. Reflecting the disquiet of his times, Boccaccio's works waver between the traditional hierarchy of old orders, expressed by means of established canons for moral teaching, and the flux and innovation of new cadres revealed through narrative autonomy. His works are often Christian allegories or moral treatises whose formal message is a rejection of terrestrial pleasures and profane passion in favor of holy rewards and sacred love. But the rejection is never quite total; a certain indulgence in earthly delights frequently creeps in to compromise the erudite plan or to color the message of moral and Christian enlightenment.

The life of Boccaccio (1313–75) spans most of the fourteenth century, and his activities and interests place him so much in the mainstream of events and ideas that his works could serve as a prism through which to study the currents of this complex period. Conversely, an understanding of the times is essential to the appreciation of his works.[6] The fourteenth century was a period of profound upheaval and transformation in Western Europe. Italy, especially, was a land of contrasts and confusion. It was the stage for many of the conflicts of the waning Middle Ages—the contest between the Empire and the Papacy, Church and State, feudalism and mercantilism, aristocracy and bourgeoisie. Intellectuals and men of letters sensed the change and displayed both optimism and uneasiness.

For Italians there was the most dramatic and disturbing fact of the so-called Babylonian Captivity. This abduction of the Papacy to Avignon, reducing it to a secular entity to be manipulated by kings, seemed to confirm a breakdown in the traditional universal Church and created a feeling of disquiet which was accompanied by an ardent desire to return the Papacy to its rightful place in Rome. Boccaccio himself had his small role in this issue, for he was sent as Florentine ambassador to Avignon, and like most of the major writers and intellectuals of the age, he remarks upon the devastation and chaos that had overtaken the eternal city of Rome, home of both ancient and Christian glory.[7] Against this backdrop was the everlasting contrast between North and South. The South was subsumed under the Kingdom of Naples, an impoverished land with a small and strong aristocracy, a large and oppressed peasantry and a meager middle class. This area had remained essentially feudal and was under the dynastic rule of the French family of Anjou. The great Angevin leader in the fourteenth century was the famous King Robert, called The Wise. He was a generous patron of the arts and the center of an illustrious court whose enlightenment, however, did not extend beyond the city of Naples. Though a Tuscan, Boccaccio lived as a youth in Naples which was an important center for Florentine merchants and bankers in that period. The rest of his life—part of his childhood and all of his adult life—was spent in Tuscany and Florence.

In contrast with Neapolitan society, Florence was a dynamic city of merchants and bankers whose wealth was based primarily on cloth trade, and was dominated by the upper middle class. It is to this class, which was essentially practical in needs and outlook, that we owe many of the great civic monuments that characterize the city of Florence; their influence on taste and artistic canons probably could not be exaggerated. Likewise, the needs of this bourgeoisie had a lasting effect on language and letters where both the use of Italian and a new kind of interest in the classics began to emerge. The need to draw up contracts and bills led to a preeminence of law, and particularly of the work of notaries. It also led to an increased use of Italian alongside Latin, and these factors in turn had literary significance. The dawn of Italian literature is closely associated with notaries, many of whom were accomplished poets in Italian. And a more participatory and broadly based literate public created a demand for works and translations in

Italian. The study of law, and especially of ecclesiastic canon law, led to greater contact with the *ars dictandi,* which was influential in the formation of Italian prose style. It also led to the study of Roman law, which in its turn contributed to a generally growing interest in ancient civilization and left an imprint of classical Latin on the developing Italian language as well. At the same time, the secular thrust of this upper bourgeoisie contributed to the emergence of an increasingly nationalistic spirit. Major figures such as Dante and Petrarch contemplated Italy as a nation, and Petrarch particularly was determined that this embryonic nationalism find expression in an appreciation of Italy's ancient heritage. This, too, further helped revive the cultivation of the classical world.

The painting of the period reflects a similar secularization. Subjects are primarily religious, but the divine is humanized. Representations of traditional religious themes become less symbolic and dogmatic, and are more literal, tranquil, and realistic. Narration becomes more important than allegory, and fidelity to nature and the human dimension predominate. With the bourgeoisie's emphasis on individuality, industriousness, and civic and social activity, traditional cult figures are personalized. They are presented as mediators for mankind and as people with real stories.

The painter who most completely represents this new spirit is Giotto. We need only call to mind the scenes he chose for the fresco cycles in the Scrovegni Chapel in Padua or in the chapels in Santa Croce in Florence to understand the emphasis on the individual and his personal relationships. Boccaccio knew Giotto and his work, and in a story in the *Decameron* in which Giotto is the protagonist, he proffers not only his admiration for the great painter, but the measure of what he considered significant in his art. Giotto, he says, had

. . . genius of such excellence that there was nothing created by nature . . . that he, with stylus, pen or brush could not paint so like it that it seemed not a likeness but the thing itself, so that many times, when seeing things made by him, the visual sense of man was deceived, taking for real that which was painted. And therefore, having brought back to light that art which for many centuries had been buried, through the error of some who had painted more to delight the eyes of the ignorant than to please the intellect of the wise, he can justly be called one of the lights of Florentine glory. (VI, 5)

Nevertheless, bourgeois mercantilism, with its industriousness, optimism, and materialism, was also accompanied by feelings of doubt and guilt, and was contested, condemned, and qualified by a rejection of wealth, best characterized and voiced by the Franciscan Fraticelli, throughout most of the early part of the century.[8] The ascetic Franciscan *paupertas,* combined with a classical Stoic spirituality, helped to foster an attitude prevalent in the early humanists—Petrarch and Boccaccio in particular—that one must eschew earthly goods and seek poverty and seclusion. The guilt and ambivalence with regard to wealth and earthly possessions, exacerbated by the preaching of the Franciscan followers in the minds of the bourgeoisie, came to a crisis in the middle of the fourteenth century through a series of disastrous events which affected Florence and its environs. Bank failures, the death of Florence's ally King Robert of Naples, a year under dictatorial rule, and the Black Plague were some of the disasters that created a shift from the hegemony of the upper middle class—and the more rational, secular optimism that accompanied it—to a greater emphasis on the *popolo minuto,* on the Franciscan strain of poverty, and on a more hieratic, dogmatic, and emotional art.[9] This latter period culminated in the popular uprising of the Ciompi, who were soon after suppressed by the urban patriciate.

Boccaccio was in touch with important centers of intellectual activity and, as he himself indicated in his epitaph, was passionately interested in all forms of literature. As a youth he became familiar with the aristocratic court of Naples, the feudal society upon which it was predicated, and the courtly French culture from which it derived. But in Naples he also knew the Florentine merchant world, studied poetry in Italian, canon law and the *ars dictandi,* and began his study of the ancients. His return to Florence brought renewed contact with Tuscan allegorical literature, which was essentially Christian and didactic, but at the same time he absorbed the earthly optimism of the bourgeoisie. With the crisis at midcentury he too underwent a change, turning to more systematic studies of the ancients, erudite Latin treatises, and a Franciscan kind of penury, and emerging, together with Petrarch, as one of the fathers of humanism.

The manifestations of these experiences in literary terms are considerable. Boccaccio's works embrace medieval and classical literature, prose and poetry, epic and lyric, Latin and Italian, popular and "high" culture. He revived the pastoral romance, attempted a modern epic, established the vernacular *ottava* as the epic stanza in Italian, and then, later in life, renewed the classical epistle and eclogue in Latin, wrote biography, helped revive the study of Greek, and began formal Dante criticism. He also affirmed in a manner unmatched by anyone before or after him the validity and variety of Italian prose. Yet what predominates in all Boccaccio's very different endeavors is the force of narration. He was a consummate storyteller. He turned his efforts in biography, literary criticism, and even the sonnet into narrative episodes; and he wrote short stories in the various guises of myth, history, and Christian allegory.

Because of the preeminence of narration, the culmination of Boccaccio's literary experience is the *Decameron,* which becomes perforce the touchstone for any consideration of his works.[10] In it he proposes narration for its own sake, and, in advocating amusement as much as improvement, his point of view becomes earthbound. The *Decameron* is Boccaccio's human comedy, "the luminous and fully human epic," that stands next to Dante's *Divine Comedy.*[11] Passing human affairs under a lens of practical causality and uncompromising humor, he captures the realities of terrestrial existence with candor, tenderness, intelligence, and bemused indulgence. These qualities, and a passionate devotion to literature, infuse all the works of this great man of letters for whom poetry was, in the full sense, a calling. We must now turn to trace the beginnings of this literary vocation.

Chapter Two
Naples

Giovanni Boccaccio was born sometime in June or July of the year 1313, the illegitimate son of Boccaccio di Chellino.[1] We know the approximate month of his birth from his letter to Mainardo Cavalcanti (*Epist.* XX) dated August 1372, in which he says, "I am in my sixtieth year." A passage in Petrarch, addressed to Boccaccio, confirms this information, "I preceded you in birth by nine years" (*Sen.*, VIII,1). The place of his birth, on the other hand, has been the subject of wide speculation. The only information available is that contained in autobiographical hints in some of his early works. But despite his indication of Paris as his birthplace, most modern Boccaccio scholars seem to agree that the father of Italian prose was born in Tuscany, either in Florence or Certaldo.[2] We know that Boccaccio's family was from Certaldo, because they appear as landholders there until the end of the thirteenth century; and it was to this small hilltop town that Boccaccio retired later in life to pursue his scholarly endeavors. By the end of the thirteenth century, his father and uncle Vanni were residents, as merchants, in the San Frediano quarter of Florence. Around the year 1314 they were living in the district of San Pier Maggiore, and by this time were probably quite successful in the economic boom that was creating the merchant fortunes of the period. During this time they may have expanded their activities on a European scale. Although there is some doubt about the name, a merchant Bocassin and his brother appear in Paris early in 1313. In any case, Boccaccio's father probably made several trips to France in the course of his career, for Boccaccio mentions such in the *De casibus* (IX,21).

The identity of Boccaccio's mother is unknown, but his father legally adopted him soon after his birth, probably before marrying Margherita dei Mardoli in 1319, and his early youth was spent in his father's house in Florence. With the idea of preparing his son to be a merchant,

Boccaccino provided for his education under the tutelage of Giovanni di Domenico Mazzuoli da Strada, whose son Zanobi was to become Boccaccio's friend and later rival for favors at the Angevin court in Naples. He received the rudiments of the trivium (at the age of seven he supposedly wrote poetry), and a basic training in Latin, in addition to becoming quite expert in arithmetic. Mazzuoli may also have introduced him to some poetry in Italian, especially the Stilnovo poets and Dante. Boccaccio's early works resound with echoes of these poets, Dante in particular, and later in life he refers to Dante as the first guide in his studies.[3]

Around 1327, Boccaccio's father took him to Naples. Boccaccino was working for the Bardi Company, one of the several large Florentine banking companies that served as arbiters of the financial affairs of the Kingdom of Naples. From 1327 to 1341, from the age of fourteen to the age of about twenty-eight, Boccaccio resided in Naples. Naturally the experiences that filled these formative years were crucial in determining his interests and sensibilities. He assisted his father in business there, and though we have no precise traces of him, we can imagine the elder Boccaccino taking full advantage of his son's training in arithmetic, and at the same time making every effort to introduce him into the circle of merchants to which he considered him destined. In the *Decameron,* stories like that of Andreuccio da Perugia (II,5) or of the Tuscan merchant Salabaetto (VIII,10) recall this merchant's world in sketches replete with trade vocabulary and exact topographical references to commercial districts.

In these same years Boccaccio frequented the Angevin court. There he became a close friend of Niccolò Acciaiuoli, an ambitious and ruthless compatriot who belonged to another great Florentine banking family and who worked side by side with Boccaccio in financial dealings between Florence and Naples. Acciaiuoli had insinuated himself into the court of King Robert of Anjou where he eventually became the powerful seneschal of the Kingdom. For Boccaccio, in later years, he was to be a painfully contradictory figure, object of devotion and resentment, of admiration and harsh criticism. But in these early years they were friends and it was probably through Niccolò, if not through his own father, who had direct dealings with the court, that Boccaccio was introduced there and came to frequent the circles of the Neapolitan aristocracy.

It would be difficult to exaggerate the influence of the Angevin court on Boccaccio's personal and intellectual development. The cultural ambience of the court and the example of its intellectuals spurred him to pursue his call to study and literature, the path to which he considered himself destined "from his mother's womb" (*Gen.* XV,10). Fired in adolescence by his innate vocation for literature and by the diverse enticements of Naples, he found the profession of merchant increasingly odious. In later autobiographical passages, he speaks of his time spent as a merchant's apprentice as "irredeemable." But when his father, who was clearly opposed to his son's literary bent, finally agreed to Giovanni's leaving the world of merchants, it was only under the strict condition that he study canon law. Thus, "wasting his time," as he again recalls in the *Genealogie* (XV,10), Boccaccio spent another six or eight years in the arid studies of the jurists. Nonetheless, this period was not unfruitful for him as a writer; for the study of canon law meant taking up his childhood studies of Latin. Here he probably gleaned new experience in the *ars dictandi* which was to prove essential in the development of his Italian prose style. The *Studio* in Naples also boasted important jurists in that period, and it is likely that through the *Studio* he came into contact with an illustrious fellow Tuscan, Cino da Pistoia, who appears to have been there from 1330 to 1331.[4] Although Boccaccio attended Cino's lessons in law, by his example alone Cino must have provided further incentive in guiding Boccaccio toward literature. He probably renewed his contact with the Tuscan poetic tradition, and especially with the revered Dante. These important influences are manifest in the frequent echoes of Dante's verses scattered in Boccaccio's early works and in a passage in the *Filostrato* where he incorporates an entire poem by Cino (*Filos.* V,62–65).

Perhaps even before beginning his legal studies, Boccaccio had begun to frequent another great center of Neapolitan culture, the royal library, which had been greatly enriched by King Robert. Here he met Paolo da Perugia, the court librarian[5] to whom he owed his first serious introduction to the classics and mythology. As author of the *Liber Genologie,* which Boccaccio transcribed in his *Zibaldone Magliabechiano,*[6] and as commentator of classical texts, Paolo was an excellent model for the kind of encyclopedic classical erudition that inspired Boccaccio. First as a model for imitation and ornamentation in the earlier works and later as the object of scholarly study in the *Genealogie,* the ancient world was never absent from Boccaccio's poetic consciousness.

Along with Paolo da Perugia, Boccaccio associated with Paolo's friend and colleague, Barlaam of Calabria, a well-known scholar of Greek (*Gen.*XV,6). These men offered him a fascinating, albeit spotty, introduction to the Hellenic world. Through them, Boccaccio acquired an interest in Greek, which was a less familiar portion of the classical heritage. While in this early period the interest is manifest mainly in the capricious form of the pseudo Greek titles he gave his works, later in life it led him to the adventure of a translation of Homer in collaboration with Leontius Pilatus. The importance of the classics and the diversity of his interests are represented in two minor works contained in another "notebook," the *Zibaldone Laurenziano.* They are the *Elegia di Costanza,* written for the death of a Neapolitan girl, in which he paraphrases the epitaph of Homonoia, and the so-called *Allegoria mitologica,* based on the first two books of Ovid's *Metamorphoses,* with variously combined elements of myth, allegory, history, and blendings of paganism and Christianity.[7]

Another figure influential for Boccaccio in this period was Dionigi da Borgo S. Sepolcro, born in Tuscany and educated in France. Dionigi probably introduced Boccaccio to the works of Petrarch and to Valerius Maximus, for he had written a commentary on this popular text. It was almost certainly due to Dionigi that Boccaccio studied Valerius Maximus more closely at this time. Possibly he even made a translation of this work,[8] thus refining his style on a Latin model.

The *Factorum et dictorum memorabilium* of Valerius Maximus was an infinitely important source of anecdotes and stories. It was one of the cornerstones of the *exempla* tradition which was in turn basic to Boccaccio's inspiration as a narrative poet. The *exemplum* stemmed from Greek and Roman usage where it was considered primarily a handmaiden to rhetoric. The orator was to bolster his argument with an example or an anecdote. In subsequent centuries the *exempla* tradition developed upon classical and Christian sources as a collection of anecdotes, a stockpile for preachers to be used in sermons to dramatize moral lessons. In the

Middle Ages the *exempla* consisted of fables, parables, anecdotes, miracles—all episodic narrative forms. Although originally the *exempla* emerged from the everyday experience of people, these experiences had been raised to a transcendental level as a paradigm for all ages, distilling moral abstractions from concrete episodes of life. If history was a means of understanding the relation between man and the divine, only the constants in a fleeting reality counted, the moments that repeated themselves with moral or emblematic value. Therefore, although based on history, the *exempla* were idealistic abstractions, no longer concerned with experience within the flow of history.

The narrative episode as an *exemplum* is behind almost all of Boccaccio's works and often imprints the works with its own tension between moral abstraction and concrete experience. His ultimate creation of the novella form in the *Decameron* has its roots in the *exemplum* but transforms it by casting it into the relativity of history. In Boccaccio's novella the emphasis turns to individual quest and narration rather than universal messages and didacticism.[9]

Along with the strong presence of classical literature there was the rich heritage of French and Provençal literature which dominated at the court of King Robert and was properly represented in the court library. Boccaccio thus became familiar with the French romances, the *fabliaux,* French and Provençal lyrics and the courtly forms of amorous casuistry from both the literature and practices of this noble French society. It is probably fair to surmise that the opulent and corrupt Angevin court offered personal as well as literary experiences, providing a taste of political and amorous intrigues and of aristocratic pleasures and diversions. This luxurious life is often represented in Boccaccio's early works: the *Fiammetta* paints a vivid picture of the court pleasures and the vacations at Baia, in the *Ameto* a narrator recalls the magnificent feasts of King Robert, and in the *Filocolo* Florio happens upon an idyllic setting where noble youths discuss questions of love in the manner of the French courts. The aristocratic pleasures of Naples came to be associated with the *topos* of the idyll, the resplendent garden in the springtime where noble youths enjoy elegant amusements. With the passage of time this theme takes on the flavor of a personal nostalgia for a lost innocence; an ideal world he had known in Naples, when youth was in harmony with Nature.

We can further assume, without trying to construct a literal biography, that the Neapolitan experience offered our author his initiation to courtship and passion. This initiation probably made him familiar in some manner with the social ambience of the court. In the *Caccia di Diana* [Diana's Hunt], one of his very early works, he furnishes a long list of noble ladies which indicates some familiarity with Neapolitan aristocracy. Years later, in his letter to Nelli (*Epist.* XII), he would boast, with a shade of the parvenu's pride, that he was brought up with noble youths in Naples, who, though noble, were never ashamed to visit his house.

Thus the years spent in Naples were of inestimable significance. From the myriad encounters there we can trace the course of Boccaccio's development as an artist. After his childhood preparation in the rudiments of Latin, and the first introduction to the allegorical and Stilnovo poetry of the Tuscan tradition, there comes his enthusiastic, though disorganized and indiscriminate study of the classical literature available in Naples, the reluctant study of canon law, and finally, the exposure to the French and Provençal traditions of courtly lyrics, popular romances, and *fabliaux*. Poetry and prose, Latin and Italian, the popular and the scholarly, epics and lyrics all inspire the intellectual fervor of his youth just as they will receive the reflective dedication of the elderly scholar.

During his stay in Naples Boccaccio wrote his first poems, some letters, the *Caccia di Diana,* the *Filocolo,* the *Filostrato,* and the *Teseida.* The letters and the poems are a chronological accompaniment to Boccaccio's life and mirror his interests of the moment, be they personal, literary, or political. They are known in their collected forms as the *Epistole* (cf. Chapter 5) and the *Rime.* Though it has been impossible to date the *Rime* with any precision, there are certain topical elements or apparent changes in mood that yield some outline of personal chronology. While those that are considered the earlier poems treat the first joys and pains of love, the pleasures of Baia and an ample use of classical and Stilnovo imagery, the later poems reveal greater moral burdens, religiosity, intellectual concerns, and the growing influence of Petrarch. One of the last poems (CXIX) seems to echo Petrarch's prayer to the Virgin, and may in fact reflect Boccaccio's attempt at self-evaluation in regard to the cultivation of the Muses and his own approaching death. Others are clearly specific, such as CXXII–CXXIV, where he defends his public reading of Dante against the accusation of casting pearls before swine.

Boccaccio's poems in the early period reveal a close imitation of his Tuscan idols, the poets of the Stilnovo and Dante. He too has his Beatrice, his *donna angelicata*. His lady is heaven-sent, she is surrounded by an admiring court of ladies, her eyes can send rays of light and love into the heart and soul of the poet which at once ennoble him and cause him to suffer. These are all conceits well established from courtly poetry down through Dante. But next to these ethereal and angelic ladies we also find earthly women. In the familiar idyllic scene we behold three angelic ladies sitting around a fountain in a green field all abloom, perhaps recounting the stories of their loves. But this idyllic setting, though inhabited by a mystical number of angelic ladies, seems to be dedicated to profane, not sacred love. Boccaccio's ladies pose themselves the question, would they flee if the lover of each should appear? and two answer that anyone who fled at such good fortune would be most unwise. The angelic beloved of tradition can also turn ugly, like any earthly lady. In a resentful sonnet that bears the insistently reiterated admonition to seize the time for love in youth (XLIV), the poet imagines his beloved with gold hair turned to silver, a wrinkled face, her beautiful eyes watery, her fair bosom flabby and her sweet voice harsh. This brutally realistic rush of misogynism characterizes Boccaccio's ambivalent view of ladies and love and his frequent inversion of exalted themes through popular realism.

Boccaccio's *Rime* have aroused less interest than his other compositions. He did not collect them as Petrarch did, and in fact burned many in a moment of repentance.[10] They have been considered mostly as illustrations of moments in his life and certain constants of his poetic sensibility. The most outstanding of these constants is narration, and in this regard it has been observed that Boccaccio's tendency toward narration is even manifest in his use of the sonnet form.[11] He makes the sonnet tend more toward the narrative *ottava* by not separating the two quatrains but rather by blending them into one poetic phrase detached from the tercets, which then remain as isolated silhouettes or outbursts.

The *Caccia di Diana* [Diana's Hunt]

The *Caccia di Diana* is Boccaccio's first substantial work. Written probably around 1334, but certainly no later than 1338,[12] this poem of eighteen brief cantos written in *terza rima* tells of a hunt of Diana in which the ladies of Naples rebel against Diana and pass over to the service of Venus. Boccaccio is following a poetic tradition of catalogs; his models are a lost *sirventese* by Dante, and possibly another by Antonio Pucci, both of which praised the lovely ladies of Florence. In the *Caccia* a narrator is wandering in the springtime, wondering how to protect himself from the bitter assaults of love, when he imagines he hears a gentle spirit calling the ladies of Naples to the great court of Diana. A hunt is organized but is interrupted when attention is drawn to another hunting party, likewise of Neapolitan ladies with their prey. As noon approaches Diana assembles all huntresses and ends the hunt, but a "pleasing lady," whose name was not mentioned, incites the women to reject Diana's authority. This exacting goddess then returns to heaven and the huntresses turn their prayers to Venus who descends and accommodates them by transforming the captured animals into handsome young men. At this point the narrator, who reveals himself a stag, beholds Venus and is likewise changed into a man.

The *Caccia* can serve as a good introduction to some of Boccaccio's narrative techniques. For one, it is structured around a list, a technique common to classical and medieval writers alike, which can take the form of a catalog or a procession. Here Boccaccio lists Neapolitan noblewomen and the animals they have caught; in the *Teseida* he will list Greek kings, in the *Ameto* the contents of a garden, in the *Amorosa Visione* heroes and heroines of the past and present. These are inchoate forms of his endeavors in later life which will be compilations of geographical sites, of famous men and women, and of ancient myths. The list offers an abundance of often indiscriminate material and constitutes what we see; it is a form of realism. But already here in the *Caccia* we find a more sophisticated device, also constant in Boccaccio's works, which considers the problem of how we see: the use of a narrator to control the reader's perception of the text. In *Caccia* this presence, the narrator-stag, takes us by surprise at the end, as does the narrator-poet in the *Ameto*. In other works the narrator is introduced at the beginning through proems and introductions, and in the *Decameron,* where perspective is most carefully controlled, the presence of the narrator has its most important implementation in the use of the framework.[13]

Considered by most critics the awkward effort of an immature author, the *Caccia* has been interpreted as an allegory, which it clearly is. The traditional interpretation maintains that it represents the rebellion of ladies, specifically Neapolitan ladies, against the strictures of chastity and the active life imposed by Diana in favor of love and the idleness required for the cultivation of Venus.[14] It presents the *topoi* most basic to Boccaccio's works. A pastoral setting in which nymphs hunt, bathe at a font, cease their activities for more important events at midday, and are ruled or governed by a lady veiled in mystery who is in some sense the poet's lady—all are *topoi* of the *Caccia,* but could describe, at least in part, the *Ameto,* the *Ninfale fiesolano* and the *Decameron* as well. The meanings of these *topoi* are at times pagan, at times Christian, at times both. For the *Caccia* the overriding classical inspiration is Ovid, but recent criticism has observed a Christian message as well, whose iconography is inspired by Dante. The link between the two is metamorphosis; for the *Caccia* revolves around mythological figures and describes Ovidian metamorphoses, but it also describes a *trasumanar,* as Dante would have it, or a Christian conversion, and appears to be not only a classical idyll but a Christian allegory.[15]

Boccaccio's debt to Dante leaps from the pages of the *Caccia* at every turn. It is written in *terza rima,* it catalogs beautiful women, it paraphrases Dante's praise of Beatrice in the *Vita Nuova* as a lady of virtue who brings salvation and to whom he will offer more fitting praise in another work, and it echoes Stilnovo conceits and Dante's verses.[16] It is also organized around a complex order that imitated Dante's use of numerical structure in which the fulcrum is the association of the poet's lady with the number nine.[17] The Venus to whom the ladies appeal at the very end becomes, in this allegorical frame, not profane love and the pleasures of lust, but sacred love and the joys of Charity, the triumph of reason and Christian virtue over bestial instincts.

The *Caccia* is a pastoral poem whose pastoral integument seems to be also classical in conception, for the allegory, in addition to being moral or anagogical, is also historical. We must remember that each of the "nymphs" following Diana, then Venus, is a specific and identifiable lady of noble Neapolitan family.[18] Their hunt, therefore, where animals become men and lovers, could very well be a literal allusion to a dimension of chronicle (namely the machinations of Venus in the Neapolitan court) that is lost on the modern reader but would not have escaped Boccaccio's contemporary audience. For this aspect of his poem Boccaccio seems to be using the allusive allegory of Virgil's eclogues, which in antiquity had established a specifically historical reality behind the words of shepherds,[19] and Virgil was a model followed closely by Boccaccio later in his own eclogues. Virgil's Arcadia provided the spiritual distance from which to reflect Rome, and thus Virgil brought the pastoral into history. In Virgil's most specifically Roman eclogues, for example I or V, where Mopsa sings of Daphnis, allegorically Caesar, the song of the shepherd has a clear "other" sense based on the everyday reality of Rome. This dual level of meaning, one literal and pastoral and the other allusive and historical, associated classical pastoral poetry with an allegorical form that served as a poetic veil for historic fact. It is an aspect fully exploited in Boccaccio's works, for the work of art, particularly in an idyllic natural setting, is always used as a means of attaining perspective on the real society behind it. So despite its apparent simplicity, the *Caccia di Diana* is not as immature or tentative a work as one might suppose. It suggests many of the constants of Boccaccio's poetics and serves as an introduction to his following works.

Most important in his subsequent works is the theme of love. All Boccaccio's works of fiction, from the *Caccia* to the *Corbaccio,* revolve around the theme of love. But what does love mean? Medieval conceptions of love, and the theories of love known to Boccaccio, present an extremely complex picture. Christian love or charity was contrasted with instinctual or natural love. The two were reconciled in marital love, in its turn contrasted with courtly love and the teachings of Ovid. All these contradictions converge in Boccaccio's works. Love is sacred and profane, it is spiritual and physical, it ennobles and it debases, it is a totally personal experience and yet a common denominator for all mankind, and often it is all of these together. Behind these antinomies it may be useful to single out two kinds of love, as Boccaccio himself does in his gloss on Venus in the *Teseida*.[20] "This Venus is double, for one can and should be understood as all honest and legitimate desire, such as the desire to have a wife to have children and such like; and of this Venus we are not speaking here. The second Venus is she for whom all lasciviousness is desired and who is commonly called the goddess of love . . ." (*Tes*. VII, 50, *chiosa*). One is the celestial Venus, the Venus of marriage and the family and sanctioned Christian love; the other is the carnal Venus or the goddess of lust and concupiscence; one is represented by Mary, the other by Eve.[21] The forms that this duality assumes in Boccaccio's works are complex, for not only does this dual love unfold within the contradictions inherent in courtly love, but there are also superimposed the tenets of the Stilnovo and, possibly, personal or autobiographical elements.

With regard to Boccaccio's dual view of Venus, courtly love presents certain paradoxes.[22] Love is spiritual and enlightening and suited only to the noble in spirit; but it is not without certain physical consolations, and it is extramarital.[23] Though this love is characterized by a spirituality that enlightens, it is also secular and does not lead to salvation. This point is made clear within the only treatise we have on courtly love, the *Art of Courtly Love* by Andreas Capellanus.[24] In the last book, after having exhausted the subject of secular love, Andreas recants with a rejection of profane love in favor of sacred love. We discover that though he has discussed courtly love for two out of three books, it is only *in saeculo bonum,* an earthly good, and is not to be confused with the eternal good of religion. The two are incompatible; thus at the end the Chaplain tells Walter, the young man to whom the work is ostensibly addressed, that this lengthy investigation should only help him to know of courtly love in order that he abstain. This recantation in Book Three makes Books One and Two what C. S. Lewis described as "truancy," a concept important to the emergence of literature that purports to be serious without being committed to Christian teaching.[25] It is exemplified by the Chaplain's manner of discussing courtly love, which depends, as one of his female interlocutors says, on "leaving the religious side of the question out for a moment."[26] For two out of three books the author, and the reader, have enjoyed a wholly secular discussion of profane love. They have played truant with regard to the salvation of their souls, but have come back just in time, at the very end, with the expedient of recantation. About a century later, with the Stilnovo poets and Dante, the antinomical relationship of courtly love and divine love will be blended in a more harmonious view. The *domina* or mistress of the courtly lover becomes a heavenly messenger sent to bring *salute* or salvation to the soul of a poet. This is the *donna angelicata,* the bearer of beatitude or Beatrice, who is central to Dante's magnificent vision and who is behind the figure of Boccaccio's beloved as well.

But Boccaccio's beloved is an enigmatic figure. Critics of the late nineteenth and early twentieth century, seeking information about her, deduced a somewhat romantic biography from what appeared to be autobiographical references scattered through his early works.[27] The tone of Boccaccio's early works, especially those in prose, seems particularly vehement and emotional, and this, they felt, justified a literal reading. The story they reconstructed ran thus: Boccaccio was born in Paris in 1313 from the illicit relations between his father and a Frenchwoman of noble blood named Jeanne (hence his name Giovanni). As a young boy he was brought to Florence, where his father had married, and in early adolescence he was sent to Naples to escape the persecution of his stepmother. As he grew up in Naples, he had his first experiences of love, first with Pampinea and then with Abrotonia (pseudonyms that appear in the works), but after eight years came the most important encounter of his life. In church on Easter Saturday he beheld Maria dei Conti d'Aquino—an illegitimate daughter of King Robert of Naples, whom he nicknamed Fiammetta—and fell hopelessly in love. After a long courtship he finally won her favors, surprising her at night in her chambers in the month of October, but she soon betrayed him and cast him into deepest despair.

Although this sequence is to be found, reworked in various guises, in all of Boccaccio's early works, as a basis for biographical reconstruction it should be viewed with skepticism. Contemporary Boccaccio scholars have dismantled the story and refocused it in the more realistic perspective of a literary play on themes that do not license a factual reconstruction.[28] First, the presence of a narrator or poet in a work, as is to be found in all of Boccaccio's fiction, does not consequently guarantee that the presence is the poet himself. The narrator is above all a means of allowing perspective. Second, many facts belie the story. The oldest biographers do not mention Boccaccio's birth in France, and documents do not reveal the existence of a Maria as a member of the illustrious and well-known d'Aquino family. Furthermore, these so-called biographical facts seem to undergo a maturing process. While, in the early works, Boccaccio's alleged French mother is a princess and an innocent maiden, in later works she is downgraded to a noblewoman and a widow desirous of new loves. In addition, the most important elements in the story conform to well-established conventions: a meeting in a church at Easter, the maiden dressed in green, the lover surprising the lady in her chamber; and the affair progresses according to all the stages prescribed by the treatises on love. All leads to the conclusion that Boccaccio, with a measure of personal sentiment, has embellished and modified whatever facts he had in order to create a literary myth.

The *Filocolo*

In the period from about 1336 to 1338 Boccaccio was working at a larger and more complex task, the composition of the *Filocolo*. Based on the story of Florio and Biancifiore, a popular legend known through two French poems of the twelfth century and possibly from a *cantare* known in Italy,[29] Boccaccio wrote the work at the alleged request of his lady. He relates that she asked him to tell the story of these two lovers so that the memory of their love might be exalted by some poet, whereas up to that time it was told only in the "fairytale-like" versions of the common people. With this work Boccaccio begins to grapple with the problem of developing a viable literary language for a popular story. The popular *cantari* came from stories told to the people in public squares by troubadours or *cantastorie,* and were based largely on the French romances, though some may have been Oriental in origin. The *cantare* was a popular genre par excellence. The protagonists were inevitably glamorous nobles, the plots were dramatic, simple and full of action, with rapid passages from one moment to the next. There was no psychological observation, little dialogue, and the events usually came to a happy conclusion. In contrast to these elemental narrations Boccaccio introduces richer psychological portraiture, greater attention to detail, allegorical structures, and an abundance of erudition.

With his characteristic penchant for Greek etymologies (often incorrect) Boccaccio calls his version of the romance of Florio and Biancifiore the *Filocolo,* the "labor of love."[30] In the *exordium* he tells us of a lady Maria whom he met in church at Easter and who has brought beatitude and light to her lover, both assertions well established by literary convention. Following an ancient *topos* he states that it is she who requested this work.[31] The dedication is here addressed to the youths who are "navigating in the winds caused by the wings of the son of Cythaerea," a circumlocution for lovers. As for the ladies, whom he will not bore with ponderous tales of ancient battles, he hopes they will learn to love one man as Biancifiore did. The dedication or proem is a rhetorical device, present in each of his works after the *Caccia,* which serves to establish the fundamental relationship of literature to the reader and to life. As a means of controlling that relationship it is a framing device and serves to indicate the purpose of the work. In the early works, with the *exemplum* tradition in the background, Boccaccio's narrators view the purpose of literature as consolation, or instruction for the purpose of consolation. In the *Filocolo* the narrator hopes to offer consolation by example to suffering lovers; in the *Filostrato* he is writing his work to relieve his own pain and possibly regain the favors of his lost beloved, and the same is true of the *Teseida*; Fiammetta, in the work of the same name, writes her story to gain the sympathy of her readers; and in the *Decameron,* when the flames have subsided, he writes out of gratitude to help those who are most needy, the idle ladies.

In the *Filocolo,* Florio, son of the first king of Spain, and Biancifiore, a descendant of a noble Roman family (though this is unknown to her), are raised together. In early childhood they fall in love. Florio's family, thoroughly opposed to their love, tries various expedients to separate them and finally sells Biancifiore to merchants, who bring her to the Orient and sell her to the Admiral of Alexandria. Florio assumes the disguise name of Filocolo and sets out to look for her. After numerous adventures he finds her and makes his way into the tower where she is held captive by hiding in a basket of flowers. The two are discovered together and condemned to death, but at the last minute the admiral recognizes Florio as his nephew and they are saved. Biancifiore is discovered to be of noble origin, they marry and all the pagan characters are converted to Christianity.

Critics generally consider the *Filocolo* a rambling medieval miscellanea that contains a bit of everything. It does indeed have an uneven rhythm, as this fairly simple story serves as an armature for a varied string of adventures, stories, and myths. These include metamorphoses of both Ovidian and Dantesque inspiration; divine interventions as in classical epics; situations resolved with magic stones, proofs of chastity, and poisonings as in Greek and medieval romances; tournaments and a court of love; prophetic dreams and symbolic visions. As might be expected the language used to express such diversity of situations oscillates between involuted mythological similes with impassioned apostrophes to the reader, and swift-moving, realistic, expository prose. The tone of the *Filocolo* lies in the "uncertainty between lyrical and narrative."[32] It is this very diversity that makes the *Filocolo* fertile terrain for an analysis of Boccaccio's poetics. As in the *Caccia,* classical myth is central, and metamorphoses, determined by both sacred and profane love, are the fulcrum. This movement of abstractions is nonetheless situated in a specific reality and, most important, the possibilities of the pastoral *topos* are for the first time dedicated to a narrative dimension.

Classical myth in the *Filocolo* is largely a rhetorical presence. Christ is the son of Jove, nuns are nymphs who follow Diana, morning is when Aurora has removed the nocturnal flames and Phoebus has dried the dewy grass, and five years of childless marriage are indicated thus, "Lelio had been with his wife Giulia, after Hymen was crowned with the fronds of Pallas and the holy torches were burned, so many times that Phoebus had five times returned to the house of the Virgin" (*Filoc.* I,5).

Classical myths turn up in the swollen rhetorical outbursts of characters of the *Filocolo.* Biancifiore, when she learns that Florio is to be sent away to study, pronounces a wailing monologue in which she evokes the examples of Ariadne, Phaedra, Arethusa, Hecuba, and others as cases of abandoned women happier than she.

More central to the classical inspiration of the *Filocolo* are metamorphoses of an Ovidian stamp. These transformations are the core of many tragic little love stories that divert the action from the two protagonists. In his travels to find Biancifiore, Florio comes upon Idalagos, who has been turned into a tree, with his beloved transformed into a fountain, and Fileno, Florio's rival, likewise metamorphosed to a fountain. Each of these metamorphoses constitutes a short story, and in fact the *Filocolo* is a love story in which most of the digressions are little love stories framed by the story of Florio and Biancifiore.[33] What kind of love does it recount?

Ostensibly Florio and Biancifiore are examples of profane love and concupiscence. The two children fall in love over a book, "the holy book of Ovid" Boccaccio calls it, the *Ars amatoria.* This work was immensely popular in the Middle Ages and was the breviary for the religion of love developed in courtly culture. The importance of the book is explained by Florio. "I believe that the forces of the holy verses, which we devoutly read, has ignited our spirits with new fire, and brought about in us what we have already seen it bring about in others" (II,4,2). The book of Ovid was a Gallehaut or go-between for lovers, and significantly Gallehaut is the subtitle Boccaccio will give to his *Decameron.* [34] The fire that burns within these two children, couched in religious language because it is the religion of love, is profane love, lust, or the worship of Cupid.

But there seems to be another message hidden in the *Filocolo,* one that refers to a different kind of love and a particular kind of metamorphosis which is not Ovidian but Christian in meaning. In a prophetic dream which foretells the entire plot of the book, King Felice sees a reverse metamorphosis, as in the *Caccia,* in which a doe and a lion cub (Biancifiore and Florio) after varied adventures are bathed in a fountain and turned into a beautiful man and maiden, finally to return home with great happiness. This dream and certain underlying numerical patterns and symmetries suggest that the apparent chaos of the plot is sustained by a structure that signifies the rejection of the worship of Cupid. This is articulated in a series of "centers."[35] In the very center of the work, the middle of the Third Book, we find Fileno, a disconsolate lover, rejecting love in a tirade against Cupid, who, he says, seizes the souls of the ignorant with tricks and brings down the valorous. Fileno berates all women as insatiable and corrupting daughters of the Devil and Eve, mother of lust and sinful love (III,34–35). Next to this center is a section which has long been considered the most important section of the *Filocolo,* the *Questions of Love.* In this rather long digression, Filocolo takes part in a court where thirteen questions of love are presented to queen Fiammetta, in the manner of the French courts, and she pronounces her answers. In the central question, number seven, an important symbolic number, Caleon asks whether or not it is to man's good to fall in love, and the queen's answer, surprisingly, is "no." This "no" is therefore a centrally placed rejection of profane love or the worship of Cupid within this episode. The episode itself is framed by a dream and a vision. The dream preceding is an ornithological representation of the author's allegedly tortured affair with Maria. The vision following the episode is clearly Christian and allegorical, representing Filocolo's conversion by a symbolic lady who enables him to perceive the three theological virtues, ladies dressed in red, white, and green. The *Questions of Love,* therefore, preceded by a tortured representation of profane love and followed by a Christian vision of sacred love, becomes an episode of conversion. It is central in the development of Florio and Biancifiore's love, which goes from lust inspired by Ovid in the first book to marriage and piety at the end and to a conversion which is paralleled by the general conversion to Christianity that takes place in the final book.

But the tension between sacred and profane love is never quite resolved in Boccaccio's works. When asked to pronounce on the value of love, queen Fiammetta begins her remarks by undermining them. She declares the court a game (as such courts were traditionally called) and says that to answer the question she must speak against the god of love to whom they are all devoted. She hopes that the god of love will recognize that her answer is forced by the game and that he will forgive her and not visit his indignation upon her. She further tells Caleon, her interlocutor and likewise a servant to love, to hear her answer but not to deviate in his devotion to Cupid. She has begun her condemnation of love by apologizing for it. This itself is a framing device. She is playing reality against a game and has established a means of controlling her audience's perception of both and of appealing to whichever frame suits her. It might also be added that though the central question seems to deny love for pleasure, the whole episode is devoted to just that and therefore constitutes a form of truancy.

Fiammetta proceeds to distinguish three kinds of love: honest love, which is that between God and His creatures, governing the heavens and earth, and through which we attain heaven; love for pleasure,

which is passionate love or lust, to which they must address themselves;
and love for utility or love joined to fortune, which fills the world but is
more hate than love (this kind of love will be amply illustrated in the
Decameron, along with the other two). Fiammetta, speaking against
love for pleasure, declares that it brings anguish and deprives one of
honor and, most importantly, of liberty, man's most cherished possession. Caleon responds with the tenets of courtly love: love ennobles, it
humbles the proud, makes the avaricious generous, the timid brave,
and so on. He bolsters his argument with examples from pagan myths
and poets—Mars, Medea, Paris, Virgil, Ovid, Orpheus were all moved
by love. Fiammetta replies, using the same myths to prove the opposite
point and adding some more of her own to demonstrate that this kind of
love is destructive, particularly of marriage, and that it crazes, debili-
tates, and corrupts. She concludes that men would certainly live
happily without it, but "we realize this damage too late; therefore, once
we have fallen into love's net, we must follow his life until the light
[Venus or Christian love] which brought Aeneas from the shadowy way
as he fled the dangerous flames, appears to us and draws us to her
pleasure" (IV,46,20). Christian, here honest, love is better, but while
we are waiting we must live with love for pleasure.[36]

Beyond the complexities of their theoretical background the *Questions of Love* have an artistic function that is essential for Boccaccio's
work. They are devoted to narration, and the entire episode, long seen
as important with regard to the pattern of the *Decameron,* must be
evaluated in this perspective as well. The *Questions of Love* are a series of
narrative episodes that stand out as a major digression in a work already
riddled with digressions.[37] One of the patterns that determines Boccaccio's narrative art is the creation of an ideal situation that will assure
the flow and enjoyment of the stories. Here, as elsewhere, he fuses the
court of love with an ideal pastoral setting or *locus amoenus.*[38] This
episode is a closed world, a microcosm removed in time and space from
the events of the embracing story, a delightful pastoral suspension of
the travail that surrounds it.

But one of the most striking aspects of Boccaccio's works, even the
more abstract like this one, is that the idyll is located geographically
and situated outside a specific frame which defines reality as a city.[39]
All of Boccaccio's fictive works include and are framed by a city. In the

Caccia there is the Naples of King Robert which recurs in the *Filocolo,* alternating with ancient Rome. In the *Filocolo* Marmorina (Verona), Naples, and Alexandria are among the cities used as cardinal points for the action; and one of the important digressions describes Caleon founding Boccaccio's native city of Certaldo. In later works (for example the *Ameto, Ninfale fiesolano,* and the *Decameron*) the city, mythic and real, becomes the basis for the perception of reality. But in the *Filocolo* is the first real example of the city as a framing device.

On his outbound trip to Alexandria in quest of Biancifiore, Filocolo meets with a ferocious storm off the coast of Naples. As the ship is tossed about, and Florio laments his fate, they are swept ashore, and while awaiting the repair of his ship, he stops to listen to the beautiful song of a group of young people gathered in a garden. The garden that arises suddenly out of surrounding shipwreck and despair places the idyll in contrast to calamitous reality (a scheme developed further in the *Ameto* and the *Decameron*) and Filocolo and his companion Ascalione soon enter into the festivities of the group. Once within, all is suspended except the common goal of pleasure. As the hot part of the day approaches, a lovely lady named Fiammetta invites Filocolo to come to a field full of trees, flowers, and shade. They are there to pass time, and there comes the proposal that they do so by discussing questions of love. As she is crowned queen, Fiammetta promises lighthearted rather than profound answers to the questions, for their court is a game. The questions are part of the traditional courtly repertory. Should a lady choose a lover who is strong, courteous and liberal, or wise (III)? Should one love a woman of lower or higher social station (VIII)? Is it better to love a maiden, a married woman, or a widow (IX)? Is it more pleasant to behold the beloved or think about her (XI)? And so forth. But it is interesting to consider how the quasi-scholastic practice of courtly dialogue, consisting of questions and answers, fares under the pen of Boccaccio, for many of the questions turn into stories. Only five questions (III,VII,VIII,IX,XI) are posed as direct questions. All the others acquire some form of narrative garb. In some, a sequence of events is essential to the question. Thus in XII, a youth in love with a maiden has an old woman arrange a meeting. When her brothers discover them together they tell him he may sleep with the maiden for a year only if he sleeps with the old woman, duplicating every caress,

for another year. The question is, whom should he choose first? The
queen's answer is the beautiful maiden, for one should not forego a
present pleasure for a future one. When one of the company objects
that men must bear present woes to attain the rewards of the afterlife,
the queen retorts that they are speaking about earthly and not
heavenly delights, and therefore one must seek what is delightful and
not repulsive; a reply which maintains the tension with her rejection
of love for pleasure. In some questions the narrative construction is
more artificial. In question V, a youth recounts a dream in which a
boat full of lovely young maidens approaches,[40] and as he chooses one
of them, Cupid shoots him with a golden arrow and the maiden with
one of lead. As he goes on his way, cursed with loving a maiden who
hates him, he meets a young man who has known requited love but is
tormented by jealousy. The question, which could have been put
directly, is, who is more unhappy? (The queen answers that the
jealous lover is more unhappy, for his love has been forever poisoned,
while the unrequited lover can still hope for perfect love.)

The overlaying of narrative devices upon moralizing questions
yields even more important narrative moments, for two of the questions (IV and XII) were later used in the *Decameron* (X,5 and 4). Both
stories are believed to be of Oriental origin and both were probably
well known in Boccaccio's day.[41] In both cases it is obvious that they
were stories to which a question was attached to make them suitable
for inclusion in the *Questions of Love*.[42] The story of the IV question
(*Dec.* X,5) is as follows: a nobleman is in love with a married woman
who resists his advances. She finally tries to rebuff him by promising
to grant her love if he complies with a request she knows to be
impossible: that he give her a flowering garden in January. The
nobleman succeeds through the devices of a necromancer, and when
the lady reveals her predicament to her husband he insists that she
keep her word. Hearing of the husband's magnanimity, the nobleman
relinquishes his right to the lady's favors, and hearing in turn of this,
the necromancer relinquishes his right to payment. In the framework
of the *Questions of Love,* the queen must decide who was more noble, the
husband, the nobleman, or the necromancer? As a story in the *Decameron* the protagonists are examples of the theme of the Tenth
Day—those who liberally or magnanimously performed some action.

Comparing the two versions we glean insight into Boccaccio's art and his development as a narrator. The later novella is generally more refined and more worldly-wise in comparison to the earlier question. In the *Filocolo,* Tarolfo's courtship and wanderings to find the necromancer—replete with geographic descriptions and a lecture on democracy—follow the dominant pattern of digression, or at least a tangential introduction to the heart of the story, which is the final interaction of the characters. In the *Decameron* the courtship unfolds in one sentence. Ansaldo, as he is called there, remains at home and sends for the necromancer, who comes and produces the garden in rapid indirect discourse. This rapidity serves to telescope the action toward the climax, which will be dramatized and drawn out. When, in the earlier version, the lady beholds the garden and presents her husband with her predicament, he enjoins her to keep her word and declares that he will still love her; whereupon she adorns herself and goes to Tarolfo. When Tarolfo asks how her husband permitted this we are told obliquely that she recounted the situation to him. In the *Decameron,* on the other hand, this is the crucial moment and it is consequently dramatized. The husband is first angered, but then, considering the purity of his wife's original intention, he resolves that she must keep her word. The anger gives plausibility to the depiction of a man who is about to give his wife to another. Nor is the husband beyond the practical considerations typical of the optics of the *Decameron,* for he is afraid that Ansaldo would use the arts of the magician for vengeance should they deceive him. He wisely advises his wife to satisfy Ansaldo chastely; that failing, he enjoins her to give herself in body but not in soul. The final confrontation between her and Ansaldo is staged with direct discourse to heighten the pathos and significance of the story, which is the personal code of honor each person is exemplifying. She tells him in tears that "neither love for you, nor the promise I made, bring me here, but only the order of my husband, who has shown more respect for the efforts of your disordered love than for his or my honor." Whereupon the nobleman frees her of her obligation.

Similar observations apply to Question XII (*Dec.* X,4). The story is again that of a man who loves a married (and pregnant) woman in vain. When he hears of her death he vows to have from her in death the kiss she would not grant him in life, and when he opens up her grave and begins to kiss and touch her, he discovers that she is still alive. He takes her to his home, where his mother revives her, and asks her to reveal her resuscitation to nobody until he has returned from his service in another town. Upon his return he prepares a banquet to which he invites her husband, and during the banquet he presents the husband with his wife and son, born in the meantime. The later version is again more attentive to plausibility and narrative drama. While the first story tells vaguely of a gentleman of the town who had a duty to fulfill in another town, the second story speaks of a member of the Carisendi family in Bologna sent as *podestà* to Modena. While in the first story the nobleman demands blind obedience from the revived lady and deflects the final dramatic moment, the returning of wife and son to their rightful master, to the privacy of another room, in the second story he constructs a subtle crescendo to the dramatic climax. The nobleman does not require blind obedience from the lady, but reveals his plan, to which she acquiesces. At the banquet he returns wife and son before all the assembled guests and even stages the magnificence of his gesture by telling a parable of the situation and having all present agree that he who saved her, and not the original husband, has the moral right to this woman and her child. The effect is heightened by irony, for messer Nicoluccio, the lady's husband, unaware of the identities hidden under the parable, rises and makes a speech approving the general opinion. Boccaccio constructs the episode to enhance the enjoyment of the situation with irony and to magnify the generosity of Gentile Carisendi, who, through this dramatic construction, is returning the lady to her husband not as his due, but as a gift from Gentile of the very thing he holds most precious.

We have taken the opportunity here to observe the development of the characteristics of Boccaccio's genius as a narrator because the special case of the recurrence of these two stories begs for comparison.[43] Furthermore, the presence of two such complete novelle in the *Questions of Love* confirms the importance of the episode as a narrative nucleus. Indeed the importance of episodic narration is confirmed throughout the *Filocolo*. The digressions to the stories of secondary characters which seem to wreak havoc on the plot become, instead, the unavowed structure of the work. Even the résumé of the development of Christianity in the last book becomes a novella. And the sizable digression of the *Questions of Love* stands as the best indication of the narrative pivot of the work.

The *Filostrato*

Like the *Filocolo,* the *Filostrato* takes up another popular romance, the story of Troilus and Criseida. Boccaccio probably knew the story from the *Roman de Troie* of Benoit de Saint Maure (ca. 1160), as well as from the translation of Binduccio dello Scelto, and the *Historia troiana* of Guido delle Colonne (ca. 1285). The date of the work is debated. Many critics tend to date the *Filocolo* and the *Filostrato* more or less contemporaneously, with the *Filostrato* possibly later, due to the stylistic progress manifest in its simplified and more concise structure, but some place it before the *Filocolo* for reasons of content and technique.[44] The story tells of Troilus, son of King Priam, who loves the pretty young widow Criseida, daughter of Calchas, a Trojan seer who has passed to the Greek camp. Through Pandarus, friend to Troilus and cousin to Criseida, Troilus succeeds in gaining her favors. When there is an exchange of prisoners, however, Criseida is called back by her father and passes over to the Greek camp, swearing eternal faith to Troilus as she departs. But the fickle woman immediately yields to Diomedes, who has been sent to accompany her to her father, and when Troilus learns of her betrayal he throws himself into battle with the intention of killing his rival, only to be killed himself by Achilles.

The *Filostrato* is largely derivative, but it moves away from many of the influences we have observed in previous works. It hovers between courtly and popular literature and deals with profane love only. Neither paganism nor Christianity forms the ideological substratum and the classical elements are at most ornamental. Though based on a pagan story, the *Filostrato* is turned into a story about love for pleasure, or lust in conformity with medieval courtly canons. In Benoit's *Roman de Troie* the story of Troilus is merely an episode, a story within a story that focuses on Briseida (Boccaccio derived the name Criseida from a mistranslation from Ovid) and her fickleness. In the *Filostrato* Boccaccio turns the situation around and concentrates on Troilus, a more suitable mirror for the feelings of the narrator, who, as he will tell us in his introduction, has been abandoned by his mistress.

The *Filostrato* virtually avoids classical references, a situation which we are led to expect from the introduction. As in all his works, Boccaccio begins with a dedication *exordium*. Here the work is dedicated to the narrator's lady, Filomena, in her absence, for whom he will tell the story of Troilus and his suffering for the absence of Criseida. The work is to serve the purpose of relieving his own pain upon his lady's departure. We find the conventional *topos* of self deprecation: the author has composed this work in simple rhymes (the work is in the popular narrative verse form of the *ottava*) in his own Florentine tongue, with a modest style, and he has found solace in the composition. To emphasize the popular and earthly scope of this work, he overturns the conventional invocation required in the first verses. He states that although other poets call upon Jove or Apollo, and though he himself used to call upon the Muses to assist in poetic creation, he now calls upon his lady, who is his Jove, his Apollo, his Muse, *in fine,* the only inspiration of his art.

Boccaccio will make this point again in his self-defense in the *Decameron,* where to the accusation that he is wasting his poetry on ladies, he replies that the Muses are ladies and, moreover, his mistresses have inspired him to write more poetry than the venerable ladies of Castalia. So the *Filostrato,* despite its source, is clearly not classical in inspiration, and we note in its style the simple and more direct rhythms of the language and the relative absence of classical references. But neither is the love story of Troilus a story of Christian love.[45] There are echoes of Stilnovo poets and their conceits, and the indispensable echoes from Dante to be sure, but they are conventional forms of rhetoric and are devoid of any religious meaning. An example of this is the following echo from Dante. Here Pandarus returns to Troilus with the news that his mission to Criseida to proffer Troilus's love has been successful: "As little flowers, bent down and closed by chill of night, when the sun whitens them, straighten and all unfold upon their stems, such in his faint strength did Troilus become, and looking up to heaven he began in a bold voice, 'Praised be your supreme power, Venus, and that of your son, Love' " (II,80). This directly recalls Dante's verses in *Inferno* (II,127–29) where the Christian pilgrim Dante is restored for a very different purpose through the intervening grace of Beatrice and the Virgin.[46] Another large debt to Stilnovo poetry is owed to Cino da Pistoia, for in Book V (62–65) Boccaccio virtually reproduces Cino's most famous canzone. Most of the rhetoric of the work and the meaning of the story, however, go back beyond the Stilnovo to courtly love.

The proem places the work in the courts of love with the common question: is it more pleasant to speak of one's beloved, to behold her, or to think about her? (cf. *Filoc.* Quest.XI). The author states that he had always deemed thinking about one's lady most delightful, adducing the very practical reason that in imagination one can do as one wishes with no harsh reality to offer contradiction. In this specific case, however, when he can no longer behold his lady because of her absence, he believes that seeing her would be the greatest joy of all; this is a fitting introduction to the story of Troilus, who was left without the sight of his lady. Sight is a conceit dominant in love poetry from the Provençal poets to the Stilnovo, and it is a binding thread throughout the *Filostrato*.[47] In the introductory verses Boccaccio invokes the "lovely light of the beautiful eyes in which love has placed my delight" (I,4); and when Troilus first beholds Criseida he finds delight in "staring at her shining eyes and angelic face" (I,28), nor does he realize "that Love, with his darts, dwelled in the rays of those lovely eyes" (I,29).

The courtship of Troilus and Criseida unfolds according to the canons of courtly love as they were exemplified in the works of the troubadours and the poet Chrétien de Troyes and codified by Andreas Capellanus.[48] The development of their love follows the four stages—uncertainty, trial, acceptance as a suitor, acceptance as a lover—and Criseida, following the preferences of tradition, is a widow.[49] She feigns indifference, and concern for her honor, but reasons to herself that time is passing and no one will love her when she is old. That one should seize the day in accordance with the promptings and order of Nature is a notion particularly dear to Boccaccio, and amply supported by tradition. In his *Art of Courtly Love* (Bk.I,Ch.6,5th Dialogue) Andreas describes an allegorical procession representing women who loved too much and too many, too little and too few, and the proper number to a suitable degree. Those who refused love have offended the most and are represented as beautiful but shabbily dressed in clothes too warm for the lovely season. They are dirty and ride unassisted on unsaddled horses covered with the dust raised by those who precede them. When the group comes to a *locus amoenus* called Delightfulness, these ladies are forced to remain in a circle called Aridity, where they sit on bundles of thorns and scorch their feet on the burning ground.[50] Boccaccio echoes the same theme in a speech made to Abrotonia in the *Ameto*, where she is urged to accept a love while she is young, and in the story of Nastagio degli Onesti in the *Decameron* (V,8), where a woman is eternally chased and torn apart by dogs for having refused her suitors. Nature teaches that love belongs to youth, and Criseida judges that since she is young, beautiful, widowed, rich, noble, and childless, it would be folly to reject Troilus, who is likewise suited for love. So she sends him a letter that is a subtle mixture of doubt, indifference, and acquiescence. In doing so she is careful to maintain utter secrecy, also essential according to the courtly canon. Their love must not be discovered. With the troubadours this derived partly from the fact that the beloved was usually a married woman, and even more from the psychological truism observed by Ovid (*Ars Amatoria*, II,387), and stated by Criseida herself, "stolen water is far sweeter than wine given abundantly" (II,74). The two lovers, especially Troilus, manifest the standard symptoms of the lovesick as observed by Ovid, and then Andreas—restlessness, sleeplessness, loss of appetite, trembling, fainting, sighing, courage in battle, and great physical strength, among others. Likewise there is the traditional and essential figure of the paranymphus. Classical literature, as well as novelle, fables, and the popular *cantari*, taught that lovers needed a go-between or a confidant or maid through whom the lover might approach his lady, be it by bribery or by more gentle persuasion, and Filostrato has his Pandarus.

Another tenet of courtly love (and not only of courtly love) is that love is democratic. Andreas defined it as an ennobling emotion that knew no class distinctions.

. . . Love is not in the habit of differentiating men with titles of distinction, but . . . he obligates all equally to serve in his, that is, Love's army, making no exceptions for beauty and birth, and making no distinctions of sex or of inequality of family, considering only this, whether anybody is fit to bear Love's armor. Love is a thing that copies nature herself, and so lovers ought to make no more distinction between classes of men than Love himself does. (Bk.I,Ch.6,Dial.2,p.45)

An exception is made only for peasants, who are rarely found serving in the courts of love; nor, says Andreas, should they be so instructed, lest they abandon their labors, which are useful to us. This last is a point Boccaccio will overturn in the *Decameron,* where all is swept aside by Nature. In the *Filostrato* he concentrates on love as a democratic force that overwhelms nobles. "The ardent flames of love did not spare him on account of his royal blood or the greatness or virtue of his spirit, nor did they have care for the physical strength or bravery that was in Troilus" (I,40).

But for all that it expounds the canons of courtly love, the overriding inspiration of the *Filostrato* is the popular *cantare.* It is a popular romance with courtly culture superimposed. It is direct, simple, immediate, and realistic, just like the popular romances. The rapidity with which events unfold is characteristic. In only two stanzas the situation is set by Criseida's father, Calchas, who, being a seer, foresees the defeat of Troy and deems it wiser to pass over to the Greeks. With equal rapidity the characters fall in love. Troilus is smitten upon beholding Criseida, and so later is Diomedes when he sees her taking leave of Troilus. Rarely does the author halt for descriptions of persons or places, nor is his narrative dotted with rhetorical outbursts or erudite references. Compared to the lofty rhetoric of the *Filocolo* and its many digressions, this work, in a humble style, moves swiftly to its conclusion. Many of the *cantare* techniques appear, for example the voice of the author anticipating the action.[51] When Criseida has just returned to her father, she is sad and firm in her love for Troilus, but "was soon to change and abandon him for a new lover" (V,14). Also common to this popular form is the use of proverbs and maxims familiar to the audience. Pandarus laughs to himself at Troilus's self-deception as he awaits the return of Criseida, repeating an ironic proverb: "Di Mongibello aspetta il vento questo tapinello" (VII,10)—poor Troilus is waiting for a cool wind from Etna. The language of the *Filostrato* is also popular in inspiration, though there are moments of strident contrast when these common terms are juxtaposed with more lofty and lyrical passages. Ladies are consoling Criseida for her imminent departure, speaking nobly of friendship and despair, when their succour is described as being "nothing more than scratching her heels when it was her head that itched" (IV,85). And harsh rhymes, with endings such as

"-aggio" or "-azzo," further contribute to making the language popular and colloquial.

Because of its down-to-earth focus, the *Filostrato* offers a different manner of character portrayal. In the *Caccia di Diana* and the *Filocolo* the characters were abstractions, not unlike the personifications of allegory. Here, though far from presenting complex psychological portraits, they are more realistic in that they move in a realm of strictly earthly passion. Troilus, like Florio, is youthful, romantic, and noble in all of his reactions; but at the same time he is portrayed as weak and irresolute. He would certainly be incapable of seducing Criseida if left to his own devices. Fortunately he has his friend and confidant, Pandarus. Pandarus is shrewd and worldly-wise (though not wholly cynical as he will be depicted by Chaucer and Shakespeare), yet at the same time is loyal and devoted, much like his forerunners in chivalric romances. In his practical assessment of human affairs he anticipates characters of the *Decameron*. He acknowledges that his cousin Criseida is an honest woman, but he trusts his own eloquence in helping Troilus to seduce her, and takes the commonplace view that all women are desirous of love, and only refrain from fear of shame.

Criseida reveals a more human dimension than either *cantari* or allegories would give her. She is at least temporarily sincere in her concern for her honor, sweet and almost maidenlike in her abandon to Troilus, and initially sincere in her despair at leaving. At the same time she is calculating in her decision to love Troilus, matter-of-fact in her acceptance of her return to her father, and naturally fickle in switching her affections from Troilus to Diomedes. It is her contradictions that make her a real object of desire, and place her far from the paragons of virtue of the traditional beloved. Because of its essentially popular inspiration the *Filostrato* is more realistic, direct, and cohesive and reveals a much more meager cultural frame of reference than other works of the early period. To be sure there are long tirades, as in the letters the lovers exchange and in Troilus's laments,[52] but the overall effect is of rapid action based on earthly love with an eye to the realities of human behavior.

The *Filostrato* is written in *ottava rima*, a narrative rhyme scheme of six alternate rhyming verses closed with a couplet, that was the standard scheme of the *cantari*. Though the story of the *Filocolo* was derived from the *cantare* tradition, and the epitaph of Topazia Giulia in the *Filocolo* is an example of *ottava rima,* the *Filostrato* is the first work with roots in the *cantari* written wholly in *ottave.* With this, the *Teseida* and the *Ninfale fiesolano,* Boccaccio gives a special form to this narrative verse scheme that was to be the basic verse for Renaissance epics. The most salient characteristic of Boccaccio's *ottava* is one that has already been observed in his sonnets: the tendency is away from verse and toward prose narration.[53] Rather than emphasizing the rhyme by having the conclusion of a phrase coincide with the end of the verse, the rests at the end of a phrase occur frequently at midverse, thereby reinforcing the importance of the logical flow of the content over the constrictions of meter. Only in the final couplet is the importance of the rhyme unavoidable, and even there Boccaccio often uses an awkward term that jars the rhythm of the stanza. Emphases on relative pronouns and gerundive and participial constructions are also elements that characterize his prose and serve to change the aspect of the *ottava.* Boccaccio's contribution to the *ottava* as a narrative verse form is that he rendered it more faithful to prose rhythms. At the same time he dotted his narration with lyrical and Stilnovo forms, particularly in personal monologues, and replaced the commonplaces and prefabricated patterns of the *cantari* with freshly invented rhymes and images.

The *Teseida* o *Le nozze di Emilia* [The Marriage of Emilia]

Again with the intention of ennobling popular forms and endowing them with a full literary distinction, Boccaccio wrote the *Teseida,* a poem in twelve books, written in *ottave* and framed by a prose dedication and sonnet as introduction and two sonnets as conclusion. The work, written in the period 1339–41, would be among the last written in Naples.[54] Although a specific source remains undetermined, the work follows the pattern of medieval romances based on classical stories such as the *Roman d'Eneas* or the *Roman de Thèbes.* Nevertheless, Boccaccio is particularly aware of the distinction between these romances and the classical epic, and his object is clearly the latter. Dante, in his *De vulgari eloquentia,* had defined the poetic categories of love, arms, and virtue and said that no one had ever written of arms in Italian. At the end of the *Teseida* Boccaccio boasts of being the first to have sung "the labors of Mars . . . never before done in the vulgar tongue" (XII,84). Supporting evidence for his intentions is found in the division of the work into twelve books and in elements such as the lists of heroes, the funeral games, and the interventions of gods, all common to classical epics. The specific model for this work was Statius's *Thebaid,* for echoes of numerous scenes and verses from the *Thebaid* indicate that Boccaccio had his Statius close at hand.[55]

The story begins with the victorious wars of Theseus in which the hero conquers the Amazons and marries their queen Hippolyta. He then conquers Creon in Thebes and takes two Theban princes, Arcita and Palemone, back to Athens as prisoners. But beginning with Book III the story centers on the love of the two prisoners for the lovely Emilia, Hippolyta's sister. The two youths behold Emilia singing and weaving garlands before their prison window one day and are struck violently with Cupid's darts. They pine and sigh but are helpless because of their imprisonment, until one day Arcita is freed, on the condition that he leave Athens and never return. After a year, unable to bear the separation, he returns in disguise under the name of Penteo and hires himself as a servant to Theseus. Emilia recognizes him and keeps her silence, but when Palemone learns of his return he is consumed with jealousy and contrives his escape from prison. He overtakes Arcita, whom he finds sleeping in a wood, and in the argument that ensues over who should have Emilia, the two friends come to blows. At this moment Theseus arrives with Emilia and their entourage, and he orders that the two princes gather their forces and return to Athens in a year's time to decide their fate in a tournament. Emilia will be awarded to the winner. Arcita wins, but Venus, protectress of Palemone, intervenes and makes Arcita fall from his horse. Although seriously wounded, he is declared the husband of Emilia; but realizing that he is about to die he exacts the promise from Emilia that upon his death she will marry his friend and rival Palemone. Arcita dies and is buried, after which all turn to the celebration of the marriage of Palemone and Emilia.

The *Teseida* is clearly not a classically epic poem. Its jousts, allegorical figures, and Stilnovo conceits bring it far closer to medieval literature. Most importantly, the narration of a love story immediately takes center stage. Even as early as the introduction the narrator belies his intention, and, once again, tantalizes us with autobiographical games. He recalls the happy times when his lady loved him, and though he realizes he has now lost her forever, he still has pleasure in remembering how she used to love to hear and read stories, especially love stories. He has now found a very ancient story, unknown to most people, treating of nobles and the subject of love, and he and his lady are veiled in two of the characters, he says. He also invites us to an allegorical reading, singling his lady out from the crowd as someone intelligent enough to understand allegories, and inviting her to read his story with a "healthy mind," a term analogous to that with which Dante invites his readers to look for allegory in *Inf.* IX. Finally he invokes the god of Love to reignite, if he can, the flame of love in his lady. Confirmation that it is a love story comes in the concluding sonnet where the poet's lady gives the work its name and calls it not only with the epic title of *Teseida,* but with the subtitle of a love story, "The marriage of Emilia."

The problem is, what kind of love story is the *Teseida?* It clearly tells of passionate and concupiscent love, for both Arcita and Palemone are delighted, crazed, tortured, and, in the case of Arcita, killed for love of Emilia. But the *Teseida* seems to redeem this kind of love, and as has been illustrated by several scholars, the key to the love story is probably in the subtitle given by the poet's lady, marriage or marital love. This is supported by both numerological and astrological patterns.[56] The turning point in the poem is Book VII, where Arcita prays to Mars, Palemone to Venus, and Emilia to Diana before the great joust. In the first two prayers Boccaccio gives lengthy descriptions of the houses of Mars and Venus, glossed (classical references in the work are accompanied by the author's glosses) respectively as irascible and concupiscible appetites. Both are dual. Mars represents both wrath and righteous indignation but, he says, it is of wrath he is speaking here. The house of Mars is a sterile wood inhabited by Discord, Fear, Fury, Death, and all manner of evil personifications. Venus is also dual (cf. above) and Boccaccio is dealing with the second Venus, ". . . she through whom all lasciviousness is desired and who is commonly called the goddess of love; and it is of her that the author here designs the altar and the surrounding things, as appears in the text" (VII,50). The temple of Venus is a delightful garden inhabited by Courtesy, Kindness, Beauty,

and Idleness as well as Flattery, Pandering, and other less idyllic aspects
of concupiscent love. After these prayers and glosses on Mars and
Venus, who represent wrath and concupiscence or, if we like, the epic
and amorous matters of the poem, the conflict of battle becomes peace,
and love turns to marriage. Marital love is even extolled not only above
concupiscent love, but above chastity as well; for although Emilia prays
to Diana, and says she would as soon enter a convent after Arcita's
death, she is prevailed upon to accept the bond of marriage. The force
governing these changes or "conversions" is Theseus, who has been
interpreted as reason, taming and governing the discordant elements of
the soul.[57] It is the same Theseus who tames strife-ridden Thebes,
which is contrasted with peaceful Athens. The *Teseida* then could be
interpreted as an allegory of the movement of the soul from concupiscence and discord to honest love (marriage) and peace; this is paralleled
by the same movement in a civic frame through the dimension of
opposing cities.

The *Teseida* contains many of the *topoi* we have learned to look for in
Boccaccio's works: an idyllic garden, catalogs of trees and geographic
sites, processions of famous figures, and astrological descriptions, but it
is also the first example of the kind of erudition that will characterize his
later endeavors. Here the matter is specifically mythography. For the
many references to classical places and persons in this so-called epic,
Boccaccio gives glosses in the text of the *Teseida* with descriptions and
stories of ancient gods.[58] These myths are little narrative footnotes that
also serve to remind us of the importance of storytelling in his work. In
the gloss on Venus, for example, he tells nine other myths or short
stories. And narration imprints once again his use of meter. In choosing
the *ottava* for his epic, Boccaccio confronts the problem of forging an
epic meter out of a traditionally popular form. The *ottava* of the *Teseida*
is loftier in tone, in keeping with the whole cultural frame which is far
more erudite than the *Filostrato*. But the rhythm of his verse is still a
prose rhythm and the patterns are like those of the *Filostrato*. The
classical model works ultimately to the same purpose, for on the
example probably of the *Thebaid*, though he does the same in the
Filostrato, he fuses two or more *ottave* into a narrative unit.[59] Yet on

occasion the popular origin shows through and the *Teseida* becomes a *cantare*. The author's résumé of the action (IV,81) and the description of Emilia with the popular cliché of a fresh rose or a lily are *cantare* techniques that remind us of the popular elements behind this epic. Like its forerunners, the *Teseida* commingles classical and medieval poetic elements in moral, lyrical, and erudite frames. The Neapolitan experience ends with this work. We must now consider Boccaccio upon his return to his native Tuscany.

Chapter Three
Florence

In the winter of 1341 Boccaccio returned to Florence. From 1338 his father no longer seems to be connected with the Bardi company, and it is also probable that Boccaccino was in financial straits and suffering from the crisis which was overtaking Florence. In the *Ameto* (Ch.XLIX), the first work written in Florence, and in a letter to Acciaiuoli (*Epist.* V), we hear Boccaccio voicing resentment of his father and lamenting his sad and miserable existence in Florence as compared to the delights of Naples. The letter represents the first of his many attempts to return to Naples, for which he hoped to enlist the support of his powerful friend. This aspiration was to endure, somewhat unrealistically, throughout his life. Several times he undertook trips to the city of his youth, often with disappointing and even humiliating results. But Naples was in the past, and in 1341 we find Boccaccio, willingly or not, residing with his father in the district of Santa Felicita in Florence. The literary currents and the events which were shaking Florence inevitably touched the young writer.

The decade 1340 to 1350 was one of major upset for the city. There was the Bardi conspiracy in 1340, the dissent with King Robert of Anjou, the fall of the Guelf bloc, the adventure of dictatorship with the Duke of Athens ruling Florence from 1342 to 1343, the insurrection of the *popolo minuto* against the *popolo grasso,* the decline of the major guilds, the growth of the minor guilds, the devastating failures of the Bardi and Peruzzi companies, the famine of 1346 to 1347, and the famous plague of 1348.[1]

In this vortex Boccaccio became Florentine again. He found himself in an ambience which contrasted sharply with the aristocratic court of King Robert. His response was to rework the forms of the courtly tradition, and to graft his familiarity with classical literature onto the models of Tuscan poetry and the world of the mercantile bourgeoisie.

The works that fall into this period are the *Comedia delle ninfe fiorentine* (*Ameto*), the *Amorosa Visione,* the *Elegia di Madonna Fiammetta* (*Fiammetta*), and the *Ninfale fiesolano.*

The *Ameto*

Boccaccio's first work of this period is an allegorical pastoral romance, the *Comedia delle ninfe fiorentine* or the *Ameto,* written 1341 to 1342. The work tells of the crude and boorish shepherd Ameto, who comes upon seven lovely nymphs while hunting one day between the Arno and the Mugnone. He falls in love with one of them, Lia, and spends his days hunting in their company. But though winter puts an end to their jaunts, during the winter months of separation his passion waxes. Finally one spring day, during the holiday dedicated to Venus, he happens upon the troop of nymphs again, and they agree to pass the hot hours of that day together, each nymph telling the story of her loves. At the end of this day, Ameto realizes that the nymphs are really the seven virtues, and he is purified and ennobled by his love for these ladies, particularly Lia, through whom the soul ascends to Paradise.

The *Ameto* is constructed on an intricate intersecting of Christian virtues, pagan goddesses, and real people. Each nymph, representing a Christian virtue, takes a lover, representing the opposite vice, and with her love transforms him. So Adiona or Temperance takes Dioneo or Dissolution, and Fiammetta or Hope takes Caleone or Despair. Furthermore each nymph is aided by a suitable goddess: Mopsa or Wisdom is aided by Pallas, Agape or Charity is aided by Venus, and so forth.

Boccaccio's foremost source of inspiration in the *Ameto* seems to be Tuscan allegorical literature and especially Dante. Dante's example is evident in the prosimetrum pattern of prose interspersed with poetry as in the *Vita Nuova,* in the use of *terza rima,* in the allegorical intent of the work, and even in the title of *Comedia.* But Dante's allegory was unique[2] and in the *Ameto* Dante's unity of history with allegory becomes polarized into personification allegory on one level and the historical allusion of the classical pastoral on the other. In this sense the *Ameto* is much like the *Caccia di Diana.* Beyond the literal and moral, or anagogical, levels of Christian personification allegory there is, as in the

classical eclogue, a level of allusions to local history. Each of the nymphs
and each of their respective lovers appears to represent families well
known in Florence, such as the Della Tosa, Nerli, Peruzzi. The modern
reader lacks information complete enough to reconstruct the facts
underlying the fiction, but the references seem carefully set. In addition
to beholding the force of Venus upon seven nymphs and a poor
shepherd, or the action of the seven virtues upon the seven vices
through the force of Christian love, we are probably also beholding the
force of love, but it Venus or Charity, at work in the lives of
fourteenth-century Florentines. In combining this allusive quality of
classical pastoral allegory with the medieval allegorical vision and the
narrative romance, Boccaccio forges a new form, the pastoral romance.[3]

The garden or pastoral setting is fundamental to Boccaccio's works
and recurs everywhere. Its meaning is therefore extremely important,
but also difficult to determine. The meanings of the pastoral setting
vary and even contradict each other. The garden is like the garden of
Eden, at once the earthly paradise of spiritual and moral order to which
man desires to return, and the beguiling and sensual site of man's
corruption and fall which eternally tempts him with temporal and
deceiving pleasures.[4] In the *Ameto* the garden takes on a broad range of
meanings within these two extremes. It represents moral order, Christian virtue, sensual pleasure (and even obscene metaphor), perspective
on society, and narrative structure. The medieval catalog Adiona gives
in her story is one kind of pastoral idyll. Here a lengthy description of a
garden exhausts botanical reality and represents a natural order that
reflects moral order and the beneficent effects of Temperance on Dissolution. Likewise in the poetic contest between two shepherds about the
proper way of tending sheep, the moral contrast between virtue and
vice is couched in classical pastoral terms. And it is, of course, within
the pastoral setting that Ameto's conversion takes place and that he
learns to behold the gathered nymphs in the proper sense.

But the garden, or the pastoral idyll, can also signify pleasure. When
Ameto first beholds the nymphs, who are described, according to
traditional canons, from head to foot, they are at once physical incarna-
tions of the virtues they represent and at the same time portraits of
ladies who are viewed by Ameto with a certain literalness and carnal
interest in penetrating their more secret parts. In the same vein, the
natural and moral order that was so beautiful in Adiona's garden is

turned to obscene metaphor in the story of Agapes (and her marriage to an elderly man is itself an overturning of the natural order), who describes her plight in bed with her husband: ". . . he tries in vain to cultivate the gardens of Venus; and seeking to cleave the earth of these gardens, which long for gracious seeds, with an old ploughshare, he works in vain; for that plough, eroded by age, moving its pointed part in a circle like a loose willow, refuses to fulfill its due office in the firm fallow" (XXXII,15).

It is also a commonplace that the pastoral setting provides an idyllic vantage point with respect to society and sharpens the perception of society by contrast. It is a means of gaining perspective, and Boccaccio's use of the pastoral vantage point in this work is indeed a treatment of perspective, both social or historical, and narrative. Perspective becomes emphatic at the end, when we discover that the narrator himself is a character in the romance who has escaped the melancholy of his own life to look on, unnoticed, at an idyllic scene that is abstracted from society but yet reflects that society in its stories. Society is pivotal, and one indication of this is the dominance of the theme of the city in the *Ameto*.[5] From their vantage point outside the city, the nymphs tell stories that repeatedly carry them back to the dimension of the polis. Each nymph begins her story from the frame of a city—Athens, Paris, Rome—and Fiammetta dwells at length on the mythic founding of Naples, followed by Lia, who tells the history of Florence. With the importance of the city as a social frame comes a moral frame as well. In the works of the Neapolitan period Boccaccio reflected more closely the courtly tradition as it emerged from the cultural models at the aristocratic court of King Robert. The *Ameto,* his first Tuscan work, takes those same models but turns to Tuscan literature and to the setting of a bourgeois city of merchants. The ideas of courtly poetry are now more emphatically interpreted in their democratic overtones, and love is emphasized as a positive force in society, capable of entering any rustic spirit and creating an aristocracy not of birth or of wealth, but of sentiment and intellect. Troilus was the son of King Priam brought low by concupiscent love; Ameto is a poor, simple shepherd ennobled by Charity.

But one of the most significant aspects of the use of the pastoral setting in the *Ameto* is its establishment, through perspective, of a frame for narration. For the first time Boccaccio's favorite *topos,* the scheme of youths in a garden, is developed as the structure of an entire work, and not just an interlude as in the *Questions of Love*.[6] Here it becomes a significant poetic structure that is predicated on digressions and stories which then do not conflict with a narrative frame, as in the *Filocolo,* but rather are the frame's fulfillment. Each nymph is there to tell the story of her love; when that is not sufficient, as in the case of Lia, who loves Ameto and has little to tell, the tangential etiological myth of Florence still serves their purpose quite well. This narrative focus produces extreme diversity. The work is studded with pagan myths, stories in themselves, most of which are, or turn into, Christian allegory. The same is true of other narrative interludes such as the pastoral contest and the symbolic visions, as of cranes and swans, or virtues and vices, which are exemplifications of the moral purpose of the work. But into the midst of mythological, allegorical, and histori-cal narration a different kind of narrative strain insinuates itself. Agapes, who is unhappily married, tells of her elderly husband and his unpleasant antics in bed with a kind of physical and psychological portraiture that sharply contrasts with the abstract detail of the catalog of a garden or the canonic description of ladies.

He has moreover, and this disturbs me more, eyes more red than white, hidden under cavernous brows which are thick with long hairs; and they are continuously watering. His lips are drooping like those of the long-eared ass, and, colorless and pallid, they offer the sight of his teeth, ill-placed and yellow, in fact rather rusty and rotten, whose number is deficient in many points. And the thin neck hides neither bone nor vein; indeed trembling often with the whole head, it shakes the withered parts. (XXXII, 15)

When this elderly man, who has been given a young bride because of his wealth, is unable to fulfill the offices of Venus or "plough her garden" as she has told us, he compensates with conversation. He tells her of the feats performed for women when he was young, and lists reasons why she should be happy with an older husband, inveighing against those who transgress the holy laws of matrimony in adultery. This kind of portraiture contrasts with the abstraction of the main characters, who are virtues, and is an example of refined and malicious humor in an otherwise humorless work. It is in fact quite curious that the extraordinary humor of the *Decameron* has no precedent in the early works of Boccaccio. The only exception is this story, which is comparable to the *Decameron* for its ironic perspective on human reality. The story obviously stands out from the allegorical intent of the work. In fact the entire *Ameto* unfolds as a contrast between a horizontal dimension immersed in history and narration and a vertical aspiration to moral truth and edification. The contrast is often surprising. Mopsa, allegorically Wisdom, when unsuccessful in wooing her lover away from his boat, bends coquettishly so as to entice him with the sight of her bosom. It is also legitimate to wonder why ladies representing Christian virtues are telling stories of adulterous loves.

The discord between the literal and allegorical levels is pervasive. Ameto enjoys the sight of the nymphs in a wholly carnal sense, and their stories in a wholly aesthetic sense. Only at the end of the storytelling do we, and he, learn that these nymphs are not desirable maidens, but really virtues, and only then does Ameto suddenly understand that he did not desire them in the proper sense. "Similarly he sees who these nymphs are who had formerly pleased his eye more than his intellect and now please his intellect more than his eye" (XLVI,3). It might be argued, as Boccaccio does in the *Amorosa Visione,* that one must know vice so as to embrace virtue, but the *Ameto* seems to be more an example of sensual indulgence redeemed at the last minute by conversion, or truancy followed by recantation, than a persistent journey through vice to virtue. Although it is a Christian allegory of the conversion of the soul, the conclusion offers curious perspective on the ultimate significance of the work, which would seem to be as much historical as theological. This Christian allegory does not conclude with the conversion of Ameto. Instead it ends with violent historical realism, as quite abruptly we are hurled from the perspective of an idyllic interlude back into the context of the narrator's difficult situation in the city. It is significant that Boccaccio does not close the *Ameto* with the dedication to an abstract beloved or lovers, as is his custom; the only case in all his early fiction, he dedicates it to a real historical personage, his friend, the prominent Florentine citizen Niccolò di Bartolo del Buono. After the Christian conversion of Ameto, we are ultimately thrown back into the bitter reality of the city of Florence.

The *Ameto* embraces the diverse elements of the classical pastoral, medieval canons, the allegoric-didactic tradition and a glimpse of bawdy realism. All these divergent strains are held together in a strange tension; but this tension is partly created by a polarization which isolates the elements on different levels. It is to be expected then, that the works immediately following should be either more didactic or more realistic, more allegorical or more literal.

The *Amorosa Visione*

Following the *Ameto* in time and in conception we have the *Amorosa Visione*, which has been dated between the end of 1342 and the beginning of 1343.[7] The inspiration is again the moral-didactic vision literature of the Tuscan tradition. The "vision" as a means of elucidating transcendental truths came from both classical sources and Christian models,[8] but again the primary model for Boccaccio was Dante, who in the *Divine Comedy* had completely renewed the "vision" genre. In imitation of Dante, Boccaccio uses the technique of a journey in which he beholds famous figures. He also uses the *terzina,* which in his hands seems more to resemble the narrative *ottava,* as well as incorporating frequent echoes of Dante's poem.[9]

The *Amorosa Visione* is a poem of fifty cantos which purports to be an allegorical vision representing the salvation of the soul. It is constructed on a giant acrostic composed of the first letters of each *terzina,* which, when put together, form three sonnets of dedication. The first two are to Madama Maria or Fiammetta, and the third is to the reader. As the first canto opens, the narrator, in a dream, finds himself in a setting familiar to readers of the *Divine Comedy.* He is lost and fearful on a deserted shore, when a beautiful woman, dazzling with light, appears to him and promises to guide him to the supreme happiness. They begin their climb and arrive at the door of a noble castle wherein the poet sees two doors, one long and narrow leading to the virtuous life, and the other open and great, promising riches and earthly glory. Each door has a suitable inscription above (as in Dante's gate of Hell in *Inferno*), and while the guide urges him to pass through the narrow door, he beholds the wide one all aglow and ringing with festivity, and he begs to enter there. The ensuing contention between the poet and his guide (the poem is in the first person) reveals the tension of the work. " 'It is true, kind lady,' I answered, 'that I have seen the gifts as they were written, but I should like to see what it is to possess them. It is not a sin to know all the things of the world, one must just leave off the evil and keep the good'" (III,28–33). While the guide is insisting that earthly goods are fleeting and deceptive, two young men emerge from the wide door and urge him to enter. They even suggest to him truancy and recantation: "'Pleasure and delight, as many enjoy, lacks not here, after which you will yet have time to climb above in your later years'" (III,55–57).

The door of earthly delights prevails, and will prevail, throughout. First the pilgrims enter a room decorated with frescoes. This room is dedicated to the glorification of earthly goods. On each of the four walls are celebrated those who were famous on earth. The first wall shows Genius, and we behold Wisdom surrounded by great philosophers on one side and poets on the other. Curiously, for a Christian allegory, all the philosophers depicted are pagans, moving only as far up as Boethius and Avicenna. The same is true of the list of poets, except for Paulus Orosius and the most notable exception, Dante. Dante is depicted as celebrated by all the poets present, and the author himself offers a panegyric in which he claims Dante as the source of all his inspiration.

The second wall depicts power. Here, Boccaccio passes in review the great kings and warriors of ancient Greece and Rome, King Arthur and his knights, Charlemagne, Barbarossa, and finally Manfred. The third wall represents wealth, and, along with Midas, Nero, Dionysius, and King Robert of Anjou,[10] we also behold Boccaccio's father, though in a more generous light than in previous works. These figures are depicted as running frantically here and there, digging and filling chests with riches. We further note that while the author declares at the beginning that the walls were painted so beautifully and so like to nature that on earth only Giotto could have performed a similar feat,[11] the movement in his descriptions belies the perception of a painted image and seems more like the recording of real events, as in the journey of Dante.

Finally, on the last wall, Love is represented by Cupid and Venus, who is described according to Stilnovo conceits as a *donna angelicata*. Love, as the title indicates, is the subject of the work. It is a journey toward Christian love achieved through the knowledge of examples of the error of profane love. But the profane love never really becomes sacred and the examples become the narrative focus of the work. The author enjoys not only the passing sight of the heroes and heroines of the love stories of antiquity, but often dwells on their stories. He views Hercules and Deianira, and in a lengthy message he imagines Deianira exhorting Hercules to return to her.[12] When he comes to Dido and Aeneas, he dwells on their love and imagines an apostrophe by the abandoned Dido. After reviewing the ancient myths he jumps closer to his own time with Florio and Tristan. Then, as we emerge from this room, he turns to his guide in a burst of enthusiasm and says, " 'Oh how valuable it is . . . to have seen these things you said were so evil! How could one ever either think or hear more worthy things than these are, or more marvelous?' " (XXX,6–10).

Next they come to the second room, wherein is depicted Fortune and the vanity of earthly goods. Although this section is shorter, it treats a theme dear to Boccaccio that is the subject of two of his later works: the fragility of human glory and the fall of famous people. Here he beholds the fall of Thebes and Troy, of Alexander, Caesar, Nero, and many others. It is this vision, and neither his guide nor the examples of hazardous love, that finally convinces the poet and sets him on the right path. Now he tells his guide that he will follow her where she will, and at last they enter through the small door. There they find a *locus amoenus*, a garden with fountains and flowers, filled with lovely ladies. Some of the ladies are symbolic, dressed in colors representing virtues. Others represent Neapolitan and Tuscan nobility, identified by their coats of arms, in an allusive and allegorical pattern that recalls both the *Caccia di Diana* and the *Ameto*. At last the narrator beholds Fiammetta, the *donna angelicata* and the symbol of *Caritas*, and as he is dazzled by his love and the vision, he seems to embrace and kiss her. While they enjoy this moral loveplay, to the ecstasy of the narrator, he tells Fiammetta of his guide and his purpose in coming. She bids him follow the guide but not to forget her. The poet then runs to the severe lady who guides him and asks that she take him to Fiammetta and nowhere else, which the guide refuses, accusing him of indulgence in profane love. They argue, and to bolster his argument he denies the sensuality of his encounter with Fiammetta: " 'If I loved only to satisfy lustful desire, in truth you would be rightly angry; but on the contrary, I love, serve, and honor her goodness with that complete charity with which one must love one's neighbor' " (XLVII,67–82). After this declaration the guide recognizes

Fiammetta as an ally and the two women hail each other as virtues while the guide bequeaths the poet to Fiammetta. This, we expect, is his conversion or its beginning.

But then the two lovers find themselves alone in a deserted garden, and with all the secrecy of illicit and profane passion, the narrator says to himself: "'. . . I do not know what I am waiting for. Why, since I am here, do I not take from this woman the delights so painfully sought? The spot where we are now seated removes all suspicion, nor could she who was following us ever find us here, nor do I believe any other could disturb us. She is willing and I also desire, therefore why seek to delay further?'" (XLIX, 13–21). Once again, despite the allegory which has Fiammetta as *Caritas* and the poet as the Christian soul, the reader labors to capture the spiritual sense of the scene. Boccaccio is clearly enjoying the sensual description of the physical possession of a beloved woman. He draws near her as she sleeps. "I held her tight in my arms; a thousand times I think I kissed her before the beautiful angel awoke. But when awake, in confusion she began to say, 'What are you doing? Oh, do not! If that lady comes what shall you do?'" (XLIX, 25–30). She indeed seems more a lady misbehaving than the first of the Christian virtues. The lover begs and insists, and "Already the lady was quiet, humbly consenting and all disposed to my pleasure, when the soul, delighted with so much good, was filled with such joy that it could no longer be contained, but broke the sleep in which I was so happily dwelling . . ." (XLIX, 38–45). As he would possess her, he wakes. We are reminded, by contrast, that Dante's ultimate vision also fell away at the very moment of attainment, but it was quite a different vision altogether. When the guide promises the pilgrim that she will take him to the lady he has seen in his dream, and will satisfy his longing, he follows her. The voice of the poet then turns to the lady to whom the poem is dedicated, declaring that he has yet to write all that he will see by following her (the analogy is with Dante's *Vita Nuova*), but for the moment he is content if he has served his lady with the high praise due her.

The *Amorosa Visione* depicts profane concupiscence not sacred love. Sacred love seems left, implicitly, to the work the author promises will follow. The journey does not embody progress toward spiritual enlightenment, but is instead a cultural venture that dwells on episodes of myth and history framed by sensual love. The narrative expedient used here is not unlike the triumphal procession.[13] It is a form particularly suited to the narration of episodes and to an anthological array of culture which permits digressions and stories by passing in review famous figures. From the list of noblewomen in the *Caccia di Diana,* to the list of Greek heroes in the *Teseida,* to the more general review of ancient and modern figures in this work, to his later scholarly reviews of myths and famous men and women, the procession of civilization is a source of continuous inspiration to Boccaccio. Sacred love, on the other hand, dwindles in importance in the very work that is dedicated to it: the *Amorosa Visione* postpones the exposition of sacred love and dwells on more earthly considerations. Ameto was ultimately converted; the narrator of the *Amorosa Visione* is recalcitrant and must at best await a subsequent work.

The *Elegia di Madonna Fiammetta* [Fiammetta]

This short novel, written before 1345, is a new literary experience in the Boccaccio corpus. It embraces a narrative dimension and a psychological refinement never before attempted in his works. It is the epilogue to the story of Fiammetta, and her swansong, for the story of her love never appears again specifically. Here, by reversing the scheme of his story, Boccaccio changes perspective with a new literary elegance. The story of the love affair of the Neapolitan noblewoman with the Florentine merchant has heretofore been considered from the point of view of the rejected suitor. In the *Fiammetta* it is the lady who has been abandoned, and it is she who speaks, addressing herself to ladies in love. The result of this inversion is what has been called the first psychological novel of modern literature. Its first-person protagonist is certainly the progenetrix of novelistic heroines such as the Princesse de Clèves, Emma Bovary, and Anna Karenina, for the entire novel is the projection of the tormented psyche of a woman in love. We return to Naples. Fiammetta, a noble lady in that city, recounts the story of her adulterous love for Panfilo, a Florentine merchant. The ostensible plot of the novel is the simple story of her seduction and abandonment—how Panfilo won her, how they enjoyed the fulfillment of their love briefly, and how subsequently he abandoned her with the promise to return, leaving her to live a tormented existence suspended between anguish and hope. The real matter of the work is the delicate tracing of her states of mind.

The *Fiammetta* is a complex literary construct.[14] It is largely indebted to classical sources. There are frequent echoes of Seneca, Ovid, Virgil[15] and frequent references to ancient heroes and myths. All of chapter VIII is devoted to Fiammetta's comparison of her fate with that of ancient heroines, where in the pattern of a procession Dido, Medea, Myrrha, Deianira, and many others seem to pass before the crazed mind of Fiammetta with their suffering. These are some of the same heroines treated in the most important classical source for the *Fiammetta,* Ovid's *Heroides.* In the *Heroides* Ovid penetrates the psychological reality behind the great love stories of classical myths and imagines letters written by abandoned women to their lovers. But Boccaccio abandons the epistolary fiction of the *Heroides* and weaves a tightly structured fabric of literary styles calculated to explore fully the tormented psyche of just one woman.

The *Fiammetta* also has analogies in Dante's *Vita Nuova,*[16] which was always an important model for Italian prose. Like the *Vita Nuova* it is divided into nine books, and like the *Vita Nuova* it tells of the birth and development of love. But the *Fiammetta* is the *Vita Nuova* reversed. While Dante's love for Beatrice was sacred and exalting, Fiammetta tells of concupiscence and destructive adulterous love. With the familiar *topoi,* Fiammetta sits in church on Easter Saturday, and glories in the admiring glances of many men, when she catches the eye of one young man, particularly attractive, graceful, and well dressed. Solicitous of her reputation, she is at first impervious to love, but her pride is finally brought low and she says that "He had from me what he, just as I, most desired, though we pretended the contrary" (Ch.I,25). The nature of their love is physical. "Certainly, if this physical possession were my reason for loving him I would confess that each time it returned to my memory it was a pain like no other; but as God is my witness, this accident was, and is, only the smallest cause for the love I bear him; nonetheless, I do not deny that it was, then and now, most dear to me" (Ch.I,25).

As physical love it takes a physical toll, and Boccaccio reverses the exalted themes of courtly love and emphasizes those of devastation.

Love is not enlightening or ennobling, it is folly and pain. Nor is it the suitor who suffers at the hands of the lady, but rather the woman who bears the pain of rejection. The wealth and aristocracy of the lady are worthless and are leveled by the traditionally democratic force of love, and the sublime beauty of the lady disintegrates as Fiammetta is consumed to the point of unattractiveness. The didactic value of the *Fiammetta* is in its description of concupiscent love to a female audience as a caution to them concerning its consequences. Everything in the work is constructed to reflect not moral order but personal disorder.

Singularly effective in Boccaccio's portrayal of the unhappy Fiammetta is the restlessness and agitation of her mental state. First she seeks solitude in which to think about Panfilo, then company in which to be reminded of him, then again she returns to her room to be alone with her memories, or she reads his letters, or she asks her maid and confidant to speak of him, or again she goes out to look among his friends and then once again seeks to be alone. This frenetic movement is accompanied by a tumult of emotions and associative thought that is painfully acute. An episode provides a good example. One day, as Fiammetta sits in the company of nuns and other ladies in a convent she is visiting in the hope of forgetting Panfilo, a Florentine merchant happens upon the company. After a swift business transaction, they begin to converse while he is waiting to be paid, and one of the ladies present asks for news of Panfilo. The matter-of-fact indifference of the transaction and the frivolous conversation set a contrasting scene for the devastating news Fiammetta is about to hear: that Panfilo has taken a wife in his own city. Conversation ensues in rapid dialogue (used effectively for the first time in this work)[17] and describes a crescendo in tragedy for Fiammetta. But there are even more subtle complications. As Fiammetta is listening to this overwhelming news, she realizes that the woman asking the questions is equally interested and even more overcome. Her pain at hearing she has lost Panfilo is compounded and overridden by the sudden discovery and ensuing jealousy of a rival closer by, whose existence was unknown to her. When finally alone, Fiammetta indulges her desolation in anguished outcries and a torrent of contradictory thoughts. She imagines Panfilo making the same vows to his wife that he so sincerely made to her; that thought leads her to relive her seduction, when he surprised her in bed, which in turn leads her to imagine him criticizing her to his wife, just as he criticized others to her. With the thought of others she renews her jealousy of the woman she has just discovered to be Panfilo's mistress as well, and then she invokes him to return for the sake of the other woman, if not for her, finally concluding that her pain would be even greater were he to return. Then she reverses her thoughts and begins to rationalize: he had to marry to please his father, and of course, not all men love their wives. She passes her days in such thoughts, but nighttime enlarges and exacerbates all her woes, and in desperation she jumps from her bed, runs to the window, and invokes Venus to send Cupid to strike Panfilo with love for her, after which she invokes Sleep to overtake her and bring her peace. But even her sleep is agitated and full of unpleasant dreams, and soon her inner turmoil takes its toll and gives outward evidence. She has lost her appetite, she is thin and pale, her eyes have purple circles around them and seem enlarged. Her husband, unaware of the cause, notices her decline and takes her to Baia. But the frivolous entertainment of society there seems even more meaningless and discouraging. Fiammetta continues to vacillate, at the mercy of contradictory news and her own self deception until, in extreme despair, she wants to kill herself.

It has been observed that the "events" of the *Fiammetta* are "non events," that every action has another negating action. Panfilo is reported to be married, then not married; he is reported to be about to return to Naples, then someone else by the same name returns instead. This would seem to indicate that the real "events" are Fiammetta's state of mind, and Boccaccio's use of language corroborates this impression. In a careful juxtaposition of styles, which are not simple indirect narration but a weaving of monologues, dialogues, and apostrophes, Boccaccio pinpoints the frenzied vacillation of Fiammetta's psyche.[18] And the literary scheme becomes the final focus of the work, its denouement; for ultimately Fiammetta finds consolation in literature as she writes her story in order to glean compassion from her readers. By penetrating behind the conceits of passion and devoting his attention solely to concupiscent love, Boccaccio has fully revealed the hazards of love for pleasure. He has at the same time entered a hitherto uncharted terrain of narrative realism.

The *Ninfale fiesolano* [The Nymphs of Fiesole]

The last work preceding the *Decameron* is the *Ninfale fiesolano*,[19] a work in *ottava rima* which, like the *Fiammetta,* effectively integrates the author's early literary experiences. It is one of Boccaccio's most beautiful and accomplished works. He blends the sensitive observation of characters in love, especially the two protagonists Africo and Mensola, with an Ovidian and at the same time Florentine myth of the story of the origin of two rivers in Florence, Africo and Mensola. In the rarefied atmosphere of a simple country idyll he sketches the delicate emotions of two adolescents as they grapple with a passion that grows from sweet innocence to maturity and fruition and finally to desperation. The country boy Africo surprises the nymphs of Diana one day as they bathe on the hillside that will become Fiesole, and while watching unseen he falls in love with the nymph Mensola. He suffers with love for her—he cannot sleep, he loses his appetite, he feigns other causes for his suffering to his concerned parents—and finally he sets out to seek her in the woods. When he finds her and gives chase, she becomes frightened. She begins to run (uncovering her legs and thus increasing his ardor), and shoots an arrow at him, but misses her mark. She immediately regrets her act and is happy to realize that she did not hurt him; but she does not want him to pursue her and she runs off. Africo offers a sacrifice to Venus and the goddess promises aid and ultimate satisfaction in his love for Mensola. She advises him to dress as a nymph and join them. This he does, and he and Mensola seem soulmates as they participate in the nymphs' games. Finally the nymphs go to bathe, inviting Africo to join them. He waits until they are all undressed and in the water, calculating that thus they will be unarmed and unable to hurt him. When he undresses and reveals himself a man they all seize their clothes and flee, but he manages to retain Mensola, who gradually yields to his love, in the end with full abandon. Nonetheless, repenting of her weakness and afraid of Diana's vengeance, Mensola resolves never to see Africo again, and when she does not appear, he, out of desperation, kills himself, coloring the river with his blood and giving it his name. Mensola realizes that she is pregnant, and with the aid of a wise old nymph hides until her time is complete. She gives birth to a beautiful boy who fully resembles poor Africo. When she is discovered and cursed by Diana she flees, and in her flight is also changed into a river. Her son Pruneo is brought up tenderly by Africo's parents and becomes seneschal to Atalante, founder of Fiesole, and father of a noble line of citizens.

The *Ninfale* synthesizes in delicate equilibrium most of the elements common in Boccaccio's early works. Most essential, however, is its popular tone. Like the *Filostrato* it is modeled on the simple *cantare* tradition and is intended to tell a story to a broad public. The action is simple and rapid. There are literally no rhetorical passages, no long apostrophes or laments, no long exhibitions of erudition. Boccaccio's love for myth infuses the whole work, which is the creation of a myth, but myth offers no superficial adornment. Aside from the appearance of Cupid and Venus, and the brief mention of Diana and Callisto, seduced by Jove (a reference immediately reduced to simple familiarity by the myth of Mugnone, another Florentine river), there are virtually no classical references in this work. That the work was intended as a *cantare* is also evident in its technique. The author's voice is often present. As the story proceeds we find expressions such as "Now I shall return to the youth we left" (30) or "Let us return a little to Mensola" (328). On occasion he addresses his characters. As Girafone, Africo's father, prepares a bath to cure his son's hunting wounds, the narrator says, "Oh Girafone, you do not know how to medicate him . . ." (159). Or, he addresses his readers: "Lest you think that there were then palaces or houses as there are now" (40). And he applies the common *cantare* technique of foreseeing future events: "By Africo Mensola became pregnant with a little boy, of such great valor and virtue, such that surpassed all others of his time, as this story further on at the end will clearly relate" (311). He also uses rustic similes, as the *cantari* did, to describe people or actions. The result is a homey simplicity. Africo apostrophizes Mensola in a passage where both the psychology and the language are crude, and the metaphors are meant quite literally: "If you flee you are more cruel than the mother bear when she has borne her cubs, you are more bitter than bile and harder than marble stones; if you await me you are sweeter than honey, than the grapes that yield sweet wines, and more than the sun you are lovely and enticing, soft and white, humble and pleasing" (104). Equally suited to the popular tone is the language the author chooses. It is the language of the simple and uneducated and has the distinct flavor of dialect to be heard in the Tuscan countryside.[20]

As a pastoral, the *Ninfale* represents a new equilibrium. As Africo seeks Mensola in the woods we are often reminded of his predecessor Ameto seeking Lia, likewise in the hills of Florence. But unlike Ameto, Africo's love is simple and direct physical passion with no moral overtones. The complex mixture of pastoral and history in the *Ameto* has here been distilled into total immersion in nature. The pastoral setting is not juxtaposed with the city as a form of escape, but instead is all embracing and includes the city by including its mythic foundations. The city of the *Ameto* was generic and included many cities. The *Ninfale* represents a more elemental attachment to Florence and to its myths. And though the story tells of the powerful love of Africo and Mensola, and the contrast between Venus and Diana, it ends with the history of Fiesole and Florence as handed down from generation to generation. It is equally clear, from the essential elements of this myth as Boccaccio tells it, that it is rooted in bourgeois society.[21] Instead of a mythic play of cosmic forces, what emerges is a bourgeois myth of love, maternity, the home and the family, a story of simple domestic sentiments. Africo's parents, Girafone and Alimena, are the backdrop against which he lives through his tragic love for Mensola. They are ever present to comfort and warn him with tender parental intuition. When he refuses to admit the cause of his suffering and says he is downcast because he could not catch a deer he wanted, his father understands his veiled speech and warns him against such deer with a family example, his grandfather Mugnone turned into a river for similar hunting. Mensola as well, for all her confusion and grief, is redeemed from her tragedy by the arousal of maternal sentiments. After the morally and physically painful ordeal of childbirth, she finds herself, almost by surprise, mother of a delightful child, and she begins to care for and caress him in enjoyment of her newly discovered maternity. Just as the tragedy of these starcrossed lovers is redeemed by the family, so is the family ultimately redeemed in terms of the polis; the infant Pruneo is returned to his grandparents, who feel they have Africo back once again, and is raised to become a major figure in the founding of the city.

The portrayal of the characters of Africo and Mensola, especially Mensola, is noteworthy. This aspect raises the *Ninfale* high above the general level of the *cantari,* where physical and psychological description were virtually unknown. Mensola is a delicate mixture of doubts and contrary emotions. The conflict arises from her vows of virginity and dedication to Diana and the irrepressible force of nature which draws her to Africo. When she shoots the arrow at Africo she is immediately sorry, then glad she has not hit him, then insistent again that he not chase her. After she has finally surrendered to Africo, she vacillates between familiarity and hostility, refusing at first to submit to him again, as if to undo what has already been done. Finally she not only gives in, but promises to return. At the same time she tries to annul this concession by refusing to leave Diana, and pretending nothing has happened. When she has left Africo she debates returning to him and decides ultimately against it, as if to expiate her sin. She thus precipitates his suicide. Mensola, portrayed with tender affection as caught between the profane Venus and the sacred Diana, between nature and society, is one of Boccaccio's most effective characters.

With the *Ninfale fiesolano* we are at the eve of the *Decameron.* In the primacy of action, economy of means, suitability of language, sensitivity to complex emotions, use of metaphor and capacity for quick and powerful narration we begin to behold the predominantly narrative focus that will be revealed in the *Decameron.*

Chapter Four

The *Decameron*

In the years following his return to Florence Boccaccio actively entered Florentine life both intellectually and politically. He developed friendships with the Tuscan lyric poets Sennuccio del Bene and Franceschino degli Albizzi, with the authors of popular literature in Italian Antonio Pucci, Giovanni Villani, and Franco Sacchetti, and with the humanists Mainardo Accursio and Bruno Casini. These contacts reflect the facets of his literary interests and probably served to confirm his adherence to the school of Dante and the Stilnovo, to renew his commitment to popular literature in Italian, and to stimulate his interest in the new intellectual circle that was gathering around Petrarch. Probably in this period Boccaccio wrote the *De vita et moribus domini Francisci Petracchi* [Life of Petrarch], the first major document of his lifelong admiration for Petrarch in which he hailed him alongside the greatest of classical authors. The government of Florence also entrusted him with various missions to other states and nations, and his success in these added prestige as a diplomat to his reputation as a man of letters. One mission of literary importance was in the year 1345–46 to Ravenna at the court of Ostasio da Polenta, where he may have tried to gather more information about the last years of Dante.

More important at this time were his translations of the Third and Fourth *Decades* of Livy. Thanks to Petrarch's enthusiasm and attention to the text, the works of Livy were of growing interest to his intellectual circle. Translations were desirable, and with Boccaccio's stature and experience in both the classics and Italian, he was a likely person to undertake such a venture. The two *Decades* seem to have been translated at different times, but there is evidence that they both can be attributed to Boccaccio. Similarities of style, the dedication of the Fourth *Decade* to Ostasio da Polenta, Boccaccio's host at the time, and the attribution to Boccaccio of translations of Livy by an early biographer all support this thesis.[1] The experience as a translator was a valuable experience that undoubtedly helped to form the "Latinized" syntax and rhythm that distinguish his prose in Italian.

We next find him with Francesco Ordelaffi in 1347 in the city of Forlì, where he began his association with Donato Albanzani, in later years a most devoted friend to both Petrarch and Boccaccio. In this period he began a correspondence in Italian (*Rime* XXXIX) and Latin verse (*Buc. Carm.* I,II) with Checco di Meletto Rossi, secretary to Ordelaffi. These Latin poems were the first of a series of eclogues written sporadically through the following years and ultimately collected as the *Buccolicum Carmen*.

In the spring of 1348 the plague struck Florence. The Black Death of 1348 was one of the greatest disasters ever to hit Europe.[2] Indeed, according to the figures of historians of the time,[3] the prosperous city of Florence (population estimated at 100,000) was reduced by half. The outcome of this devastating period for Boccaccio was the death of many dear ones: Villani, Casini, Albizzi, Sennuccio, and more important, his stepmother and then his father. Boccaccio was in Florence at the time, and remained there, now head of the family, to administer his modest inheritance and the tutelage of his stepbrother. At this juncture, approximately between the years 1349 and 1353, Boccaccio wrote the greatest of his works, the *Decameron*.

The *Decameron*

As is evident from the Greek title, the work is structured around the number ten. It is a collection of one hundred short stories told by ten youths in ten days. Following a pattern set by Martianus Capella, Boethius, Bernard Silvestris and more immediately Dante, the work intersperses prose and verse, but the prose constitutes the essential text and the poems or ballads have mostly an ornamental function.

The *Decameron* begins with a Proem. Recognizing that for him the flames of love have already subsided, the author nonetheless feels dutybound to make his contribution to humanity out of gratitude for the help offered him by friends in moments of amorous suffering. Since those same friends have no need of his help if they were able to help him, he will offer it to those who seem most in need, namely the idle ladies. For while men, when they are lovesick, can hunt, fish, ride, or do business and thus distract their minds from melancholy thoughts at least for a while, women are confined to their chambers and restrained by the wills of fathers, brothers, and husbands. Therefore, in the case of women in love, the only women that interest him, he says, their thoughts cannot help but be melancholy. He thus dedicates his work to the idle ladies to offer them both amusement and useful advice as to what to seek and what to avoid, while helping them to pass the time. An introduction follows, beginning with a powerfully realistic description of the plague. His record of the course of the disease, from the appearance of boils in the armpits or groin to the virtually inevitable death that followed three days later, is one of the most complete and authoritative descriptions we have of the Black Death.[4] In the wake of the pestilence came the total breakdown of social and normative structures, a disintegration carefully recorded by Boccaccio. Some people thought it best to keep to their houses, to avoid all human contact and all indulgence in luxury; others felt that carousing and feasting were the only course to take in face of such disaster, and still others abandoned all family and possessions and simply fled the city. Thus brother forsook brother, husband wife, and even parents their children. Nor were the dead given proper burials or ceremonies, but rather were heaped together like so many carcasses. "And the affliction and misery of our city had become so great that the venerable authority of the laws, both human and divine, was debased and almost completely dissolved because the ministers and executors of such were all, like other men, either dead, or ill, or so bereft of assistants, that they could perform no office. Wherefore, it was permitted to each man to do as he pleased" (I,Intro.,23).

In this situation, one Tuesday morning, three noble young men and seven noble young ladies, all related to, or acquainted with each other, happen to meet in the church of Santa Maria Novella. They discuss their plight, and one of the ladies, Pampinea, observes that he who honestly uses his reason does no wrong; and wherefore natural reason dictates that each human being must defend himself, it is appropriate that they flee the plague-ridden city and preserve their own lives. They agree to remove to a villa in the hills of Florence,[5] where they will establish their own society and await the subsiding of the pestilence. This they do, installing themselves in a luxurious setting enhanced by servants, fine food, wines, music, and all manner of pleasure. They design to pass their time in refined enjoyment, walking, singing, dancing, talking, and finally decide to give a certain order to their days by withdrawing into the shade of an idyllic garden during the hot midday where they can tell stories to pass those hours when it would be folly to go about. Thus the *Decameron* achieves the full development of the *topos* of noble youths telling stories in an idyllic garden (*locus amoenus*) that was sketched in Boccaccio's earlier works.

The ten youths agree that a king or queen will be elected each day to determine the topic of the day's storytelling and govern the activities of that day. Pampinea, the queen of the First Day, decrees that the theme be free. Filomena, for the Second Day, chooses the fortunes of those who ultimately attain unexpected felicity after many misadventures. Neifile, on the Third Day, elects the fortune of those who acquired a much desired thing with effort, or, having lost it, recover it. The Fourth Day is known as the tragic day, for the melancholy Filostrato chooses the theme of those whose loves had a disastrous end. Fiammetta on the Fifth Day chooses the good fortune of lovers after various misadventures, and Elissa for the Sixth chooses those who have avoided loss, danger, or scorn by some witty remark. On the Seventh Day Dioneo, the ribald rogue of the group, chooses stories of tricks played by ladies on their husbands for love or deliverance from danger, and whether or not the husbands detected them. The Eighth Day, under Lauretta, is devoted to tricks people play on one another, and the Ninth, under Emilia, is once again a day whose theme is free. The Tenth Day, under Panfilo, treats those who have acted with liberality or magnanimity, at the end of which the company conclude their sojourn and the author offers his conclusion.

The youths who compose this company are a delicate balance between real people and symbols. They seem akin to the nymphs of the *Ameto,* who represent specific ladies of Florence as well as abstract virtues, for they appear emblematic of qualities: Dioneo, the most fully portrayed, is pleasure-seeking and witty, Filostrato is serious and somber, Emilia is wistful and shy, Pampinea is wise and serene.[6] We do not know who they actually were, but in hints of family relationships and ownership of the villas the company occupies, we sense some historical reality behind them. At the same time they are functions of the stories. Unlike Chaucer's pilgrims in the *Canterbury Tales*, who are often more interesting than their stories, here the focus is on the tales, and the tellers remain in the background.

It is curious, however, that relatively few of the tales are original. Boccaccio declares this himself in his conclusion: ". . . but even if we did want to suppose that I was both the inventor and writer of these stories, which I am not . . ." (Concl. 17), and the narrators in the group indicate that they are drawing from a common stockpile of well-known material. In the Sixth Day Elissa declares that during the day's narration, two of the stories she wanted to tell have been taken from her by other members of the group (VI,9,3). Yet despite the painstaking efforts of numerous scholars, very few specific sources have been identified for the stories.[7] Most seem to be freely rendered from the vast medieval repertory of stories, romances, anecdotes, and parables derived from Oriental, Greek, Latin, biblical, and French sources, and many seem to develop from local chronicle.[8] Boccaccio sweeps from the bawdy, bourgeois, anticlerical spirit of the *fabliaux* to the didactic and edifying tone of the moral *exempla*, transfiguring his varied sources to conform to his own exigency of telling a good story. Because the themes of each day are essentially principles of organization (many stories could be subsumed under several of the themes) we will direct our discussion not to an analysis of the stories day by day, but to a consideration of what we believe to be some of the underlying messages of the work.[9]

What is most striking about the *Decameron* is that it is conceived wholly in terms of terrestrial reality. The tension with theological didacticism and with classical erudition is gone; gone also is any kind of personal vehemence or emotion. Boccaccio's narrator states in his Proem that for him the flames of love have subsided and his aim is now to help those in need. The tone he adopts for this is one of bemused attention to the remarkable variety of life on earth. The *Decameron* is a broad lens on a particular society, an open work that defies characterization as "moral" or "immoral," "Medieval" or "Renaissance." There are stories that delight and stories that teach; many do both and some do neither. It does not appear to hide dogmatic allegorical messages,[10] for the powers Boccaccio sees behind this real world are not transcendental virtues, but immanent forces, not divine love, but Nature. And men do not achieve their destiny through a Christian ascent to God, rather they suffer the capricious whims of the earthbound figure of Fortune. With the reality of this world determined by the morally neutral forces of Nature and Fortune, positive existence is predicated on intelligence and enhanced by creativity. One of the fruits of wit and creativity is the work of art which must create and obey its own laws; and just as the artist devises his work, so can men influence their lives with artistic flourish. The prime instrument of this creativity in Boccaccio's *Decameron* is language, a creative force applied in life as well as narration.

Instead of considering the virtue of the Church, Boccaccio chooses the virtue of the layman; rather than contemplate the individual who encounters a preordained design in this and the next world, he observes autonomy and self-determination in life on earth; for social stratification based on birth, or even wealth, he substitutes an underlying democratic order based on wit and love; and for the work of art as an essentially didactic instrument he substitutes a work created on its own terms (in this case, narration) and dedicated to utility, but above all to pleasure. The results are, as members of the company declare at the outset, honest pleasure, which for the reader can be both amusing and edifying.

The framework. The primary instrument of the moral and aesthetic suppositions of the *Decameron* is what is commonly referred to as the framework, meaning specifically the placing of the storytelling in an idyllic setting removed in space and time from plague-ridden Florence. In grouping his stories within a framework Boccaccio is first of all obeying an artistic imperative of order. It helps to organize the stories, to comment upon them, and to give the author control of his material. But Boccaccio is using this principle of order in a much more stunning manner, for it is also a principle of perspective.[11] He is controlling our perception of the stories and guiding us to read them as works of art intended for enjoyment. The framework is meant to do for the stories what a frame does for a painting, namely isolate it as an object of beauty.[12] Boccaccio does this first in the Proem by dedicating the stories to idle ladies for their pleasure and then in the Introduction by removing the youths and their tales from the possibility of moral judgment.

The intentional portrayal of society in the plague as having lost all civil and moral order places this small company beyond conventional criteria of right and wrong. In this perspective, the miniature society of noble youths is determining, and it is organized in terms of honest pleasure. Upon arrival at the villa, Dioneo gives the tone: ". . . I do not know how you intend to dispose of your cares; as for me, I left mine within the gates of the city whence I came a short while ago with you" (I,Intro.93). And Pampinea's reasoning in proposing storytelling is wholly based on the greatest pleasure for the greatest number:

As you see the sun is high and the heat great, and nought is to be heard but the cicadas in the olive trees, wherefore to repair elsewhere at this moment would be foolhardy. Here it is cool and pleasant and there are, as you see, game tables and chess boards and each can enjoy himself as he deems most delightful. But if you want to follow my advice, we should pass this hot part of the day not in games, in which the loser is vexed while neither the winner nor the onlookers glean great pleasure, but in storytelling, which, as one person narrates, gives pleasure to all. (I,Intro.110–11)

In this manner the narrator establishes his freedom and creates a particular vantage point. The framework removes him from social, moral, and literary conventions, and within its space he devises a form which reflects values akin to the dynamic optimism and practicality that dominated a bourgeois mercantile society.

The Merchant World and Realism.   The realism of the *Decameron,* acknowledged by all generations of critics, stems from the mercantile society that emerged in the late Middle Ages. These hundred stories have been called "the mercantile epic"[13] because they focus on the activities of everyday life and reveal the openness and fluidity of social and moral structures that were a result of the economic thrust of the commercial revolution.[14] The importance of the sea,[15] and the mobility of characters over the Mediterranean area through the intervention of pirates, wars, crusades, or their own personal drive to seek their fortune or change their destiny, reflect the vital flux of commerce. The picaresque rhythm of Greek and medieval romances and the archetypal narrative patterns with origins probably in Oriental sources (for example, mistaken identities and recognition scenes) are among the techniques particularly suited to the representation of this flux. Families are divided by strokes of Fortune and the necessities of trade. Therefore Andreuccio (II,5) can believe he is recognizing a long-lost sister, or conversely Madam Beritola (II,6) or Griselda (X,10) can be in the presence of their children and not know them. More specifically, the mercantile realism of the *Decameron* is based on the society of Florence. Boccaccio is representing areas important to Florentine cloth trade and banking in the great diversity of cities and lands—Rome, Naples, Bologna, Lombardy or Northern Italy, Sicily, France, England, Flanders, Greece, Arabia.[16]

The flow of mercantile adventure is counterpoised with a more homespun dimension, for the burgher's mentality of concreteness and plausibility in which Boccaccio immerses his stories yields rich detail about life in this period and a new measure of realism in literature.[17] In the story of Simona and Pasquino (IV,7) we behold the organization of wool manufacture as the companies distribute the prepared wool to spinners and then pick it up and deliver it elsewhere to be woven. Dioneo (VIII,10), in telling how the Tuscan merchant Salabaetto was tricked out of all his money by a Sicilian lady and then tricked her into returning the same amount and more, describes the organization of docks, deposits, and customs in merchant ports, as well as sensuous details of the wiles and charms used by a prostitute to enchant her victim. Indeed, every character has a name and there is archival evidence that most really existed, though the tales are not in most cases biographical.[18] Boccaccio weaves stories around historical figures close to him in time such as Charles of Anjou, Boniface VIII, Gian di Procida, Giotto, and countless others. Several stories appear to be based on anecdotes or events that were part of life in Florence. The entire Sixth Day and large parts of the Eighth and Ninth take place in Florence and its environs. In these stories, for most of which no standard source has been found, we seem to close in on daily life in this mercantile center. We see the haughty genius of Guido Cavalcanti

(VI,9), the gluttony of Ciacco and the wrath of Filippo Argenti (IX,8) as recorded also by Dante, the proverbial ugliness of the Baronci (VI,6), the gullibility of Calandrino, and the endless resourcefulness of Buffalmacco and his friends (VIII,3,6,9;IX,3,5). Boccaccio also provides detail, particularly for Florence and Naples, on houses, civic monuments, clothing and the appurtenances of daily life. Despite their sources then, the stories of the *Decameron* are wholly immersed in history that is, with few exceptions (only V,1;VII,9;IX,9;X,8 are set in ancient times), contemporary, or nearly contemporary to Boccaccio.

But the stories have more than just a circumstantial basis in real time and space. They unfold within a totally practical attitude regarding human motivation and the meaning behind events. With a wry smile of indulgence, Boccaccio views all human affairs as having an underpinning of explicable causes. The practical natural reason that brought the group of storytellers to the country is the lens through which life is projected. Simona and Pasquino are together in a garden (IV,7). The simpleminded Pasquino rubs a sage leaf on his teeth to show Simona its hygienic qualities and dies. When he is followed by the even simpler Simona, who does the same to illustrate his action and also dies, we are not left with the tragedy of inexplicable death (indeed none of the stories in Fourth Day is really tragic for this reason) for the sage bush is dug up and a venomous toad is discovered underneath. When Monna Giovanna's son, who is ill for desperately wanting Federigo's falcon, finally dies (V,9), the author comments that it was "either from melancholy because he could not have the falcon, or for his illness which would have brought him to such an end anyway." The same realistic eye is cast on human motivations. When Gilbert hears that his wife, Dianora, has required a garden in January from Messer Ansaldo before granting him her favors, and that Ansaldo has produced such a garden, he insists that she keep her promise and go to him, not only because he is a man of honor, but also because he fears the revenge of Ansaldo, and the arts of Ansaldo's necromancer, should she refuse (X,5).

The practical realism of this merchant society, with all its social and moral implications, is yoked to a nostalgia for the ideals of an old feudal world, with which it is sometimes in conflict.[19] One of the most

insistent themes is the contrast between an abstract, aristocratic view of
love and the economic imperatives of new wealth, or, in other words,
the conflict between love and money. We see many a high born but
impoverished young lady married to a bourgeois but wealthy man,
with the consequent antagonism. "She, therefore, finding herself, of
high lineage, married to a wool manufacturer, and being unable to
mitigate her scorn, since she esteemed no man of low birth, however
rich he might be, worthy of a noble woman; and seeing that still, with
all his wealth, he was capable of nothing more than devising a mixed
cloth, or preparing a fabric or discussing thread with a weaver, decided
to refuse his embraces . . ." (III,3,6).

Older men, with their wealth, can buy pretty young wives, as does
the elderly judge of Pisa, Riccardo di Chinzica (II,10). But, Boccaccio
reminds us with an amused smile, Nature is more potent than money,
and Riccardo's wife, annoyed with her elderly husband's excuses of
religious holidays so as not to tax his failing strength in sexual endeavors, runs away with the younger and more able Paganino. And
love, even purely physical love, is not to be sullied with money, as
Boccaccio told us in the *Teseida,* where he said love for money was more
like hate. One of the cleverest and nastiest tricks of the *Decameron* is that
played by the German soldier Gulfardo (VIII,1) on Ambruogia, when
he discovers that she wants money in exchange for her love. The trick is
born of his disappointment at her baseness and consists of his borrowing
the money she wants from her husband, giving it to her in exchange for
her favors, and then announcing to the husband, in the presence of his
wife, that he has given to her the money he owed the husband.

Nature and Fortune.   The forces behind this world of merchants are Nature and Fortune; it is they that govern the terrestrial
realm.[20] Pampinea calls them "the two ministers of the world"
(VI,2,3–6). We see that Nature is the very basis of the *Decameron* right
from the Introduction, for it is Nature, which is morally neutral, that
produces both the plague and the idyllic pastoral setting to which the
group withdraws, in keeping with man's most basic virtue, "natural
reason." Boccaccio further couples the meaning of his framework with
the force of Nature in the Introduction to the Fourth Day. In this
section he uses the framework to defend himself from supposed criti-

cisms of his licentious stories.[21] The defense answers to several accusations: that he is too fond of ladies, that he praises them, that he is too old to devote himself to such nonsense, that he should rather spend his time with the Muses, that he should worry about earning a living and not waste time with literature, and that his stories do not conform to fact. The accusations are serious, but Boccaccio answers them with irrepressible humor.[22] He is fond of ladies and always has been, he says; and his age means nothing, for like the leek, though its head be white, the tail is green. Moreover, respectable men such as Guido Cavalcanti, Dante, and Cino da Pistoia also offered pleasure to ladies in their works. As for the Muses, the Muses after all are ladies, so in weaving his tales he does not stray too far from Mount Parnassus. Furthermore, ladies have inspired him to write thousands of verses, but the Muses nary a one. And those who worry about his income, need not, since he is not reduced to begging bread.

To defend his right to serve ladies Boccaccio tells a story well known in his day. The Florentine citizen Filippo Balducci, a widower with a small son, decides to devote himself and his son to the service of God and thus withdraws to a hermit's life outside of Florence. He is careful to raise the child in holy worship, far from all worldly vanity. When the son is eighteen, seeing that his father is aging and ill-fit for the journey he periodically makes to Florence on business, he proposes that the father take him to the city and show him what need be done so he can relieve his father of this chore. Balducci judges that by now, the son's character is so well established that the city ought not afford any temptation for him; thus they make their journey to Florence. The young hermit is fascinated by everything—palaces, churches, houses—and he plies his father with questions. But as they walk they pass a group of women, particularly beautiful because they are dressed for a wedding, and the son immediately questions his father about them. The father admonishes him to look away, for they are evil, and hoping to mitigate their power by calling them by another name, he says they are goslings. "Wonderful to tell! the lad, who had never seen one before, forgetting the palaces, the oxen, the horses, the donkeys, the money, and all else that he had seen, immediately said: 'Father, please let me have one of those goslings'" (IV,Intro.,24). The young man does not comprehend how evil things can be so beautiful, for they are even more beautiful, he says, than the painted angels his father had so often showed him. " 'Oh' he says, 'if you love me, please let us take one of these ducks up there and I will give her some pecking.' And the father said: 'I will not; you do not know whence they peck!' and he suddenly realized that *nature was more potent than his art* and he regretted having brought the boy to Florence" (IV,Intro.28–29; italics mine). The "moral" of this story contains perhaps the overriding theme of the *Decameron*. Nature is omnipotent, and all moral or social constriction against Nature is doomed to failure. Nor should one even try, the author says. ". . . I and others who love you ladies act naturally, to whose laws, that is of Nature, whosoever wants to offer opposition would need powers too great, and oftentimes would work not only in vain but to his own serious disadvantage. Such powers I confess that I do not have, nor in this case, do I wish to have them; and if I had them I would lend them to others rather than use them for myself" (IV,Intro.41–42).

The sources of Boccaccio's conception of Nature are complex, but it is probably fair to say that Nature is equatable predominantly with Eros, as the story of Filippo Balducci illustrates. Eros in turn is most frequently the sexual drive, but not always. The love for an exalted woman that derives from courtly tenets and their Christian counterparts, which was so much an inspiration for Boccaccio's early works, also has its place in these stories. But if Nature is Eros, Eros must then be reintegrated in Nature as the instrument of fertility, for the sexual drive is part of man's participation in a natural order. It is a primordial force meant to guarantee the preservation of the species, and as such it has no moral valence. In the *Romance of the Rose,* the great allegory of the thirteenth century which influenced so many succeeding works, including those of Boccaccio, Jean de Meun describes Nature thus: "Dame Nature . . . forges . . . individual entities to save the species' continuity against the assaults of Death, who ne'er attains the mastery, no matter how he speeds, so many reinforcements she creates . . ." (77,1591ff.).[23] In this context, the many restrictions imposed by the Church or social convention (as with an old man married to a young woman, source of many mismarriages and comic adventures in the

Decameron) defy not only the laws of human appetite, but contravene a basic order intended to insure survival. And the question of survival is vital to the whole situation of the *Decameron* which takes place in the midst of a plague. We recall that in arguing for withdrawal from plague-ridden Florence (or death) to the countryside, Pampinea defined "natural" reason as self-preservation.

Love as the driving force of the natural order is overwhelming and incoercible. Neifile declares that ". . . among the other natural things, that which least admits advice or constraining action is Love, whose nature is such that it is more likely to consume itself than to be mitigated by any action" (IV,8,4). Most important to the natural order is the fact that the proper time for love is youth, albeit Boccaccio does not exempt the more mature from the effects of Love's darts, and the young are repeatedly pitted against the old to recall this lesson to them. Giannotto is a nobleman, though this is unknown to all, and has fallen in love with the noble Spina. He thus defends their love to her father: ". . . I committed that sin which is part of youth and which, should we try to remove it therefrom, we would have to remove youth itself; and this fact, if the old wanted to recall having once been young themselves and wanted to measure their faults with that of others and that of others with theirs, would not seem so serious as you and others make it" (II,6,54).

Because the laws of Nature, or Love, are ironclad, the virgin or the ascetic violates Nature. Far from punishing the lustful with eternal torments as Dante did with Francesca da Rimini, Boccaccio, in one of the rare stories that mention the afterlife, shows a woman who had refused to yield to a lover on earth being punished into eternity (V,8). The punishment is that she is eternally rent apart, eaten by dogs, and resurrected, only to begin the process again, for *not* having given her love to a lover.[24] We have already seen how futile were the attempts of Filippo Balducci in constraining the instincts of youth in the name of religious zeal. For Boccaccio the greatest offender in this sense is the Church. Nuns, priests, hermits, and the religious in all garb are targets for merciless satire and downright diatribes, not only for their corruption but because of the impossibility of their kind of virtue. Even in the lives of lay persons the Church is placed as antagonistic to Nature, for sexual abstinence is invariably in the name of religious commitment. The elderly but rich Riccardo di Chinzica (II,10), married to a young but poor maiden whom he cannot satisfy sexually, makes his excuses by alleging holidays and saints' days as a reason for abstinence most of the year. And there are numerous other such religiously inspired husbands whose spiritual bent gives their wives desired opportunities with other men.

Of course Boccaccio also heaps his sarcasm and humor on the practices of the clergy themselves. In the Third Day (III,10), the licentious Dioneo tells what is probably the most obscene story in the *Decameron,* constructed on one sustained religious metaphor, in which the practices of hermits are brutally satirized. Alibech, a naive fourteen-year-old girl in the city of Capsa (Tunisia), decides on an impulse to become a Christian and is told that the most acceptable way to serve God is to become a hermit. She repairs to the desert and tries to enlist the aid of various hermits, but because of her beauty and their fear of temptation, she is turned away. Finally she comes to Rustico, who allows her to come into his hut as a trial to his constancy. But he soon abandons this plan, and finding that she is as innocent and as simpleminded as she seems, he proceeds to seduce her. He has them both undress and kneel to pray, and when he undergoes the "resurrection of the flesh" he explains that he has the devil, that she has Hell, and what most pleases God is putting the devil into Hell. After some initial discomfort, Alibech begins to enjoy herself and claims to understand now the words of those holy men in Capsa who said that the service of God was sweet. In fact, she often admonishes Rustico for being slothful, for after all, she has come to serve God, not to remain idle. Poor Rustico, who lives on herbs and water, is hardput to satisfy her religious zeal, so when Neerbale comes from the city to take her home and marry her for her inheritance, Rustico is much relieved. When Alibech tells the ladies in the city how she served God, all laugh and assure her she will be able to persevere with her religious devotion in the city as well. The expression becomes proverbial and Dioneo enjoins the ladies of the company to serve God in like manner.

Boccaccio's criticism of the clergy derives in some measure from popular sources. The *fabliaux* and popular poetry were full of less than

virtuous clergymen; likewise a major work such as the *Romance of the Rose,*
along with sermons and treatises, resounds with the same righteous
indignation and diatribes against the hypocrisy of priests. Yet
Boccaccio seems even more determined than most to execrate this
portion of society. The introduction to the story of Frate Alberto (IV,2),
a priest who is ultimately caught and punished for seducing a vain and
foolish Venetian lady, expresses the wish that the same punishment
might be called down upon all lying priests. And with wry irony,
following the only story in the *Decameron* about a clergyman who acted
virtuously (X,2), all members of the group judge such an example
nothing short of a miracle.

The state of the Church is summed up in the second story of the
Decameron. Giannotto di Civignì, worried about the salvation of the
soul of his dear friend Abraham the Jew, tries in all possible guises to
convert him to Christianity. Abraham resists, but finally concedes that
he will convert only after he has been to Rome to see Christ's vicar on
earth and his brothers, the cardinals, and has studied their habits and
behavior. At this, Giannotto, familiar with the corruption of the
Church, despairs to himself of ever converting his friend. But Abraham
goes, and returns, and declares that he is now ready to convert. To
Giannotto's surprise, he affirms that if the Christian faith can survive
and prevail despite the diligent efforts of its representatives to disobey
its every rule, it must be the true faith. The Church is corrupt because
the practices it requires are contrary to Nature, which transcends all
human instruments. By the same token it is important to observe that
Boccaccio is anticlerical but not anti-Catholic. As in this story, the
Church grandly survives the corruption of its priests.

The handmaiden of Nature is Fortune. The figure of Fortune,
particularly compelling for Boccaccio and recurrent in all his works, is a
personification of the human condition. It embodies the difficulty of
juxtaposing man's vitality and capacities against a background of
inscrutable and uncontrollable forces.[25] For Boccaccio the rotating
wheel of mercantile fortune was ever present in repeated instances of
fortunes quickly made and lost, including the example of his father,
who suffered many upsets in the precipitous events of those years. He
also had occasion to contemplate political fortunes, which he will deal

with later in a letter to Pino de' Rossi. Finally, Fortune will appear codified and catalogued in his later works, the *De casibus* and the *De-mulieribus,* which treat mostly the misfortunes of famous men and women.

In the face of mutable Fortune, man's virtue on this earth consists in perceiving matters as they are, and in applying his intelligence or wit so as to understand the machinations of Fortune, or of Nature, and use them to his advantage. This is the "art of living."[26] The artist's narrative is a means of doing the same, for when faced with the plague, a hard blow from both Nature and Fortune, the group withdraws to the country to tell stories within a framework devised to guarantee their narration. Within the work, from the consummate performance in the first story of Ciappelletto, who actively invents his identity and his destiny in the face of adversity, to the last story of the extreme submission of Griselda, who devises her destiny from humility and passivity, we find a series of lessons about man's ability to act on earth when confronted by Fortune's whims.

A good example of this, again within the bosom of the Church, is Masetto da Lamporecchio. Masetto hears of a job as a gardener in a convent, and hoping to have the job and enjoy the nuns as he pleases, he feigns dumbness. He is immediately hired, not only because he is strong and hardworking, but because, being dumb, he will not waste time chatting with the nuns. Two of the nuns, curious to experience the quality of the male animal, seduce the willing Masetto, and followed shortly after by their sisters, they all come to an agreement to share him, unbeknown to the abbess. But one day the abbess herself beholds Masetto asleep in the garden (for he labored so much by night that he could work very little by day), and seeing him all uncovered, she falls prey to the same desire. She closets herself with him, though the nuns complain bitterly that the gardener is no longer working, and finally, between the abbess and the nuns, Masetto is so put upon that he decides to speak. "Madam, I have understood that a cock may very well serve ten hens, but that ten men can ill satisfy one woman; and I am expected to serve nine, which I cannot sustain for anything in the world" (III,1,37). The abbess is amazed that he can speak, but with ready wit he explains that he was mute not from birth, but from an illness, and that God has just now wrought the miracle of returning his speech to him. He then explains his predicament to the abbess. She, with characteristic common sense, reflects that to let him go would be to besmirch the name of the convent; so she gathers all the nuns, and by common agreement they determine to present Masetto's regained speech as the merit of their patron saint. In addition they will appoint him steward and will order matters so that he can bear the burden of their service. In the course of his service, the author says, he procreated not a few little "monklets," but all was discreetly arranged, and in his old age Masetto retired, rich and a father, without having suffered the pains and expense of rearing children. Such is the just recompense on this earth for the man who wisely uses his wits and gives Nature her due.

The most remarkable example of a man using his wits to his own advantage is in the very first story of Ser Ciappelletto da Prato. Musciatto Franzesi, a merchant who is detained in Italy in the company of the brother of the French king, hires Cepparello of Prato to handle his business and make good his credits in Burgundy. Cepparello, called mistakenly Ciappelletto by the French, is the worst man who ever lived. He is guilty of every sin punished in Hell—he falsifies documents, bears false witness, sows scandal, commits homicide, blasphemes, visits taverns and brothels but never churches, is guilty of lust, sodomy, gluttony, and theft. While in Burgundy, guest of two Florentine usurers, he falls ill, and so as not to cause trouble to his hosts by dying without the last rites, he has them call a priest so that he may make his final confession. A friar comes, and this rogue who has not only ignored the teachings of the Church but purposely violated most of them, gives a virtuoso performance of piety. He claims to have gone to confession every week, yet he begs the friar to confess him as if he had never been. He claims to be a virgin, to have subsisted only on bread and water, and to have donated his inheritance to the poor. Not content with this travesty of the sacrament of confession, he persists and produces such absurd piety that he turns the tables and chides the friar for making too little of his sins. He has grown angry seeing young men walk in the way of the world, he claims, and after inadvertently cheating a customer and seeking for a year to return the money, he donated the amount to the poor. When he says he once carelessly spat in the church, the friar laughs and says that friars and priests spit there all the day, whereupon Ciappelletto chides them for disrespectful behavior. Finally Ciappelletto begins to weep and refuses to confess one final sin. The friar encourages him, yet he still refuses. Again the friar coaxes and again he refuses. At last, following this crescendo, we come to the climax of this already incredible confession, the *reductio ad absurdum*—Ciappelletto once cursed his mother, his sweet mother, he says, who carried him in her womb for nine months, night and day!

This story was certainly put first for a reason. It exemplifies the meaning of the work as established by the Proem and the Introduction by offering a character who is at once free from the established conventions of society (here common morality and the Church) and able to create himself in total stylistic freedom.[27] The story itself tells us that Ciappelletto is beyond the established order. The two brothers eavesdrop on Ciappelletto's confession and remark: "What man is this who neither by old age, nor illness, nor fear of death, to which he knows he is near, nor of God, before whose judgment he expects to be shortly, can be removed from his usual evil ways, nor be made to not want to die as he has lived?" (I,1,79). Ciappelletto spoofs the most sacred aspects of the Church, the mainstay of the society from which the group of storytellers has withdrawn, and with his irreverent confession he affirms the autonomy of artistic creation beyond all moral concerns. He is an artist, who in this case is creating himself in absolute freedom, and enjoys his performance for its own sake by extending his confession far beyond what is required to achieve the absolution he supposedly seeks. This is the first in a series of virtuoso performances in the *Decameron.* Just as Ciappelletto indulges more than necessary in making his confession, so does fra Cipolla (see below) delight in saying more than he needs to in order to convince the people of Certaldo (VI,10), and so does Lydia not only comply with the three impossible requests of her lover, but adds an additional feat of her own and makes love to him before her husband's eyes (VII,9). Conversely, in the name of virtue, Gualtieri pushes Griselda further than necessary to test her devotion (X,10). In Ciappelletto's story the author even outdoes his character, as it were, for news spreads of the great piety of his confession and he is venerated as Saint Ciappelletto. Panfilo, the teller of this story, wryly observes that the story redounds to the glory of God, for He hears our prayers even if they are proffered through false saints.

As we saw in the above story, the use of one's wit need not only be for the gaining of some advantage. Like art, wit and humor can be enjoyed for themselves, and a characteristic particularly of Tuscan humor, the tricks people play on one another, is the theme of the Eighth Day. Among the most famous stories is that of Calandrino and the heliotrope (VIII,3), one of the four stories in which the Florentine painters Bruno and Buffalmacco play tricks on their simple friend Calandrino. The story unfolds in Florence, as do many of the stories in the Sixth and Eighth Days, and Boccaccio is lavish with detail. Calandrino is in the church of San Giovanni observing paintings and intaglios of the tabernacle that have just been put above the altar when, as his friends have arranged, he overhears their conversation about a miraculous stone called heliotrope. They confuse him with double talk about a fabulous land of macaroni and parmesan cheese, and finally entice Calandrino to seek this stone, varied in size, they say, but always black in color, which has the miraculous power of making its bearer invisible. Calandrino is anxious to set out, but his friends, calculating their prank, prevail upon him to wait until Sunday. They venture out Sunday at mealtime, so as to encounter almost nobody, and the two friends convince the customs agents to let Calandrino pass the city gates unnoticed. In the riverbed of the Mugnone, Calandrino of course finds many dark stones and, just to be sure, gathers them all till he is quite laden. At this point his friends behind him not only pretend not to see him, but even stone him, feigning that they are just throwing stones into empty air. Calandrino returns home, exhausted from carrying so many stones, and when his wife not only sees him, but scolds him for being late, he flies into a rage. Since all things lose their virtue in the presence of a woman, he believes that she has removed the charm from the stones. He beats her soundly and his friends arrive to find him tired and in despair, with his house full of stones. Relentless in their prank, they admonish him for having left them in the riverbed, and Calandrino, gullible and irate, explains that he had found the heliotrope and had become invisible, but that all had been ruined by his wife. He is about to beat her again when his friends, hardly containing their laughter, convince him that the stone has lost its power through God's will so as to punish him for not allowing his friends to participate in his good fortune.

Nature and Fortune are both proverbially blind; they are therefore both democratic. The democracy of love and of intelligence is a commonplace, and literature of all times has represented the vindication of a lower social order upon a higher in the name of natural gifts. Nonetheless, it is probably fair to say that in viewing his world as hinging upon these two forces, Boccaccio is emphasizing the interaction of various social strata, and this interaction was particularly evident in a period of upheaval and transition such as the fourteenth century in Florence. The *Decameron* offers repeated instances where the natural gifts of the lowborn transcend social distinctions.[28] Love, of course, knows no class. Lisa, the daughter of Bernardo the chemist, has fallen in love with King Peter of Aragon and says to him: ". . . in the very moment I fell in love with you I realized that you are a king and I am the daughter of Bernardo the chemist, and that it was ill suited to me to direct my love to such lofty heights. But as you know better than I, no one falls in love according to due election but according to appetite and pleasure" (X,7,40–41).

Thus Girolamo, son of a rich merchant, from childhood loves Salvestra, daughter of a poor tailor; and despite his mother's efforts to the contrary, he ultimately dies for love of her, and then she for him (IV,8). Gostanza's hand is refused to Martuccio because he is too poor. But after various journeys and adventures, Martuccio improves his position by using his wits and giving shrewd advice to the king of Tunis. He then rediscovers the lost Gostanza and can now return home to marry (V,2). And the examples could be multiplied.

Boccaccio answers Andreas Capellanus's assertion that love among peasants is the mere coupling of animals.[29] Although love prefers rich palaces and idle nobles, it can often be found among poor rustic laborers. In introducing the story of Masetto, Filostrato says he will disprove the theory that ". . . the hoe and the spade and rough food and discomfort exempt workers of the land from erotic appetite and make their wits and intellect dull" (III,1,4).

As with love, intelligence or wit are also gifts of Fortune which are distributed indiscriminately among all men. We have seen members of various classes using their wits, but there are also specific examples of confrontation between classes where the lowborn outwit or outshine the noble. When a groom sleeps with the wife of King Agilulfo (III,2), the King discovers the betrayal and cuts the groom's hair in his sleep so as to identify him the next morning. The shrewd groom quickly cuts the hair of all the other sleeping men in the same manner and confounds the King while saving his own life. Again the examples could be multiplied.

Fortune also intervenes to assist the simple. The Venetian cook Chichibìo (VI,4), aided by Fortune, shows greater wit than his master and thus saves his own life. The nobleman Currado Gianfigliazzi brings home a crane he has hunted and tells Chichibìo to prepare it for some guests. While it is cooking, Brunetta, the chef's girlfriend, comes by and wheedles a leg of the crane from him. When the crane is brought to the table with one leg, Currado calls Chichibìo and asks for the other, to which Chichibìo readily replies that cranes have but one leg. Currado is enraged, but Chichibìo perseveres, hoping to dissipate his master's wrath. Currado insists, however, that Chichibìo go out with him the next morning to show him that cranes have only one leg. Thus they do, and Chichibìo is now hard put to bolster his story. Luckily they come upon some cranes standing on one foot as they do when sleeping, and the Venetian chef happily points them out to Currado as proof of his point. Currado is not to be duped and he shouts "Hoho," whereupon the cranes lower the other foot. Currado turns triumphantly to Chichibìo, who, ". . . almost beside himself, not knowing himself whence the answer came, replied, 'Yes, sir, but you did not shout "Hoho" to the crane last night; for if you had, it would have put forth its other leg as these have done'" (VI,4,18). Currado finds the chef's reply so witty that he lets him go.

Intelligence and love ennoble the spirit and give innate dignity to common people. This is the case of the Florentine baker Cisti. In introducing this story, Pampinea remarks upon the inscrutability of the ministers of the world. ". . . I cannot determine which does a greater injustice, Nature by giving an ugly body to a noble soul, or Fortune by giving a lowly trade to a body endowed with a noble soul" (VI,2,3). Cisti, though he is prosperous, is not well born, and will not presume to invite the nobleman Geri Spina with his illustrious guests, the papal legates, to his table to taste his fine wine. Yet he wants very much to offer the wine, so he contrives a situation in which they request the wine of him as they pass by in the heat of the day. He gladly complies and they are duly impressed. Shortly after, when Geri Spina is giving a dinner for his guests and sends a servant for a small amount of Cisti's fine wine, that each of his guests may have half a glass with the first course, the servant takes it upon himself to overstep the limits of courtesy and brings Cisti a large container to fill. Cisti sends him back to his master with the cryptic message that the servant has been sent not to Cisti but to the Arno river. When Geri Spina hears the message he asks to see the container the servant brought and recognizes the justice of Cisti's message. Cisti, innately dignified and noble in spirit, knew how to keep his place, but expected others to do the same, and the nobleman Geri Spina immediately recognized this through a common bond of sensibility that momentarily transcends social position.[30]

In the first story of the Fourth Day the noblewoman Ghismonda, daughter of the prince of Salerno, gives a veritable disquisition on the insignificance of high birth. Ghismonda is widowed in youth and returns to the house of her adoring father. When she realizes that her father ignores "the nature and might of the laws to which youth is subject" (IV,1), especially a young lady who has known the pleasures of the marriage bed, and that he has no intention of remarrying her, she willfully determines to fall in love with his valet, Guiscardo. She contrives their meeting and they take their pleasure, until, one day, her father discovers them, Heartbroken and furious, he has Guiscardo taken and imprisoned and confronts first him, then Ghismonda, with his discovery. Ghismonda rebels against his accusation of having taken a man beneath her station.

. . . for you, following more the common opinion than the truth, more bitterly admonish me, saying that I have chosen a man of low condition, almost as if you would not have been vexed had I chosen a nobleman. In this you do not realize that you are not admonishing my sin, but that of fortune, who often exalts the unworthy, leaving the most worthy in low estate. But let us leave off this and look at the principles of things. You will see that we all take our flesh from the same flesh and our soul with equal powers, equal strength and equal virtue from the same Creator. It was virtue that made the first distinction among us, born, as we were, all equal; and those who possessed and used the most virtue were called nobles and the rest were not called thus. And although contrary custom has since hidden this law, it is still not effaced or spoiled by nature or good manners; wherefore he who acts virtuously clearly shows himself a gentleman, and should anyone call him differently, it is he who calls and not he whom he denotes who is in error. (IV,1,38–40)

When, to punish her transgression, her father has her lover strangled and his heart brought to her in a cup, this strong-willed lady pours poison over the heart and unflinchingly drinks the contents.

It is important that we remember this lofty aspect of Boccaccio's art, particularly in view of the distortions of six hundred years of criticism. Not all his stories are roguish, or obscene, or even funny. He himself says there are stories that delight and stories that "sting" (Concl. 19). Into the nonprurient category fall many of the pure adventure stories (Second Day), many of the unhappy stories (Fourth Day), and all of the stories of the Tenth Day, which tell of magnanimity and nobility. Friendship, for example, does not only mean camaraderie or playing tricks, but can also be a lofty bond among men that represents loyalty and self-sacrifice, as in the story of Titus and Gisippus (X,8).

The outline of this story comes from the *Disciplina clericalis* of Pietrus Alphonsus, but is greatly expanded by Boccaccio. The story, one of very few in a classical setting, takes place in ancient Rome. Titus, the noble Roman, is sent to study in Athens in the house of Chremes where he shares a tutor with Chremes's son, Gisippus. The two boys grow up together in utterly devoted friendship; but when Gisippus is to be given Sophronia for a wife, Titus beholds her and falls hopelessly in love. Of course he does not dare reveal his feelings to Gisippus, but his health wanes from lovesickness and, pressed by Gisippus, he finally reveals the cause. Gisippus, out of love for his friend, convinces Titus that he instead must have Sophronia, but that this must be done by a ruse. Gisippus brings her home as his wife, but Titus slips into her chamber and she, thinking he is Gisippus, accepts him as a husband. When Titus must return to Rome, and wants Sophronia with him, the ruse is revealed, but Gisippus is reviled by the Athenians for what he has done.

By way of explanation, Titus harangues the Athenians with great eloquence, justifying himself, the marriage, and the noble bond of friendship that joins him and Gisippus. He then departs for Rome. Gisippus, however, is soon reduced to poverty and desperation, and being exiled from Athens, he makes his way to Rome, hoping to find Titus. Titus passes by one day, but does not recognize the poverty-stricken Gisippus, and Gisippus, taking this as intentional shunning, wanders disconsolately, yearning for death. Shortly after, he is witness to a murder and gives himself up as the murderer by way of finding death without suicide. But as he is being tried, Titus happens by, recognizes him, and to save his friend promptly tells the judge it was he, not Gisippus, who committed the murder. In hearing this multiple confession the judge becomes convinced that neither man is guilty, and finally, moved by the noble sacrifice of these two men, and by the devotion they show each other, the true murderer is conscience-stricken and confesses. The judge then absolves all three, whereupon Titus takes Gisippus home, restores him to health and wealth, and gives him his sister for a wife.

On the Fifth Day (V,9), under the theme of good fortune befalling lovers after diverse dire or disastrous adventures, comes a most touching story of love. Federigo degli Alberighi is consumed by love for the widow Monna Giovanna, and he consumes all his wealth in trying to win her love, which she refuses. Reduced to poverty, he retires to a small country house where he lives simply with only one possession, a prized falcon. Monna Giovanna and her young son spend summers on an estate near Federigo and the son befriends Federigo and particularly covets his excellent falcon. The boy falls ill and reveals to his mother that could he but have the falcon, he feels he would rapidly recover. The honest Monna Giovanna is hard put, for aware of Federigo's love for her, she knows the falcon would be hers for the asking; yet she dare not deprive him of his last possession. Finally maternal love wins out and she pays a visit to Federigo. Ashamed because of his extreme poverty, and desperate to honor his guest properly, he sees no other resource but his falcon, whereupon he wrings its neck and has it prepared as a fitting meal for such a lady. When the meal is over, with much apology Monna Giovanna tells him the reason for her visit, at which Federigo starts to weep, not because he must part with his falcon, as she surmises, but because he cannot comply with her request. He explains what has happened, and after chiding him for killing so fine a falcon for a lady's breakfast, she inwardly commends him for the magnanimity of his spirit which poverty had been powerless to impair. The lady returns home and her son dies shortly after. When her brothers urge her to remarry, she says she would prefer not, but if she is to marry, it will be only to Federigo. The brothers laugh and protest that she is rich and he has nothing, to which she replies: "I'd rather have a man without wealth than wealth without a man" (V,9,42).[31] The dignity, courtesy, and sensitivity with which these two characters behave are a constant element in Boccaccio's human comedy.

Love therefore means not only sexual satisfaction but ennoblement, as in the courtly ideal, and self-sacrifice. The story of Cimon (V,1) describes the transformation of a rustic soul akin to that described in the *Ameto*. The well-born Cypriot Cimon is ignorant, uncouth, and impervious to all teaching. One day he beholds Iphigenia asleep on the grass and falls in love with her. What the efforts of parents and tutors could not achieve, love does in a flash, for Cimon becomes the most refined and intelligent of men, a personification of the courtly tenet that love ennobles and enlightens.

We have seen in the story of Federigo that love also evokes self-sacrifice, but perhaps no story illustrates this more clearly than the last story of the *Decameron,* the story of Griselda (X,10). Gualtieri, the marquis of Saluzzo, is urged by his people to take a wife. He agrees on the condition that she be of his choosing, and he proceeds to choose Griselda, a peasant's daughter. He insists that she come naked from her father's house, symbol that he has taken no dowry and owes her nothing. They marry, she is installed as the mistress of his household and proves to be an obedient and devoted wife, adored by all. In good time she is delivered of a daughter, healthy and beautiful, but her husband, because of some inexplicable harshness, decides to try her patience with long and cruel sacrifices. With the excuse that his people object to Griselda's low birth and to the fact that her first born is a girl, he sends a servant to take the child to be killed. In truth the child is sent to Bologna to be raised by a relative. Griselda, ever humble and liege to her lord's wishes, masks her suffering and relinquishes the child. Soon after, she gives birth to a son, who, with the same excuse of the mother's lowly birth, is also taken from her. The patient Griselda again replies that her husband's pleasure is her pleasure.

But Gualtieri is not yet satisfied, and as a final test of her obedience he pretends to repudiate her and send her back to her father so he may take a new wife. He counterfeits the necessary papal dispensation and makes ready to send her back with her dowry, namely naked. Griselda bears even this affront with extreme dignity, asking only that since her body has borne his children it might not be exposed to the public view, and that as a token for her virginity, which was her only dowry, she be allowed to cover her body with her shift. Though moved to tears by her humility, the perverse Gualtieri persists. He grants her wish and Griselda departs. But even this is not sufficient and Gualtieri perseveres. When his new wife is to arrive he calls upon Griselda, because she is familiar with the household, to set the wedding feast, and though these words are all knives in her heart, she consents. Gualtieri, creator of this cruel destiny, continues with artistic flourish. He presents his beautiful young bride, who has come with her younger brother, and asks Griselda her opinion. The pathos surrounding Griselda culminates with her response. She replies that while she finds the maiden beautiful, young, and well bred, she hopes Gualtieri will spare her the tribulations inflicted upon his first wife, who was simpler and more robust and hence more able to sustain them. Gualtieri then discloses the trials to which he put Griselda and reveals the young maid and her brother to be their very own children. Reuniting the family, he lived happily with Griselda, honoring her always.

The trials of Griselda, which seem exaggerated to us even as they did to Boccaccio, are an example of the popular theme of the unjust persecution and trial of a woman recurrent in many guises in the literatures of different lands.[32] For Petrarch it was one of the few parts of the *Decameron* that really pleased him; so much so that he translated the story into Latin (*Sen.* XVII,3) to give it the greater dignity he felt it deserved. Thence comes Chaucer's version (*Clerk's Tale*), and indeed the Griselda story has been among the most popular of all in the *Decameron*. But the story of Griselda must also be seen in terms of the *Decameron* itself to understand its distortion or exaggeration. It is first of all the conclusion to a crescendo of examples of virtue; for in the Tenth Day each narrator seems to vie with the others to excel in stories of magnanimity.[33] Furthermore, just as Ciappelletto in the first story is the quintessence of evil, a *reductio ad absurdum,* likewise is Griselda for virtue. If we find Ciappelletto more credible and realistic than Griselda, that may be because vice is more engaging and believable than virtue. But both stories, carefully placed at either end of this human comedy, reveal the same patterns and techniques. In both cases the dynamic of the story is pushed beyond credible limits simply for the enjoyment of narrative flourish, and in both we find extreme examples of men freely creating their own destinies. We can surmise that Boccaccio placed Ciappelletto and Griselda at either end of his work as emblems of the extreme limits within which human experience on earth is contained.[34]

The primary virtue they reveal is that of individuals creating their own destiny in the face of adverse Fortune. But the terms of this virtue are lay, not ecclesiastic.[35] Indeed, in the society of the *Decameron,* virtue is only lay and never ecclesiastic. In the first story a member of the vital new merchant class destroys through derision the broadest base of traditional society, the Church. In the last story, and indeed in the whole last day, morality and human dignity are based on lay examples, culminating with Griselda. At every possible moment between Ciappelletto and Griselda the Church is debased, mocked and denied, as we have had occasion to observe. There is only one example of a virtuous clergyman (X,3), and that is judged by the company to be simply a miracle. But the *Decameron* is not only devoted to the satire of the Church, as was the case in many of Boccaccio's literary forbears. It does envision moral order. What is substituted for the moral order bequeathed by the Church, is a new morality that stems from the lay world and is based on a juxtaposition of the realistic needs of an open mercantile society with the lay ideals of love and friendship inherited from the old courtly culture and the classical world.

Curiously enough, this new order is often presented in terms of traditional ecclesiastic rhetoric. It has its priests and its martyrs. The elder Natan (X,3,30) seems like a high priest of the lay cult of virtue as he lifts Mitridanes to his feet, embracing and kissing him and addressing him as "my son" while absolving him from the "sin" of an excessive desire to excel in liberality. Griselda is a feudal Job or a Madonna of humility, "virgin" and martyr to the cult of the power of love and sacrifice for one's fellow man here on earth.[36] These characters, and many others, form a new "priesthood" that Boccaccio is substituting for the many clergymen he has vituperated. It is in this sense that the *Decameron* retains something of the *exempla* tradition. As Boccaccio says in the Proem, the stories offer, in addition to amusement, "useful advice" about what to seek and what to avoid here on earth.

Narration. The *Decameron* offers detailed observation of a mercantile society within the flow of history, and grafts a new ethos upon the old. The form chosen to express this is one eminently suited to the open development of ideas and events in time, prose narration. It is fitting then that the work affirm the supremacy and vitality of narration; and so it does. Narration becomes one of the themes treated in the *Decameron* as the frame narrators repeatedly comment on the stories. And the fact that the author states that the stories are not original, and even gives a synopsis of the action before each story, emphasizes that what is important is not only what he is telling, but how he tells it. This is confirmed by the story he places in the important central position of the whole collection (VI, 1), which is a story about how *not* to tell a story. The first story, about Ser Ciappelletto, is really a story of a man narrating himself, or creating himself through narration. And though the *Decameron* is "realistic," and in every case Boccaccio is careful to place his action among real people and in history, what immediately becomes important in the stories is the narrative thread and not the historical reality or the depiction of daily life. Even love, the subject of so many stories, is never analyzed in detail, but is instead described with rather standard formulas and considered only insofar as it produces action and adventures.[37]

This emphasis makes the *Decameron* a veritable tour de force of narrative techniques, and the variety and sophistication of patterns, rhythms, and language is indeed remarkable. In some stories Boccaccio strings together a series of adventures, in others he dramatizes a single moment; in some he makes incredible circumstances and coincidences seem real, in others he makes real and commonplace situations seem incredible. Some stories focus on the psychology of a single character, while in others the protagonist is an object moved by events. The author asks us to observe this variety, for as Fiammetta introduces her story of Andreuccio, which tells of a series of mishaps (II,5), she remarks that her story differs from the previous one, because whereas the mishaps of Landolfo Rufolo (II,4) probably took place over the course of several years, her story took place in one night. The variety of techniques is underscored by the variety of rhythms in which long stories are interspersed with short. The longest, about the tortuous and premeditated revenge of a student upon a widow, is about twenty-eight pages long (VIII,7), and the shortest, about the quick retort of a woman to a king, a little over one page (I,9). Other tales use devices such as a story within a story or the embellishment of a song. Because of this diversity the *Decameron,* though it is a collection of short stories, really represents a variety of literary genres that go from the picaresque adventure story to the psychological novel, from the *exempla* to kitchen comedy and even the high comedy of classical theater.[38] In all cases it is the delight of telling a story and the concern for telling it well that guarantee that style, rhythm, and language are carefully pitched to express the essence of the tale.

The story of Titus and Gisippus (X,8) for example, is really a lofty disquisition on friendship; when Titus has harangued the Athenians in a magniloquent rhetorical passage,[39] the importance of the speech is enhanced by its immediate contrast with the rapid narration of a series of events. Direct and indirect discourse are likewise artfully juxtaposed. A story which emerges more as theater than narration, because of the use of direct discourse, is that of the nightingale (V,4). Caterina loves Riccardo, but she is so closely guarded by her parents that the two cannot meet. She finally hits upon the expedient of sleeping on the balcony over their garden so that Riccardo can visit her there. One night in May, Caterina complains to her mother that she cannot sleep for the great heat.

"Oh my daughter, how is it hot? On the contrary, it is not hot at all." To which Caterina replied, "My dear mother, you should say 'in my opinion' and perhaps you would then be correct; but you should remember how much warmer young girls are than older women." Then the woman answered: "My dear daughter, that is true; but I cannot make warm and cold weather as the seasons give it to us; perhaps this next night will be cooler and you will sleep better." "May God will it," said Caterina, "but it is not common that toward the summer the nights grow cooler"; "Well" said the woman, "what would you like us to do?" (IV,7,16–20)

The maiden proposes to sleep on the balcony where she can hear the song of the nightingale, Riccardo visits her, they take their pleasure, and the next morning Caterina's father discovers the two of them asleep on the balcony, she with the "nightingale" in her hand. After the necessary admonition and apology it is arranged that the two will marry. This is a good example of a linear plot fleshed out and turned into highly entertaining comedy through the use of dramatic dialogue.[40]

Language. The *Decameron* is clearly the culmination of Boccaccio's linguistic experience and a most extraordinary phenomenon in its time. All the imbalances of the early works have disappeared; gone are the apostrophes and the lists of pagan myths, gone are the echoes of his favorite authors, gone are the discordant and complicated Latinisms. While giving Italian a "classic" form, the *Decameron* refines the use of dialect and popular language. Whereas in the early works dialect or colloquialisms were used rarely and inappropriately, for example Neapolitan forms in the mouth of the Florentine shepherd Ameto, in the *Decameron* they are used purposely to enliven the narration. Chichibìo, the Venetian cook, answers Brunetta's request for the leg of the crane by chanting in Venetian dialect, *Voi non l'avrì da mì* ("You will not have it from me," VI,4,8). And there are examples of Sienese forms and Sicilian dialect.[41]

As could be expected, colloquialisms and proverbs are frequent in the mouths of Florentine characters. An old lady, expounding the importance of enjoying youth, advises the wife of Pietro di Vinciolo (V,10,15) and says that she must pay her husband tit for tat (*pan per focaccia*), that when you are old no one gives you fire for a rag (*fuoco a cencio,* to light one's hearth), and she illustrates the prevalent attitude toward old ladies with a proverb: The young ladies get the sweet morsels, the old can choke (*Alle giovani i buon bocconi e alle vecchie gli strangugli-*

oni). And Dioneo concludes the story of the Tuscan Salabaetto's revenge on the Sicilian lady with a proverb of Tuscan pride: He who must deal with Tuscans needs both eyes (*Chi ha a far con tosco, non vuole esser losco,* VIII,10,67). The story in which a country priest seduces Monna Belcolore (VIII,2) is perhaps the most notable example in the *Decameron* of rustic colloquial language. The entire story comes from the popular tradition and is animated by rustic terms, songs, lively conversations, and images and references from country life. The gifts offered are garlics, beans, or onions; the priest plays on Belcolore's simplicity by mixing Latin with a measure of nonsense; and the mispronunciation of words that is common among the uneducated, is recorded (*boto* for *voto,* and especially the use of legal terms, *parentorio* for *perentorio, pericolatore* for *procuratore,* and others).

Boccaccio everywhere suits the language to the speaker and to the great variety of situations he creates for his characters. The Proem, parts of the Introduction, the defense of the Fourth Day, and the Conclusion offer examples of variegated and refined expository prose with all the rigor and complexity of Latin. The narrative of the stories is usually more direct and returns to greater rhetorical flourishes when the subject or speaker requires. Ghismonda's speeches on the real significance of nobility and birth (IV,1), or the stories of the Tenth Day, whose theme is magnanimity, have a more lofty tone. In the story of Titus and Gisippus (X,8), Titus speaks first to himself in an inner monologue and later to the people of Athens with all the rhetorical devices required by good Latin style. The language suits both the speaker, a noble and educated Roman, and the subject, love and friendship; but the burden of classical references and echoes, so weighty in Boccaccio's early works, is gone.

The *ars dictandi* and the development of Boccaccio's prose. The most important vestige of classical culture in the *Decameron* is one that is much less obvious, nor is it totally classical; it is the influence of Latin in forming Boccaccio's prose. Much of the Latin style that served as his model derived from medieval lyrical schemes and medieval literary canons, particularly the *ars dictandi.* Along with the avid study of the classics early in his life, he also devoted several years to the study of canon law while in Naples, and it is there that he probably developed his knowledge of the epistolary style or *ars dictandi*. The *ars dictandi* was in some ways based on the example of the ancient epistles, but it had developed particularly in connection with the *ars notaria* and the administrative needs of notaries and clergymen; and it began to flourish toward the eleventh century. The techniques of prose style as Boccaccio could have studied them were basically four: the Roman, the Tullian, the Hilarian and the Isidorian. The Roman or Gregorian style (the name comes from Pope Gregory VIII, who, on the example of Alberico da Montecassino, codifier of the *ars dictandi,* introduced it into the Roman Curia) consisted primarily of the *cursus,* a technique of cadences which particularly concerned the end of a sentence, but was often applied within the sentence as well. The *cursus* had been used by the ancients for special effects, but it then became more common in early Christian authors, finally developing as a canon of Latin style. The Tullian style had no foot cadence but concerned primarily figures of words and thought. The first sources of the style are Cicero's *De inventione* and the pseudo-Cicero *Rhetorica ad Herennium,* a treatise believed to be by Cicero and very popular in Boccaccio's time. The characteristics of this style are series of figures of speech—metaphor, hyperbole, apostrophe, and so on, in a vast and exhaustive catalog. The Hilarian style, from Hilary of Poitiers (ca. 300–ca. 367), was a rigorous rule regarding rhythmic prose. The effect was much like that of the *cursus* and the Hilarian style was abandoned, probably because of its difficulty. Most popular of all was the Isidorian style, developed by Isidore of Seville. It stipulated several techniques. One was rhymed prose; another was parallelisms, where the sentence was arranged in parallel parts, each beginning with the same word. An almost fanatic repetition of words characterized this style, as well as a fondness for plays on words and etymologies. The Isidorian style triumphed by the end of the eleventh century and was used widely by hagiographers, preachers, mystics, theologians, and philosophers. There is evidence of this style in the works of Anselm, Peter Damian, Aquinas, and many others, right down to Dante. In addition to the dictums of the Isidorian style, treatises on the subject, such as the *Poetria* of John of Garland, indicated many important stylistic specifications—that of placing key words at the beginning or end of a sentence, keeping long words for the end to achieve greater dignity, and the use of conjunctions to join clauses. Even a superficial look at Boccaccio's prose, where the sentences most often end with verbs and almost always begin with conjunctions, yielding the impression of one long sentence, will reveal how closely he observed these canons.

Another important influence in the formation of early Italian art prose was the translation of classical Latin works, which began to flourish in the thirteenth and fourteenth centuries. In translating the revered classics, writers were careful to keep a distance from the common vernacular tongue, and with the page of classical Latin before them, they helped to infuse the developing Italian with Latin structures. Boccaccio was one of these, and in his translation of the fluid, ample prose of Livy, which was suited to his own stylistic rhythm, he molded much of his Italian style. In fact we find a blending of classical prose with medieval canons in his translations of the Third and Fourth *Decades,* where he applied the *cursus.* [42] The use of the *cursus* is in fact applied in all of Boccaccio's Italian prose. In general we find it in the more rhetorical parts of his works such as proems or introductions, oratorical tirades, or, as in the *Decameron,* in the more rhetorical stories of the Tenth Day.

Boccaccio's Italian prose was formed by more than just adherence to the forms of the *cursus,* however, for we find him amply using etymologies, plays on words, and parallelisms, all techniques prescribed by the Isidorian style. Greek etymologies determine many of his titles: the *Filocolo,* etymologically constructed to mean "labor of love," or the *Decameron,* based on the number ten. Etymologies are behind the names of characters: in the *Ameto,* Agapes represents Charity, her lover Apiros is the cold one, and Fiammetta and Panfilo in the *Fiammetta* and the *Decameron* are qualified as lovers, to name just a few. Equally popular in the early works is the Isidorian technique of plays on words (*bisticci*). An example in the *Ameto* runs thus: ". . . they returned to the first place, less fruitful than the one they had left, and to the one they had left, they left as a name . . ." (XXXV,16). But in the *Decameron* the use of this technique is refined, as in the case of the scheming wife of Ferondo (III,8), whose scheming is made evident by her speech: "Father, you must not doubt of it, for I would rather die than say to anyone something you said to me that I should not say" (III,8,12).

Boccaccio also used the technique of anaphora. Again examples are frequent in the early works. A notable instance can be found in the *Fiammetta* where three consecutive sentences begin with the word "Alas!" and end with the words "such a day" (XXVI,p.74). And the Introduction to the *Decameron* offers a good example of this rhetorical device: "O how many great palaces, how many lovely houses, how many noble dwellings previously full with families, with gentlemen, with ladies, were left empty even of servants! O how many memorable generations, how many abundant patrimonies, how many famous riches were left without a proper heir! How many valorous men, how many beautiful women, how many handsome youths . . ." (Intro.I,48). But he also applies this lofty rhetorical technique to a plebeian scene. Fra Cipolla's servant Guccio is characterized as *tardo, sugliardo, bugiardo, negligente, disubbidiente, maldicente, trascutato, smemorato, scostumato* ("lazy, filthy, lying, negligent, disobedient, foul-mouthed, reckless, witless, and mannerless," VI,10,17).

Together with these established stylistic elements that became integrated into Boccaccio's prose during his literary apprenticeship, there are other fundamental structures that came to characterize his style. His syntax is generally tightly knit and slow in unfolding, with a complex subordination of parts. It can often set a whole scene in one sentence and leisurely reflects the rambling of idle storytellers. This structure is achieved by the particular use of verbs and word order. The verb commonly comes at the end of a sentence, a rule he learned from the *ars dictandi,* and he very often places the adjective before the noun (significant in Italian where the adjective normally follows the noun)[43] so that rather than determining the noun, it is mostly ornamental. A rather extreme example can be found in the *Ameto*: ". . . and there, tired out from the *long way* and the *heavy weight* and the *overwhelming heat,* desirous of rest, he laid down his *rich burden* under a *leafy oak,* and stretching out his *tired body* on the *new grass,* he opened his *burly breast* to the *sweet breezes*; and having removed the *dirty sweat* from his face with his *rough hand,* he refreshed his *dry mouth* with the *wet fronds* of the *green plants* . . ." (III,7; italics mine).

The use of the gerund and of the present participle is also basic to Boccaccio's sentence structure.[44] The general effect in both cases is that of slowing down and prolonging the sentence, and his use of these verb forms is widespread compared to Latin. He extends the use of the gerund to certain forms that become common usage only after his example. A case in point is the gerund form preceding the main verb such as: "Wherefore, marveling at this, he said to himself . . ." (*Ameto* III, 10). The same effect of slowing down the sentence is achieved by other techniques, for example the common occurrence of inversions as we have seen with adjectives and nouns, and even more strikingly with the inversion of past participles with the auxiliary. There is also the separation of the auxiliary from its past participle and the use of the accusative with the infinitive.[45] All these techniques are present in the *Filocolo,* are exaggerated to greater intricacy in the *Ameto,* are modified in the *Fiammetta,* and finally culminate in the *Decameron* where all the stylistic experiences are harmonized in a myriad of registers so that the language is in every instance suited to the narrative essence of the event.

Boccaccio's Italian is so complex and carefully hewn that it is not surprising that language emerges as one of the protagonists of the *Decameron.* The use of language is the subject of an entire day (the Sixth); and in many stories language is action that determines the outcome of events; the storytellers discuss the art of using language, and of course metaphor, especially for obscenity, is largely the basis of Boccaccio's humor. In his conclusion he coyly protects himself behind the veil of language by appealing to the ambiguity of metaphor. He declares that his stories are not unfit for virtuous women, for ". . . there is none so unseemly herein, that, if said with the proper words, is unsuited to anyone; the which rule I believe has been fittingly observed" (Concl. 3). It is not reprehensible to use words of common currency such as "hole," "pin," "mortar and pestle," "sausage," "bologna," and other similar terms. Even St. Michael is depicted as striking with a sword, St. George with a lance, and Christ is put on the cross with nails. Evil, the author pleads, tongue in cheek, after this list of phallic symbols, is in the mind of the reader.

The proper or improper use of language also identifies persons and determines events. Alatiel's incredible adventure (II, 7), which puts her in the bed of nine different men before finally bringing her to her destined husband as a virgin, unfolds, at least in part, because she cannot speak the language of her captors. Without language she becomes an object, and she returns mistress of her fate only when she meets her father's friend, a man to whom she can speak. Simona's death (IV,7) is ultimately due to the fact that she cannot speak properly. Unable to explain to the judge how her lover Pasquino died, she is taken to the site of his death, and in order to communicate what she has been unable to convey in words, she too rubs her teeth with the sage leaf and dies, just as Pasquino did. Masetto's good fortune with the nuns (III,1) turns first on his ability not to speak (dumbness makes him an innocuous object rather than a person) and finally on his ability to speak well at the opportune moment. And Filippo Balducci pays tribute to the potency of language in the Introduction to the Fourth Day in thinking he can mitigate the power of women over men by not calling them by their proper name.

The Sixth Day, we have said, is based on language used cleverly at an opportune moment. Representative of this theme is the last story about a famous demagogue, Fra Cipolla, who comes to Boccaccio's hometown of Certaldo (known for its *cipolle,* "onions") to give his yearly sermon. He is a popular orator, as good as Cicero or Quintilian, and the simple people of Certaldo so enjoy his sermons that they give generous alms. This particular year Fra Cipolla has promised to show the people a feather left by the Angel Gabriel when he came to make the annunciation to Mary in Nazareth (the story is a marvelous spoof of the mania for relics that consumed the faithful, a common theme of the period). Thanks to the negligence of Fra Cipolla's servant Guccio, a rascal with no redeeming qualities, two young friends of Fra Cipolla are able to play a trick on the friar by stealing the feather he plans to reveal and replacing it with a bunch of coals. The friar dramatically introduces his feather and flips open his box. But when he sees the coals, and realizes the trick, he closes the box, gathers his wits, and proceeds to a brilliant speech, devised on the spot, to hoodwink his simple audience. He presents the coals as the relic of St. Lawrence, roasted on the grill, and as a miracle wrought by God because St. Lawrence's day is soon to be celebrated. His speech is a masterpiece of rhetorical nonsense and the whole story denounces the shrewd worldliness of the clergy and the naive credulity of the faithful. Though caught in an embarrassing situation, this man of quick wit decides to enjoy himself and to enhance his presentation by staging it with a tale of his exotic journey to the

Orient. To impress these folk with the places he has visited, he in fact transforms the names of the familiar streets of Florence and other places in Italy, adding a measure of nonsense, as if they were the exotic lands of the East. For the patriarch of Jerusalem he concocts the name *Nonmiblasmatesevoipiace* (do not criticize me if you do not mind"), formed on the pattern of names in allegorical poems. To this he adds the marvelous, and totally absurd things he has seen abroad: Maso del Saggio cracking nuts and selling the shells by retail, or, in the Abruzzi, hogs clothed with their own entrails (sausages). The nonsense culminates with his list of the relics he saw: some of the rays of the star that appeared to the Magi, the jaws of death of St. Lazarus, some of the sound of the bells of Solomon's Temple, some of the sweat of St. Michael battling with the Devil, and, climaxing his use, and abuse, of language by satirizing the mystery of the mass in a linguistic parody, he lists among the relics one of the ribs of the "*Verbum caro fatti alla finestra,*" literally, "Verbum caro come to the window," which is a play on the central mystery of the Incarnation *verbum caro factum est* (the word is made flesh). This fantastic and irreverent list brings him to the coals of St. Lawrence. Fra Cipolla shows his coals and the people of the town are so pleased by the friar's sermon that they are even more than usually generous with their alms. Beyond the wry social commentary, this virtuoso performance is a tribute to human wit. The real protagonist of the story is language, which is the most refined instrument of wit, and therefore a fulcrum of man's experience here on earth.

The extraordinary perfection of the *Decameron,* the total harmony of purpose and technique that it achieves, is unusual not only in the works of one author, but in all of literature. The nineteenth-century critic Francesco DeSanctis called it "not a revolution but a catastrophe,"[46] a hyperbolic expression of its extraordinary significance. It gave literary expression to an entire society, transfigured the meaning of the work of art, created a new literary language and certainly offered, then as now, great mirth. If all Boccaccio wrote before it seemed in some sense to develop toward this magnificent climax, all that came after emerges as a sharp break. Boccaccio abandoned popular literature, renounced humor, turned from Italian, and became the more ponderous scholar revealed in his later works. It is to these that we must now turn.

Chapter Five
The Later Years

The Black Death is one of the greatest disasters in the history of the West. In Florence it concluded a decade of upheaval—the failure of the great banking houses, the experiment in dictatorial rule, the change in the composition of the government from an oligarchy dominated by old wealthy families of the Major Guilds to larger representation of the lower middle class in the Minor Guilds—and marks a period of significant change in the culture and politics of the city.[1] In the aftermath of the plague there was mass migration from the territory of Florence into the city to fill the gaps created by the Black Death. These *homines novi* ("new men") easily gained economic and social position in a society torn asunder by plague and famine. They married, received irregular inheritances, and profited by all kinds of irregular trades, thus gaining position in the city government as well. Contemporary chroniclers criticize the government as being composed of inept boors[2] and Boccaccio in a letter scorns the leaders come from "hick towns" (*Letter to Pino dei Rossi,* 1118). This upheaval produced significant changes in the painting of the period after the plague that seem to reflect the entire cultural humus of Florence.[3] In the first half of the fourteenth century a flourishing and expanding economy, conducted on an international scale by a prosperous oligarchy, produced artistic activity that was best exemplified by the work of Giotto. The emphasis was on human emotions and man's relation to man. The world was contemplated empirically and quantitatively with a burgher's interest in family and civic virtues. But after the plague the situation abruptly changed. The leading families that remained seemed to welcome the support of a hierarchical Church, and in their feelings of guilt (in the Introduction to the *Decameron* Boccaccio suggests that perhaps the plague was sent by God to make men pay for their sins) sought ways of repentance and self-flagellation. The basic incompatibility of merchant activity with the Church condemnation of usury had always been a source of guilt for most great merchants and accounts for many commissions and endowments. The guilt for which the upper class sought penance seemed to coincide with the more traditional tastes of the now more dominant *homines novi*, who had never taken part in the cultural activities of the first part of the century. The result was more intensely religious, more traditional and more hierarchical art forms.

In the midst of all this upheaval Boccaccio too appears to have undergone a change. Though we must beware of constraining any body of creative activity within too rigid a pattern, it is fair to say that after the *Decameron* (if we except the *Corbaccio*) he never wrote a fictive, amorous, or humorous work again. He does seem to reflect moments of crisis, both intellectual and religious, in turning to study and scholarship with new moral concerns and very different attitudes. He first wrote the *Corbaccio*, which destroys the themes of all his earlier works, and then devoted himself to scholarly compilations, eclogues, and epistles. This final third of Boccaccio's life is characterized by its seriousness. The theme of love as a great source of inspiration disappears or becomes misogynistic tirades; the pastoral themes become Latin eclogues; his narrative power is turned toward myths, history, and moral *exempla*; and his interest in Italian is implemented in a scholarly commentary to the *Divine Comedy*.

The decade following the plague marks a period of various diplomatic activities for Boccaccio. It is the time in which he was most involved in Florentine politics. He carried out well-remunerated missions and extended his literary activity and influence, before retiring finally to Certaldo. In 1350 he went on a mission to Romagna, though we do not know to whom he was directed. We do know however, that in this year he was also in Ravenna to give ten gold florins to Sister Beatrice, the daughter of Dante, as homage on behalf of the Florentine government to its great poet who died in exile. It was in the same period that Petrarch passed through Florence on his way to the Jubilee in Rome, an important event for the circle of his friends and disciples in Tuscany, which included Boccaccio. This brief visit to Florence, when poets and scholars gathered around him to hear the precious news of his literary activities, definitively established the "school" of friends of Petrarch in Florence with Boccaccio as its senior member. From Rome Petrarch wrote to Boccaccio (*Fam.* XI,I), addressing his letter *Johanni Bocchaccii de Certaldo discipulo suo* ("from Petrarch to Giovanni Boccaccio of Certaldo, his disciple"), thanking him and his colleagues in Florence for their friendship and tribute.

In 1351 Boccaccio returned the visit to Petrarch as a representative of the Florentine government, bringing the offer of a chair in the recently established Studio of Florence. Petrarch refused the offer but Boccaccio was able to enjoy his hospitality and to participate in the literary activities of his *magister.* He took particular interest in the texts Petrarch had collected and was continually unearthing, and he began to copy avidly some of these treasures. They probably spoke of their Italian works as well. As Boccaccio read some of Petrarch's Italian verse[4] he may in turn have showed Petrarch some of his latest efforts, the *Amorosa Visione,* the *Decameron,* and possibly the material he was gathering for the *Genealogie,* including the defense of poetry. It is certain that Boccaccio maintained his interest in Italian all his life, and just as Petrarch was his mentor in the study of classics, it is possible that Boccaccio nourished Petrarch's interest in writing in Italian.[5] Nonetheless, with extreme modesty, he always held himself beholden to Petrarch, *inclitus preceptor meus Franciscus Petrarca cui quantum valeo debeo* ("my venerable teacher Francis Petrarch to whom I owe whatever I am worth"), he writes in a letter in 1372 (*Epist.* XVII). As much as an intellectual guide, Petrarch was also a moral preceptor to whom Boccaccio turned in moments of personal difficulty and religious crisis.

In 1351 Boccaccio also went on a mission to the Tyrol which took him through northern Italy and possibly Friuli (he places a story in the *Decameron* [X,5] in Friuli), and in 1354 he was sent to Innocent VI in Avignon. In 1355 his old friend-enemy Niccolò Acciaiuoli, now arbiter of the Kingdom of Naples, was in Florence to request aid against the operations of Durazzo in Naples. This visit was preceded by various expressions of bitterness and resentment toward Acciaiuoli on the part of Boccaccio (*Epist.* VII,VIII), perhaps because of the former's total neglect of Boccaccio's overtures regarding a position in Naples. At the same time his old friend Zanobi da Strada, now secretary to Acciaiuoli, had been crowned poet laureate in Pisa following the example of Petrarch, an event which had aroused indignation in the literary circles of Florence and especially in Boccaccio (*Buc.Carm.* VIII; *Epist.* VIII).

Despite all these contrary currents, Boccaccio appears to have under-taken a trip to Naples at this juncture, of which we know only what is veiled in the *Eclogue* VIII. Acciaiuoli, in the midst of crises in the Kingdom, apparently had little time or desire to accommodate Boccaccio. Thus the poet was left to visit with his old friends and those of Petrarch, such as Barbato da Sulmona, Giovanni Barrili and Zanobi. The most positive result of this unfortunate trip was Boccaccio's visit to the library at Montecassino where he consulted, copied, and even acquired some precious ancient texts.[6]

The *Corbaccio*

It is probably to this same period that we must assign his last fictive work in Italian prose, the *Corbaccio*.[7] This vitriolic little work is something of a surprise coming from the pen of the author of the *Decameron,* and coming straight upon the hundred stories which were such a masterly moment of equilibrium and benign amusement at the ways and wiles of mankind. It can perhaps best be understood as a palinode (or a *remedia amoris*), a formal literary farewell to the amorous and impassioned themes of his foregoing works which had found their inspiration in the many guiles of women and the infinite paths of love.[8] The *Corbaccio* is a bitter and sarcastic diatribe in which Boccaccio turns on women in violent misogynistic tirades that accomplish a vivid and cruel destruction of femininity and passion. The title of the work, long debated as to its meaning, comes possible from an ancient source and the *exemplum* tradition, according to which the crow (*corvo*) dresses in peacock feathers to win a beauty contest.[9] The work returns to the vision genre. It is narrated in the first person by the protagonist, who fell in love with a lovely widow (in his destruction of love Boccaccio continues with the traditional dictum of courtly love by which love is preferably to be directed toward a widow) only to be repulsed and mocked by her publicly as she scorned his advanced age and his plebeian origin. Despairing at first, his wrath finally abates, and he is con-templating revenge when in a dream the defunct husband of the widow appears to him and reveals the true nature of the woman in the most grotesque terms. The work ends with the narrator's intention of aban-doning similar adventures for the consolation of religion and the more honorable activity of study, which perfects man.

The abrupt harshness of the *Corbaccio* has led some critics to believe it was inspired by an actual similar experience in the author's life. The evidence for this seems tenuous and inconclusive,[10] but the *Corbaccio* certainly does mark a departure from the literary activity that has gone before; and this is confirmed particularly by the scholarly intention that runs throughout. If the *Corbaccio* can be considered a farewell to the Muse of his youth, it is not surprising that it reverses and destroys his erstwhile inspiration of love. It is written as a moral *exemplum* in which love does not ennoble, it debases, it does not enlighten, it crazes. The moral tension that characterized the juxtaposition of honest love with lust in the early works, and that was cast outside of the framework of the *Decameron,* here becomes resolved in a firm rejection of love as lust. The *donna angelicata* of the spiritual tradition becomes an amoral and repulsive widow. Woman is an "imperfect animal, excited by a thousand passions unpleasant and abominable even to recall, much less to discuss" (p.496), and men should seek them, as they do latrines, to take care of their physiological needs, and then flee. And love is a ". . . blinding passion of the spirit, deviator of the intelligence, fattener, nay depriver of memory, dissipator of earthly faculties, spoiler of the bodily forces, enemy of youth and death of old age, mother of vice and inhabitor of empty bosoms, a thing without any reason, any order or any stability, vice of unhealthy minds, and suppressor of human freedom" (p.495). The tone is clearly impassioned. The serene and bemused smile of the *Decameron* is gone, and in its place is bitter sarcasm. Boccaccio harshly denounces women who, "If they hear a mouse roaming in the house, or the wind moving a window, or a small stone that falls, they become all agitated and blood and all strength abandons them . . . but . . . they have and do run around the roofs of houses, palaces and towers, summoned or awaited by their lovers" (p.500). The very antics that delighted and attested to wit in the *Decameron* are turned to proof of the baseness of women here. It is also interesting that for the first time shame comes into Boccaccio's work, and the narrator feels dishonored and reviled by this widow who points him out and mocks him to other women.

With indignation he also accomplishes the physical destruction of female beauty. We are at the opposite pole of the stylized yet sensuous descriptions of the early works where blond hair, pink cheeks, red lips, pearly teeth, and white necks and shoulders gave promise of hidden charms. With singular brutality the shade of the widow's husband reverses the standard descriptions of female pulchritude and concludes with a metaphorical description of the widow's private parts:

. . . The gulf of Setalia, hidden in the valley of Acheron, under its dark woods, often full of strange animals and rusty and frothy with an unpleasant foam; yet I shall tell of it. The mouth, through which one enters the port, is such and so great, that however big the mast of my little boat, it was never such, whenever the tides were low, that a companion, with a mast no smaller than mine, could have entered without my even realizing it. Oh, what am I saying? The army of King Robert, at its largest, could easily have entered there without trimming sail or raising rudder. . . . And I will not speak of the bloody and yellow rivers that descend from there in turn, riddled with white mould, and often as unpleasant to the nose as to the eyes, so that I must speak of something else. What shall I tell you further on the street of Evil-hole, placed between two raised mounts, from which, at times, now without thunder and now with, just like Etna there emerges a sulphurous fume so fetid and unpleasant that it infests the entire neighborhood? (533)

Boccaccio's gift for realism and his use of metaphor for humor is at its most violent, and most vile, in this passage. The misogynism that was an undercurrent to the *Decameron,* but was balanced there by pleasant recollections of love, and respect for the intelligence of women, emerges more markedly in this work, and will continue in subsequent works, drawing amply on medieval asceticism as well as classical sources. At the end of the work the shade of the husband asks the author to pray for him, since his widow clearly does not, and the author emerges from a dark valley to a luminous, idyllic hilltop where he feels himself freed from the fetters of the vile lust of the valley and ready to help others through his writings. But as has been aptly observed, the *Corbaccio* may point to piety but it treats lust.[11] The rejection of lust is immanent, not transcendent; as in the *Amorosa Visione* the ultimate religious conversion never occurs. If we can speak of a conversion, it is earthly, and more specifically, literary.

During the course of his journey through the "labyrinth of love" or the "pigsty of Venus," as he calls it, the shade of the husband exhorts the author to greater circumspection. Reminding him that he had rejected the marketplace his father wanted to impose on him in favor of study, the husband's shade admonishes him that his studies should have taught him the dangers of love. He exhorts him to follow his inclination to increase his fame through study, seeking quiet places and avoiding the vile ways of women. The arguments used in the Introduction to the Fourth Day of the *Decameron* are overturned. There, to the accusation that he is too old to bother with women and that he should follow the Muses instead, the author had saucily replied that men, like leeks, may have white heads, but their tails are green; and that furthermore, the Muses are women. Here the arguments against his age and for his studies are repeated, and this time they essentially hold. Love and the antics required by love are for the young. For a man of the author's age the most rewarding activity is study.

Thus the *Corbaccio* effects a reversal in the Boccaccio corpus and gives expression, through a literary form not unlike many of his preceding works, to a new direction more than of piety, of scholarship. The value of the study of literature, even pagan literature, is an attitude Boccaccio will reiterate and expand, along with Petrarch and other humanists. It is in fact study, particularly of ancient texts, that is the touchstone of Boccaccio's subsequent efforts. The years 1355–60 witness an intense literary activity during which he delineated his scholarly treatises in Latin, the *De montibus,* the *De casibus virorum illustrium,* the *De mulieribus claris,* and the *Genealogie deorum gentilium.*

The *De montibus*

The *De montibus* synthesizes in a scholarly form an interest in geography that threaded in and out of Boccaccio's early works. The action of the *Filocolo* roamed from Spain, to Italy, to the East, and back, and so did the tales of the *Decameron,* while the stories of the *Ameto* traced specific itineraries in the Mediterranean.[12] In the *De montibus* he organizes his geographic material into a medieval compendium, a reference work in which he lists in alphabetical order, the mountains, woods, fonts, lakes, rivers, swamps, and seas familiar to him.

The work begins with a disparagement *exordium* in which he claims he wrote it only to fill his idle hours. But the literary polish of the introduction (he uses the *cursus*), the fact that younger contemporaries such as Coluccio Salutati list this among his important contributions, and the fact that he found a similar *exordium* in classical sources, indicate that this disparagement is clearly a rhetorical device.[13] The work was, however, a reference work, along the lines of the *Genealogie,* to which it has often been considered an addendum, and offers a fairly detailed list of geographic sites in Europe, Asia Minor, North Africa, and even India. The places referred to are mythological, historical, and biblical, with somewhat longer descriptions afforded to places in Italy and sites important to classical mythology. Boccaccio often describes the flora and fauna of an area or interjects other information he considers important. The Mount of Olives, for example, is qualified as the place where Christ, the Son of the true God, taught his disciples; and in describing the Arno River he mentions the birthplace of the revered Petrarch.

What is probably most significant about the work is that it is not literally a geographic treatise, a treatment of geography as phenomenology. Boccaccio, for example, neglects contemporary geographic reports (an obvious source would be Marco Polo), thereby virtually eliminating any serious consideration of the Orient, and keeps to places mentioned in classical literature and in Scripture, or places cherished because of contemporary literary idols such as Petrarch. The *De montibus* in effect contains the glosses necessary to a reader of classical literature, such as Boccaccio himself, and the places mentioned gain their geographic reality and significance through a literary tradition. In this sense, despite its aspect of medieval compendium, the *De montibus* is a humanistic treatise.[14]

The *De casibus virorum illustrium* [The Fates of Famous Men]

Another erudite work, but one with a more moralistic intention, is the *De casibus virorum illustrium,* written 1356–60[15] and revised in 1373. The *exordium,* which in his early works committed the poet's efforts to the aid of his fellow men, usually those in love, here has a specifically political tone worthy of the civic humanists.[16] "As I sought some utility I might offer the state with the efforts of my studies, I came upon a subject richer than I expected. . . ."[17] In order to be useful to society he wants to write against the excesses of persons in power, but has decided that the power of stories is more likely to persuade them than a moral treatise. So using *exempla* he will illustrate to them what God or, as they believe, Fortune, accomplished against those who rose too high. Though he reverts from the diversion of the novella in the *Decameron,* where Fortune reigned, back to the moralizing *exempla,* wherein he reads God's message, Boccaccio nevertheless remains a narrator. For Boccaccio the moralist, *exempla,* the vicissitudes of men and women in all ages battling with good and ill fortune and offering support to posterity by their example, are a most effective and congenial way to convey a message, for they are storytelling. Indeed, all of Boccaccio's erudite works have that much in common with the *Decameron*; they are all some form of storytelling, be they myths, history, biography, or literary criticism.

The *De casibus,* which treats of women and men, reworks in a scholarly guise Boccaccio's favorite theme of the fragility of human happiness and power, and the capriciousness of Fortune's wheel. The work begins with Adam and Eve and rehearses in more or less chronological order the disasters afflicting the major figures of the Old Testament, ancient Greece and Rome, medieval kings and heroes down to his own time with Walter of Brienne, tyrant of Florence. Some of the contemporary events were directly familiar to him, and many of his sources for this work (Paolino Veneziano, Paolo Diacono, and others) are known to us from Boccaccio's notebook, the *Zibaldone Magliabechiano.*

The *De casibus* is loosely organized on the by now familiar pattern of a vision or a Triumph where the famous figures of history seem to parade before the author. Between one story and another the author frequently passes in review other unhappy rulers and occasionally offers an apostrophe on virtue or against vice. The story of Adam and Eve evokes a discourse against disobedience; that of Samson, predictably, against women; that of Cicero against those who criticize rhetoric, and so forth. The moral importance of the work is voiced by Petrarch who intervenes in Book VIII to exhort Boccaccio to finish his endeavor (Petrarch also wrote a work on the lives of famous men, and the numerous editions of Boccaccio's *De casibus*[18] attest to the popularity of the theme). Petrarch affirms the importance of work in raising man closer to God, and the value of culture for the past and the future. He asserts that just as those of the past have helped us, we must help posterity.

In this vein it is interesting that Boccaccio brings his work into his own time. The latest event recorded is the battle of Poitiers (1356). He tells of Charles I of Anjou, of Jacopo, Master of the Templars, whose death he know of almost first hand from his father, and finally comes to two stories he did know first hand: Walter of Brienne, Duke of Athens during his year long rule over Florence, and Filippa, a plebeian woman at the court of King Robert of Naples who rose in position only to be cruelly indicted and killed. This master of realism spares us no details in describing the torture and dismemberment of these victims of Fortune, as if to discourage his readers from such foolish ambitions through fear of punishment. Though the *De casibus* is an erudite work that looks to the past for instruction, much like the *Decameron*, it is also rooted in the contemporary world of its author.

The work concludes with an address to rulers to open their eyes to the examples given above and not only fear the torments, but realize how mutable Fortune is and how impotent human beings are before her. Whenever Fortune appears to offer stability she is preparing deceit; therefore, as protection against her whims, the powerful should revere God, follow wisdom and virtue, preserve true friendships, take advice from the prudent, and seek glory and honor with humanity and justice. In comparison to the *Decameron* we detect a difference in tone with regard to Fortune. In the earlier work it was implied by example that man was to use his wits to turn Fortune's blows to his own advantage, an advantage that was certainly earthly and often material. Here a certain vitality and daring have been sacrificed to prudence, and we are directly advised to revere God and follow wisdom and virtue.

The *De mulieribus claris*

Similar in conception to the *De casibus* is the *De mulieribus,* which was written in 1361 and revised in 1362 in order to dedicate it to Andrea Acciaiuoli, the sister of Niccolò. In the dedication he explicitly says that he has lately withdrawn to the country (in 1361 he moved to Certaldo after leaving the house in Florence to his half brother) and free of cares he has written a work in praise of women, more for the pleasure of friends than for the utility of the republic. He thus contrasts the intent of the *De mulieribus* with the *De casibus* which preceded it, making it, like the *Decameron,* essentially "women's" literature. As in the dedication of the *Decameron,* he hopes it will comfort Andrea in her leisure and please her with examples of virtuous women and pleasant stories. He hopes also that she will ignore any lasciviousness, made necessary by the stories themselves, and will only gather the praiseworthy examples. He says in the Introduction that he will speak of pagan and not Christian women, for Christian women have already been glorified by others and their faith made them virtuous. Also, many have written of the virtue of men (and he cites Petrarch's work on famous men) but none have written of women, who are all the more to be praised when virtuous, given their natural weakness of mind and body.

The work begins with the story of Eve, and in one hundred and four biographies passes in review famous women down to Queen Johanna of Naples. Here too Boccaccio relies closely on the chronicles of his time as well as on his favorite classics, Livy, Tacitus, Valerius Maximus, Ovid. Moralistic vehemence characterizes the work. At the end of almost every story is a moral maxim or an exhortation to virtue. After telling of Ipsiphyle, who saves her father from the general homicide agreed upon by the women of the island of Lemnos, Boccaccio inserts an apostrophe on filial love. The example of the wives of the Minyans, who by exchanging clothes with their imprisoned husbands allowed them to go free, inspires a sermon on conjugal love. A concession is made to human passions following the story of Pyramus and Thisbe, who in Boccaccio's view met a tragic and unjust death because "Love is a sin of youth but not detestible for those who are not married; and theirs could have ended in marriage" (XIII, 12). Sexual passion is an affliction common in the young but must be tolerated, for it is Nature's stimulus to procreation and therefore acceptable, especially if it can develop into honest love, or marriage. For the rest Boccaccio is a stern judge of mores. Venus is described as obscene and those who believed her the daughter of Jove were fools who could not resist the obscenities of a woman. This Venus is clearly lust, in no way reconcilable with love of God or honest Christian love of a woman. The scene of Europa kidnapped by Jove while playing alone evokes an apostrophe against letting women walk about alone. The story of Megulia Dotata, a Roman girl called *dotata* ("dowried") because of her ample dowry, calls forth a denunciation of excessive dowries. And a decree of the Roman Senate allowing women to wear jewels and ornaments calls forth imprecations against this frivolity which destroys the wealth of men and increases that of women. But, the author sighs, what can be done? The times are effeminate and men are the slaves of women.

The scholarly concerns that characterize his later works, especially the *Genealogie,* are also present here. In the early part of the work, where he tells of the ancient goddesses, we are reminded of the *Genealogie* in the precision with which he collates the various versions of the myths. For Semiramis, Ceres, Minerva, Venus, and others he meticulously lists the different stories of their origins and accomplishments. For Venus, for example, he prefers the version in which Adonis was her first husband, and after his death (as a widow even Venus complies with the courtly canon) she falls into such a libidinous frenzy—be it from the corruption of her mind or the natural disposition caused by the climate of the island—that in her lust she even destroys her beauty. From an affair with a soldier, discovered by her husband Vulcan, came the credence regarding her adultery with Mars. Thus Boccaccio carefully denies the divinity of the pagan gods by giving the myths a euhemeristic interpretation: the gods were real people whose identities and lives were magnified over the ages until they became divinities. This in itself is, characteristically, a choice of the most realistic approach to pagan myth.

Boccaccio's interpretations of myths sweep from the practical realism of euhemerism to the abstract reaches of allegory. The Greeks' belief that Minerva was born from the head of Jove is called a ridiculous error and, he says, to make the story of her perpetual virginity more credible, they invented the fable that Vulcan had long fought with her but was defeated. But Vulcan, he says, was allegorically the fervor of carnal concupiscence defeated, obviously, by reason. In the same vein, Circe's conversion of men into beasts is seen, not surprisingly, as representing passion that deprives men of their reason and thus of their humanity.

Never lacking in the scholarly works of Boccaccio is the praise of letters. In an apostrophe on the glories of Italy he claims that Latin has taken some of the glory from Hebrew and Greek and now dominates all of Europe. It is through Latin, or language in general, he says, that we preserve the memory of the great human and divine acts, that we know of events that we were unable to witness, that we offer our prayers and hear those of others, that we establish and maintain friendships, and that we learn about God and our world. This exaltation of letters becomes even more emphatic when, in one of the lives, that of the Roman poetess Cornificia, Boccaccio reverses his usually misogynistic attitude and praises those women who emerge by their intelligence to study the great poets. Therefore, he says, women who have no faith in their own powers should feel ashamed. If they did not believe they were born only to satisfy the needs of men and bear and nurture children, they would have access, along with men, to all the means of study that have made men glorious.

The *Genealogie deorum gentilium*

To this same period (ca.1355–60) belongs the most significant work accomplished on the *Genealogie*. Though he had been working on a similar idea as early as 1350, it is only at this point that it takes a more definitive form, finally to be enlarged and corrected toward the end of his life, between 1371 and 1374. The *Genealogie* is a vast encyclopedic compendium of classical myths, written in Latin and dedicated to King Hugues of Cyprus, at whose request it was allegedly written.[19] It is divided into fifteen books, the last two of which are a defense of poetry. It is in fact the value of poetry that underlies the entire undertaking[20] and dictates both the presentation of the myths and the impassioned defense of ancient myth and poetry at the end. The work is conceived, like his other scholarly works, as a medieval speculum. Though he mentions Ovid, Statius, Homer, Plato, Virgil, and other ancients, his material on myths is drawn more heavily from medieval compilations of classical works such as Apuleius, Servius, Macrobius, Martianus Capella, Rabanus, and Fulgentius. For his use of allegory and his arguments in defense of poetry he is indebted to the Church Fathers Lactantius, Augustine, Jerome, Isidore, Gregory, and to apologists closer to his own time, Albertino Mussato and Petrarch. He also acknowledges his debt to the contemporary scholars Paolo da Perugia, Barlaam, and Andalò del Negro (XV,6).

But compared to these sources Boccaccio's work distinguishes itself for its large scale and scope. He assembles a wide variety of myths and legends within the order of a genealogical tree. Drawing on Theodontius[21] and Lactantius, he declares Demogorgon to be the progenitor of all the gods. From Demogorgon's nine offspring he catalogues the entire pantheon. With numerous identities for Jove, Venus, Hercules and others in between, the classification moves from the abstract reaches of Night, Earth, Pain, and Labor down to the historical realm of Achilles, Aeneas, Romulus, and Remus. His manner of proceeding is that of medieval scholarship and his tools are etymology and allegory. Showing off his knowledge of Greek, he occasionally quotes in Greek and translates into Latin,[22] and it is from both Greek and Latin that he derives his etymologies. Most often however, with scholarly punctiliousness, he lists other sources for his etymologies. One such list occurs for the name Hercules. According to Leontius, he says, it comes from *hera* ("earth") and *cleos* ("glory"), while Paolo da Perugia derives it from *eri* (Latin, *lis*: "fight") and *cleos* ("glory"), and Rabanus from *heruncleos* ("fame of strong men").[23]

Likewise for his allegories, some are derived, some original. An original allegorical reading is offered for Pasiphae. "Pasiphae, daughter of the Sun, is the soul, child of God; her consort, Minos, is human reason, which governs the soul and leads it along the right path. Venus, her enemy, is lust; the bull represents the pleasures of this world, and from the union of the soul with pleasure is born the Minotaur, the vice of bestiality" (IV,10).[24] Boccaccio is here using the allegorical mode, an extremely complex exegetical tool which will also be the basis of his defense of poetry. The allegorical mode here referred to is the fourfold medieval manner of interpretation which Boccaccio applies, by way of example, in his discussion of the myth of Perseus.

The first meaning is the superficial, which is called literal. The others are deeper, and are called allegorical. To make the matter easier, I will give an example. According to the poetic fiction, Perseus, son of Jupiter, killed the Gorgon, and flew away victorious into the air. Now this may be understood superficially in its literal or historical sense. In the moral sense it shows a wise man's triumph over vice and his attainment of virtue. Allegorically it figures the pious man who scorns worldly delight and lifts his mind to heavenly things. It admits also an anagogical sense, since it symbolizes Christ's victory over the Prince of this World, and his Ascension.[25]

We will have occasion to observe a similar use of the allegorical mode in other of his later works.

While the *Genealogie* was an essential handbook for almost two centuries, the defense of poetry in Books XIV and XV is by far the more interesting section for our age. Here again, Boccaccio offers little that is original except perhaps a more complete and more impassioned discussion of a very old question. The question, to oversimplify greatly, concerned the relation of myths and poetry to reality and consequently to morality and to theology. Upon this depended in turn the role of the poet. Central to the issue is the equation of myth and poetry, an equation that for Boccaccio embodied classical culture; hence the truth of the myths and the truth of poetry were the same problem.[26] But how could pagan myths, or poetry based on pagan myths, have any moral or theological value for a Christian?

A solution to the problem of the relationship of poetry to theology and reality had been offered by the Greeks themselves in regard to Homer. The issue of the moral value of poetry culminated with Plato[27] and was solved with the expedient of allegorical interpretation.[28] Thus poetry answered to philosophy. Homer's real meanings were hidden under the surface of his poetry. On this Greek model, allegory was also applied to the Old Testament, and from Jewish biblical allegory came Jerome, Augustine and Christian allegoresis with regard to Scripture. Indeed it was under the rubric of biblical allegoresis that pagan myths came into Christian iconography. Pagan myths therefore could reveal some of the same truths as Scriptures; and just as a biblical poetics (Jerome) justified poetry as divine (the prophets were poets, the argument ran, and Christ used parables to reveal the truth), so were pagan poets considered inspired prophets who either purposely buried their real meanings below the surface, or were led, unconsciously and by divine inspiration, to infuse their works with Christian significance.[29] This is the *theologia poetica,* the justification of pagan poetry as possible Christian theology[30] and its poets were the *prisci poetae,* superior men inspired by truth, though unbeknown to them.

It was the early Christians, such as Varro and Augustine, who helped to establish the arguments as to what truths the myths may conceal. Augustine in the *City of God* (18.14), described the gods as "(a) eminent men deified by legend; or (b) deified forces of nature and human life, 'elements of this world which the true God made'; or (c) 'creatures who were ordained as principalities and powers according to the will of the Creator,' that is, the angels both good and fallen."[31] These divisions correspond to the allegorical levels recognized by medieval exegetes and by Boccaccio. The first is historical or euhemeristic, the second moral, and the third allegorical.

The above arguments for poetry (poetry is a divine right from heaven, myths tell the same truths as Scripture, poetry is a second theology) are repeated by Mussato in his epistles,[32] by Petrarch (*Fam.* X,4) and by Boccaccio in the fourteenth and fifteenth books of his *Genealogie.*

Boccaccio begins his defense by attacking four categories of detractors of poetry. The first and weakest are the wealthy "viveurs" who are barely worth consideration in their hedonism. The second group is the imperfectly educated, those who put on ponderous airs although they possess only a very superficial acquaintance with the matter. Third are the jurists, against whom he refutes the accusation that poets are poor, with a defense of poverty. Finally there are the educated and presumptuous clergy. His arguments are many, and he digresses, but among the most important are his definitions of poetry and his view of its purpose. Poetry he says is "fervid and exquisite invention." It comes from the Greek word *poetes* which, he says, in Latin means "exquisite discourse" (the etymology is from Isidore and is incorrect). Poetry proceeds from the bosom of God and contains a component of furor, which distinguishes poetic creation from the notion of craft or mere rhetoric, and leads poets to seek secluded spots in Nature for their creation. Furthermore it has its origins in the religious instinct. In tracing the origins of poetry, Boccaccio straddles the classical and the Christian world by giving arguments for poetry as the invention of the Hebrews and the Greeks (XIV,8).

The essence of poetry is to veil truth in a fair garment of fiction (*fabula*). Fiction therefore "is a form of discourse, which, under the guise of invention, illustrates or proves an idea."[33] Boccaccio discusses four kinds of fiction: the kind that lacks all appearance of truth, as in Aesop's fables; the kind that mixes fiction with truth, as in certain myths; the kind that is more history than fiction, as in the description of Aeneas tossed by the storm (which however hides a moral message); and the fourth kind contains no truth at all and is just old wives' tales. The first three kinds of fiction are all to be found in Scripture.

The purpose and power of poetry are to edify and improve the reader, and since poetry bears the truth in pleasing garb it can both please the unlearned with its appearance and stimulate the learned with its hidden truth, improving both the while. Therefore poets cannot be liars for it is the very contradiction of poetry to deceive, and bad poetry and bad poets are not germane to his discussion for the very reason that being bad they are therefore not a stimulus to virtue as poetry by definition must be.

Poetry then is not a deceptive inducement to sin as its detractors would have it, but rather the source of noble sentiments which turn men away from the desire of vain earthly goods to the contemplation of the divine. In the Stoic and Christian elements of this argument we have the beginnings, although not original with Boccaccio, of the attitudes toward the classics and lay piety that were to nurture the following generations of humanists. And in the enthusiasm of his defense we have the measure of Boccaccio's passionate commitment to literature.

The *Trattatello in laude di Dante* [Treatise in Praise of Dante]

Boccaccio's interest in the classics never overcame his awareness of the importance and potentialities of the Italian language. Contemporaneously with these Latin treatises he wrote the *Trattatello in Laude di Dante* in praise of his revered master in Italian.[34] This work has come down to us in three versions. The first belongs to these years between 1355 and 1361, and the others, more concise and less impassioned revisions of this earlier work, to a later period.[35] The first version is as much an encomium and spiritual biography as a record of Dante's life. It seems a combination of classical biography, medieval hagiography and the art of narration as exemplified in the *Decameron*.[36] The events of the life of the Florentine bard serve to praise him, making an *exemplum* of his life, and to offer digressions to related themes. The initial purpose of this work seems to be that of serving as a political *exemplum* (as in the *De casibus*) and revealing the serious shortcomings of the Florentine government in the example of Dante's exile. But he soon wanders far afield. Boccaccio says he will write in Italian lest his work be in discord with most of Dante's works which were also in Italian. Dante's origins are told as part of a brief history of the city of Florence, which includes a prophetic dream and an eloquent declaration of Dante's importance as a poet, theologian and philosopher. We are told of Dante's love for Beatrice, of his public activity, his exile, his studies and writing, his importance for Italian literature, and his death. There follows a series of apostrophes and digressions interwoven with more biographical detail. Dante's death in Ravenna evinces a diatribe against Florence, wherein, after several examples of the glories brought to ancient cities by their outstanding citizens, Boccaccio exhorts Florence to request Dante's remains, but predicts that the request will not be granted.[37]

There follows a physical description of Dante, along with his habits, his tendency, proper to all poets, toward solitude, and his love for glory. From the question of glory Boccaccio departs on what he himself recognizes as a rather long digression on the origin of poetry. This discussion, moving from the etymology of the word poetry to the sources of ancient religion, reiterates the arguments found in the last two books of the *Genealogie* and to be found again in the *Esposizioni* (Commentary) to the *Divine Comedy*. He then returns to a description of Dante's character as disdainful and proud. And following a traditional interpretation of some of Dante's poems and certain passages of the *Commedia* as confessions of his proclivity for lust, he justifies lust as a weakness common to all men. He bolsters his argument with many great examples, and concludes that while he cannot excuse it, he also cannot condemn it.

Boccaccio relates many of the apocryphal stories and anecdotes concerning Dante and his *Commedia*. One of the most famous is that the composition of the *Inferno* was interrupted by his exile after Canto VII, hence Canto VIII begins, "I say, to continue. . . ." Another anecdote concerns the dream that came to Dante's son Jacopo as to whether or not Dante had finished the *Commedia* and the whereabouts of the missing cantos. Boccaccio also discusses the question of language and defends Dante's choice of Italian for his *Commedia* with the arguments expounded by Dante himself in the *Convivio* (I,vi), namely, that he would thus help all citizens and not just the learned, and would demonstrate the beauty of Italian. He concludes his treatise with mention of Dante's other works—the *Monarchia,* the ecologues written to Giovanni del Virgilio, his poems and the *De vulgari eloquentia*—and finally he returns to the prophetic dream that came to Dante's mother, mentioned at the beginning of the work, and draws to a close with an allegorical interpretation of this dream.

In this biography Boccaccio's intellectual passions seem to converge on the life of Dante. The importance of poetry, philosophy, and the contemplative life; his adoration of Dante, not only as a contemporary model of all these virtues, but as a pioneer in the affirmation of the Italian language; and his indignation at the political situation of Florence, also represented and deplored by Dante, are themes he has reiterated again and again. Even Boccaccio's recurrent misogynism rears its head here. In recounting Dante's marriage to Gemma Donati, Boccaccio pauses for a diatribe against wives and matrimony as he did in the *Corbaccio* and will again in the *Esposizioni.* Nor is a touch of wry narrative realism lacking in this intellectual and encomiastic biography. When he describes the divine and mystically significant meeting of Dante and Beatrice, he takes a singular view of this theological love. He does not fail to observe that as we all see from experience, at a party, the sweet sounds, the general gaiety, the delicacy of food and wine common at parties, open the spirits of even the full grown to all sorts of pleasure, wherefore they might be expected to have all the more effect on the young.[38]

The *Buccolicum carmen* [Eclogues]

Boccaccio wrote sixteen eclogues, most of which are extremely difficult to date.[39] It appears that in writing these verses in Latin, with the names and the allegory traditional to classical pastoral poetry, he was consciously following the example of Virgil and Theocritus, and probably more immediately Petrarch.[40] In one of his surviving letters, written probably in 1374 to Fra Martino da Signa, Boccaccio glosses his sixteen eclogues and recognizes only these three poets as his models in this genre. He was therefore purposely sidestepping, as did Petrarch, the more immediately familiar form of poetic contest, the *tenzone.* [41] The *tenzone* was a form of poetic correspondence in Italian where one poem required the response of another, often using the same rhyme scheme. Something similar was carried on in Latin by Dante and Giovanni del Virgilio which, despite its classical elements, seems to have been purposely ignored by Boccaccio in his *Buccolicum* as being too close to the *tenzone*. Instead, each of his eclogues (he followed a similar form in Italian in the contest between the two shepherds in the *Ameto*) contains both sides of the argument, as it did in classical pastoral poetry.

The eclogues, in the order in which Boccaccio arranged them, appear to trace the spiritual and intellectual itinerary of their author. The first two are strictly personal and sentimental. "Galla," the first, parallels the last eclogue of Virgil, and speaks of Damon (Boccaccio), who tells Tyndarus (unidentified and perhaps created simply as an interlocutor) of his love for a nymph whose love has been stolen by the shepherd Pamphylus. Likewise in the second, "Pampinea," Palemone laments his love for the unfaithful Pampinea. In the sentimental outbursts on perfidious love and the recurrence of names familiar from earlier works, some have been tempted to glimpse Boccaccio returning to the story of his early loves.[42] Once again, he is probably abstracting the emotional essence of his own experiences (after all, there is nothing original about love and betrayal) and expressing it as it had already been expressed by his models in the classical pastoral form.

Eclogues III through VI, under the allegorical veil of pastoral poetry, reflect events precipitating around Boccaccio. "Faunus" (III) tells first of Francesco Ordelaffi, Boccaccio's host in Forlì, and then of the horrendous events in the Kingdom of Naples with the assassination of Andrew of Hungary. "Dorus" (IV), "Silva cadens" (V), and "Alcestus" (VI) continue to relate the sequence of horrors in Naples, commiserating with the fate of this great state, recounting its restoration and offering an encomium of the Angevins. Eclogues VII ("Iurgium") and IX ("Lipis")—separated by VIII ("Midas"), which is a personal attack against Niccolò Acciaiuoli, seneschal of the Kingdom of Naples and onetime friend of Boccaccio—treat the issue of the Emperor Charles IV of Luxembourg and the sentiment of the city of Florence against his descent into Italy. On this matter Boccaccio was sent to Avignon in 1365 by the government of Florence to offer their support to the Pope against the Emperor. Eclogue X ("Vallis opaca") is a mysterious eclogue in which the shepherd Licida is called up from Hell to speak with

Dorilo, who laments his cruel destiny. An obscure prophecy at the end has led some to think Boccaccio was referring to his disastrous visit to Naples at the request of Acciaiuoli.[43]

Eclogues XI through XVI reveal greater serenity and a more philosophical frame of mind. "Pantheon" (XI) represents the Saints Peter and Paul and the Church, where the Church is seen as united despite the efforts of the Devil to take away the flock (to Avignon). "Saphthos" (XII) presents the issue of poetry. Saphthos (Poetry) is removed from the masses to maintain her purity. Aristeo (Boccaccio) wants to enjoy her, as Silvanus (Petrarch) has done, but Aristeo is reproached for writing in Italian and with praise of Petrarch, Boccaccio excuses his works in Italian as youthful folly. Eclogue XII ("Laurea") continues the celebration of poetry, conducting the argument in terms familiar from the Introduction to the Fourth Day of the *Decameron* and the defense of poetry in the *Genealogie,* namely, the affirmation of the value of poetry above the mundane activity of business.

"Olympia" (XIV) is one of the few documents in the Boccaccio corpus that truly reveals something of his private life, for it represents his illegitimate daughter Violante (Olympia), who died before she was seven. The only other mention of Violante is in a letter to Petrarch written in 1367 in which he says he saw her for the last time when she was five and a half years old. This is the most tender and religious of the eclogues. It begins with the dramatic staging of a servant calling Boccaccio (Silvius) to arise to come see a flame. The flame is Olympia in a celestial vision and the father, doubting his vision and finding her grown up, converses with her. She indicates the children near her as his other children—Mario, Giulio, and the little sisters—who we know only from this indication. The children then sing the praise of Codrus (Christ) and the history of Christianity, and the eclogue ends with Olympia comforting her father about gaining Heaven.

Eclogue XV ("Philostropos") is a spiritual conversation between Philostropos (Petrarch) and Typhlos (Boccaccio) in which the former admonishes the latter for his indulgence. Petrarch tells him winter (old age) is coming and warns him against his love of Criside (wealth) and Dione (lust). Petrarch describes beatitude in Christ, whereupon Boccaccio shows repentance and is helped by Petrarch to undertake the mystic road. The last eclogue, "Aggelos," is a conversation between

Apenninus (Donato Albanzani, grammarian, teacher, and friend to Petrarch and Boccaccio to whom the *Eclogues* are dedicated) and Aggelos, the poem itself. This poem treats a bit of everything— Boccaccio's admiration of Petrarch, his unfortunate trip to Naples, his tendency toward lust, now corrected, his love of freedom and his life of poverty in Certaldo. It offers the reflections of an old man taking stock of his life. Thus in the later eclogues we find Boccaccio renewing the classical pastoral form with arguments of a different nature. Beyond the classical lament on love and the veiled reflection of contemporary events through allegory, Boccaccio uses the eclogue as a philosophical mouthpiece to express his religious aspirations and his belief in the importance of poetry.

Petrarch and the Greek Translation

At this point we must turn to something that has already become evident as a pivotal force in the second half of Boccaccio's life, his friendship with Petrarch. In this long and deep association, based on mutual admiration and affection, we find many of the roots of the cultural renewal called humanism. The friendship was characterized by Boccaccio's humility before Petrarch and Petrarch's generosity toward his admirer. Boccaccio repeatedly turned to the older man for guidance, acknowledging Petrarch's spiritual and intellectual influence on him as determining factors in his work. Petrarch, in turn, never ceased to offer Boccaccio stimulation and hospitality. On several occasions Boccaccio did visit Petrarch and each of these visits yielded an exchange of ideas and a fruitful collaboration in the discovery and transcribing of texts.

From just such a visit in 1359 probably was born the great project of translating Homer into Latin from the Greek texts in Petrarch's possession. Petrarch had already requested of Leontius Pilatus, a Calabrian of Greek origin who passed himself off for Greek, that he begin the translation. Boccaccio returned to Florence full of enthusiasm for the project, and with his influential position probably spent the next months in an effort to bring this Leontius Pilatus to the Studio in Florence. His efforts were successful; Leontius came to Florence and was received as a guest in Boccaccio's house. Despite his horrid appearance and boorish manners (*Gen.* XV,6) Leontius did know some Greek, so

Boccaccio tolerated him in order to learn some of the language and finally know Homer. Leontius began giving lessons at the Studio and at the same time worked on the translation, closely followed and encouraged by the friends of the Florentine circle and through letters by Petrarch.[44] In the two and one-half years spent in Florence he translated and commented the *Iliad,* the *Odyssey,* and works of Euripides and Aristotle. The translations and the accompanying commentaries were incomplete and of average quality, but they were, if nothing else, a pioneering effort in the rediscovery of the classical world, especially Greek. It is in this connection that the modest Boccaccio displays a trace of pride when he says: "It was I who first returned the books of Homer and other Greeks to Etruria, where they had not been for many centuries; and not only to Etruria but to the nation" *(Gen.* XV,7). Classical literature, for the most part synonymous with Latin authors, now begins to be conceived and understood in a new perspective of the continuity of Greek and Latin culture.[45]

In this harmonious friendship, as we know of it from their letters, there appeared to be only two points of disagreement. The first is the question of maintaining personal freedom as opposed to dependency upon great lords and courts. In a letter to Petrarch (July 18, 1353) Boccaccio, who had procured an invitation to the Studio in Florence for Petrarch (1351), which the latter had refused, expresses his dismay that Petrarch, after long preferring Provence to Italy, has made his return to Italy only to enter the services of the Visconti in Milan, particularly because of the Visconti threat to Florence and the tyrannical nature of the Archbishop of Milan. Under the veil of a pastoral setting, Boccaccio accuses Petrarch of having relinquished his freedom, and expresses his concern as to how Petrarch, the great seeker of solitude, will fare surrounded by the multitude of a court.[46] To guarantee the personal freedom he so cherished, Boccaccio, by contrast, insisted on living out his life in poverty in Certaldo rather than accept any such offer, even that of his dear friend Petrarch.

The other matter of disagreement was the poetry of Dante, around which revolved the question of the use of Latin versus Italian. For Petrarch, more thoroughly committed to the importance of Latin and classical culture, despite his repeated attention to his own works in Italian, the question was not so thorny. For Boccaccio, torn between, on the one hand, his admiration for Petrarch and his love of the classics, and on the other, his adoration of Dante and his interest in popular literature, it was much more difficult. In the second half of his life, the period of Petrarchean influence, the conflict seemed more acute. He wrote biographies of ancients and moderns in Latin (*De casibus, De mulieribus*), but also wrote a biography of Dante in Italian. He wrote Latin letters in the classical epistolary style and classical eclogues in Latin, but also wrote sonnets in Italian and a commentary on the greatest Italian poem, the *Divine Comedy*. And while he spent a great deal of time copying ancient texts for himself and Petrarch, he also took time at the very end of his life to recopy his *Decameron*. [47] In a letter following Boccaccio's visit to Petrarch in 1359, after which he sent him a copy of Dante's *Commedia*, Boccaccio wrote his host accusing him of not appreciating Dante's poetry. That letter is lost, but we know of it from Petrarch's reply (*Fam.* XXI,15), which is ambiguous and offers only rather oblique compliments to Dante's work. Petrarch hails Dante as a friend of his father's (they were sent into exile at the same time) and admires his singleness of purpose despite all his adversities. He claims he did not read Dante in his youth so as not to have his style in Italian influenced. Dante, he says, certainly deserves the palm of "vernacular eloquence," but he himself abandoned Italian poetry early in his youth lest it be ruined in the mouths of the ignorant. Therefore, he can hardly be considered envious of one who devoted his entire life to something that for him only occupied his early years.

The same issue of language is implicit in one of Petrarch's last letters (1373) in which he speaks of the *Decameron*. He claims he has not read it, for he has more serious occupations demanding his attention. But he does approve of Boccaccio's self-defense in the book and excuses the licentious parts on the basis of Boccaccio's age at the time he wrote it, his subject matter, and the audience to which it was directed. He has read mostly the beginning and the end and was greatly struck by the last story of Griselda; so much so that he has learned it by heart, has told it to others, and has seen fit to translate it into Latin for the benefit of those who do not know Italian. He says he is telling the story as Boccaccio told it, but in his own words, and he is sure Boccaccio will be happy to have such a translator. Finally, he offers a moral purpose: not that women follow the example of Griselda, which is impossible, but that men imitate her fortitude in the service of God.

In 1362 a monk visited Boccaccio, claiming to represent the Sienese Pietro Petroni, who had just died in odor of sanctity, with the exhortation to both Boccaccio and Petrarch to abandon their profane studies and turn to sacred matters before impending death overcame them. Rather upset by this visit, Boccaccio wrote to Petrarch proposing to burn all his writings and offering to sell his library to his friend. Petrarch answered, with olympic calm (*Sen.* I, 5) that he should not make hurried decisions. He warns his friend that many lies are hidden under the veil of religion and sanctity, and that while the word of Christ is true, it must be ascertained that this is the word of Christ, for prophecies at the moment of death were common among the pagans as well, and they did not know the word of Christ. That death is approaching is axiomatic for all human beings, especially the elderly, but rather than fear death we must try to correct life. In this connection he finds the prohibition of poetry the most objectionable of the monk's exhortations, especially when made to an expert who finds all his moral solace therein. And, he argues, if such prohibitions had been made to Christian scholars such as Lactantius, Augustine, or Jerome, where would Christian thought be? Educated men can separate the true from the false in pagan works and to such a spirit letters are not an impediment but a comfort. Always avid for books however, Petrarch adds that if Boccaccio still wants to sell him his library he will be happy to purchase it at whatever price he fixes. [48]

Petrarch's arguments are important because they are part of the *theologia poetica* under whose rubric he, Boccaccio, and many of the humanists who followed them, defended their scholarly interest in pagan literature and, we might say, assuaged their own consciences as Christians. Religious scruples were certainly at least a contributing factor to some of the changes in the latter part of Boccaccio's life. In 1360 he received papal dispensation with regard to his illegitimate birth in order to receive Church benefices. We have no documentary evidence of his taking Church orders, but this document, and the fact that Church vestments appear in his will, have led many to believe that in this period he received some ecclesiastic benefice from Innocent VI.

The *Epistole* [Letters]

An important document of Boccaccio's life and thought, albeit incomplete, are his letters. The survival of the letters has been haphazard. Although they are mentioned by scholars at the end of the fourteenth century, those scholars probably did not know many more letters than we do. Unlike Petrarch, Boccaccio did not collect his letters, nor did recipients collect them, as happened with Petrarch and other friends in their circle. Some of the oldest letters Boccaccio preserved in his *Zibaldone,* the letter to Fra Martino da Signa accompanied the *Buccolicum carmen,* the letter to Barbato da Sulmona was found in Barbato's collection of his correspondence, three or four survived singly and scattered, and another half-dozen were collected by an unknown scholar a few decades after Boccaccio's death. In the case of two of the letters, among the longest and most famous, the original Latin letter was eclipsed by the Italian translation and only for one do we have a fragment of the Latin original. The letters attributed to Boccaccio today are twenty-six, including an early letter with a part written in Neapolitan dialect, and another more recent attribution. [49]

Boccaccio's letters were originally in Latin and like those of Petrarch are to be considered literary exercises. They take the occasion of the letter to offer philosophical observations and an example of epistolary style. The early letters follow the medieval rules of the *ars dictandi* and reveal a rigorous use of the *cursus*; the letters after 1350 show the influence of Petrarch, and recall classical models. We can imagine that Boccaccio wrote personal and business letters, probably in Italian, but those were not intended for public consumption, as were the Latin epistles, and have not survived.

The earliest letters are heavily rhetorical and burdened with classical images. One of the first (*Epist.* II) dated 1339, believed to be addressed to Petrarch, whom Boccaccio did not know personally at the time, depicts Boccaccio in Naples drawing inspiration at the tomb of Virgil when a woman appeared to him. He immediately fell in love, and with great rhetorical flourish he describes how Fortune mistreated him in his love and how he was delivered by a friend who advised him to follow virtue and the teaching of Petrarch to free him of his affliction. Petrarch, he says, derives his genius from Saturn, his placidity and wealth from Jove, jocundity from Venus, and so forth, including excellence in grammar, geometry, and music drawn from Aristarchus, Euclid, and Boethius among others. Through Petrarch's teaching Boccaccio hopes to decorate his brow with the Apollonian helmet, his left hand with the Athenian shield, the right with the Minervan rod and rise to understand Pluto's Hell and the Primum Mobile. These numerous classical references and the long, rhetorical nature of his sentences are characteristic of his early style.

Other letters help us to understand better some of the events and vicissitudes of his life. Some are documents of his early friendship, and later enmity, with Zanobi da Strada and Niccolò Acciaiuoli. In one to Zanobi (*Epist.* VIII) he defends himself from Niccolò's accusation that he is *Iohannem tranquillitatum*—a friend in time of tranquility, but unavailable when events take a different turn.[50] Other letters concern the study of literature, texts, poetry, and the glory of letters. Still others document aspects of his friendship with Petrarch—he describes a visit to Petrarch, he discusses the information on the life of Peter Damian that Petrarch had requested (*Epist.* X),[51] and in one of the last (*Epist.* XXIV) he mourns the death of his beloved friend to Francesco da Brossano, Petrarch's son-in-law.

One of the most famous of the letters, come down to us in the Italian translation, is the *Letter of Consolation to Pino de' Rossi*.[52] In 1360, after several years of relative calm and well-being for Florence, and for Boccaccio as well, the city was once again disturbed by factional strife. In reaction against Guelf terrorism spreading in the city, a conspiracy was planned in which several of Boccaccio's friends took part, Pino de' Rossi among them. The conspiracy was discovered, and while some were condemned to death, Pino de' Rossi and others were condemned to exile. It is on this occasion that Boccaccio wrote the famous consolatory letter (1361) in which he condemned the factionalism that was ruining the city, although, faithful to Guelfism, he did not specifically condemn the Florentine government.

The letter consoles Rossi with examples of exile among the ancients and sustains the opinion of ancient philosophers that since man is born a citizen of the world and not of a particular city, exile is meaningless. The poverty consequent upon exile evokes the familiar discourse in praise of poverty based essentially on the assertion that the life of the poor man is more carefree and stable, or more immune to the caprice of Fortune, than that of the rich. As for family concerns, it is easier to raise honest children in privation, it is easier to sustain misfortune in old age, and if he is lucky to have an honest wife—though few men do—he can have no greater consolation in his misfortune. The keynote to this letter is the *exemplum*. For each assertion and its opposite, Boccaccio comforts his friend with examples from the ancients, telling him to take consolation in the community of human experience. At the close of the letter he describes his own life, perhaps as an example as well, in his self-imposed "exile" in Certaldo, where he was growing used to the "coarser clothes" and the "peasant food."

Boccaccio did venture forth from Certaldo on other occasions subsequently. Shortly after the consolatory letter he was invited by Acciaiuoli to Naples, where he was received in a most humiliating manner, as described in his letter to Francesco Nelli (*Epist.* XII,1363). He proceeded from there to Venice to visit Petrarch, but refused Petrarch's invitation to remain with him. In 1365 he was sent to the Pope in Avignon by the Florentine government and again on a mission to Rome in 1367. In 1368 he made what was to be his last visit to Petrarch in Padua, and in 1370 a final trip to Naples, this time invited by Queen Johanna and warmly received by his friends there. He ultimately returned to Certaldo, whence we hear him writing, after 1373, about his ill health, his work on Dante, and, in a curious letter for the question of his attitude toward the *Decameron* in his later life, about his early works. This letter (*Epist.* XXI) is addressed to Mainardo Cavalcanti, and in it Boccaccio exhorts his friend not to allow the women in his household to read his licentious works (he calls them "domestic trifles") lest they be corrupted. This disparaging attitude toward his early works, an attitude of moral scruples as to their rectitude and intellectual scruples as to their cultural value, represents one aspect of Boccaccio's ambivalence in the latter part of his life. The other aspect is represented by the fact that in his very last years he saw fit to recopy the *Decameron*. In this he was not unlike his mentor Petrarch, who disparagingly called his sonnets *nugellae* ("trifles") but carefully arranged them into the *Canzoniere*.[53]

The *Esposizioni sopra la "Comedia" di Dante*
[Commentary to Dante's *Comedia*]

Boccaccio's last literary endeavor was the commentary on the *Divine Comedy* of Dante. In 1373, upon petition of certain citizens, the government of Florence approved the public reading of Dante and called upon its most prominent poet to inaugurate the first *Lectura Dantis*. Thus these last years were also spent rereading and commenting on his "first leader and light in his studies." He had completed Canto XVI and had barely begun Canto XVII of the *Inferno* when illness curtailed his work.

It is axiomatic that criticism reveals as much about the critic and his cultural ambience as about the work he discusses, and Boccaccio's *Esposizioni* are no exception. The attention of the humanistic scholar to pagan myths and etymologies is accompanied by the scruples of the medieval exegete to allegorize them; the deep feeling for the greatest Italian poet, and his most important work in the vernacular tongue, is qualified by an apology for Dante as an accomplished Latinist; and erudite prose and rhetorical discourse are juxtaposed with simple storytelling.

The critical method Boccaccio applies to the *Divine Comedy* is a time-honored one deriving from Servius, Boethius, and more immediately, St. Thomas and Dante himself, and it is a reading based on allegory. He begins in his *accessus* with a discussion of the title, the causes of the work, a brief life of its author, and a consideration of its meaning. The work is of course polysemous and for each canto he will expound the literal and then the allegorical senses. But his treatment of the meanings of the work is a somewhat confusing problem. Boccaccio holds the idea, as we observed in his discussion in the *Genealogie,* that all great poetry is polysemous. And in the specific case of Dante's poetry, Dante's own exposition of the levels of meaning of poetry in the *Convivio* (II,i) and in his *Letter to Can Grande* give even more significance to this thesis. The confusion, however, arises first from the lack of clear distinction between the allegory of poets and the allegory of theologians, where the former yields "moral" truths while the latter yields "moral" and "Christian" truths. Though he at times extracts Christian or theological truths in his interpretation, Boccaccio's reading of Dante's text is essentially "moral" or the allegory of poets. In fact he divides his discussion of each canto into the literal and the allegorical. This is itself a distortion of Dante's *Commedia* seen through the lens of Boccaccio's poetic theories. In his interpretation of great poetry as allegorical, Boccaccio's assumption is that the literal level of the poem is a fictive veil for supernal truths. This leads him to a violation of the literal level of Dante's poem, much of which he ignores in its historical and moral importance, by denying its literality. And he compromises the originality of Dante's allegory which is based on the premise that his fiction, his literal story line, is not a fiction at all.[54] Paradoxically Boccaccio then devotes more attention to the literal level of the poem, with the result that much of the historicity and factuality of the *Commedia* are allegorized while certain very striking aspects of the allegory are not revealed.

Boccaccio's points are frequently based on *auctoritas*. He summons an array of pagan authors, early Christian commentators, medieval exegetes, and examples from Scripture. He justifies Dante's depiction of souls as corporeal on the grounds that Virgil did the same in the *Aeneid* (*Espos.,Inf.* VI,17); while the authority of early Christian commentators helps him with the tangles of allegory. Augustine guarantees against excessive allegorical interpretation when he says that not all that is narrated is to be construed as having another meaning (*Espos.,Inf.*I,2,92). On the other hand Boccaccio argues from biblical exegesis for his interpretation of many figures in the *Inferno* as polysemous. In his discussion of Canto VII he justifies his dual interpretation of Cerberus as representing both gluttony and avarice with the commonly accepted opinion that figures in the Bible could have several meanings. The serpent he says, by way of example, represents the Devil in Genesis and the Apocalypse but in Numbers signifies Christ; likewise does a stone mean now Christ, now sinful men.

Boccaccio's literal exposition is often paraphrasing. He tells us that "running through the air" means "flying" (*Espos.,Inf.* VIII,14) and that "on the tip of a mountain" means "on top" (*Espos.,Inf.* XII,11). For certain poetic devices he offers a rather literal discussion. He explains that in a verse such as "She pushed me back . . . to where the sun is silent" (*Espos.,Inf.*I,60)[55] or "I came into a place mute of all light" (*Espos.,Inf.*V,28), the line makes no literal sense because the sun does not speak, nor can a place be silent of light. But this is "acrylogia," he says, on the authority of Isidore, and can be excused as a figure of speech.

Another important exegetic tool Boccaccio employs here, as in the *Genealogie,* is etymology. At the end of Canto IX, when Dante beholds the punishment of the heretics in flaming tombs, Boccaccio records the various terms used by Dante for tomb—*sepolcri, avelli, arche, tombe, monimenti.* In his zeal he even produces other words for the same— *locelli, tumuli, sarcofagi, mausolei, busti, urne*—not even mentioned by Dante. For each word he gives an etymology (e.g., *sepolcro* from *seorsum pulchro,* "separated from the beautiful," because of the corruption of the body) taken mostly from Isidore. In his discussion of Canto V and the circle of the lustful he subjects love, the muse of his youth, to similar scholarly consideration. Carnal sin can be committed in five ways and is called variously fornication, rape, adultery, incest, and sodomy. An etymology is presented for each (for example, *adulterium*: *alterius ventrem terere*) as the text of Dante becomes a pretext for a humanistic scholar.

The *Esposizioni* are also studded with rhetorical and moralizing disquisitions. In Canto I, as a gloss on the word "poet" he expounds upon the truth of the pagan poets, the importance of Petrarch, the significance of poetry in the Bible, and the arguments in the defense of poetry we have observed in the *Genealogie.* The misery and pettiness of avarice, familiar to Boccaccio from his early contacts with the merchant world, call forth a vivid portrait of the miser and an imprecation against that sin in his discussion of the very first Canto. The explanation of the circle of the lustful (*Espos.,Inf.* V) contains a denunciation of mores and manners of dressing, and finally the execration of the corruption of women in a misogynistic tirade.

The many myths and historical figures that people the *Divine Comedy* call forth digressions that are more clearly narrative interludes. It is, in fact, in these latter instances that we recognize once again the permanent genius of Boccaccio. The story of Francesca da Rimini, enlivened with dialogue and embellished with dramatic detail, stands out as a delightful little novella; and the same is true of his narration of the vicissitudes of the life of Dante or of the classical myths.

The *Esposizioni* are rich for a number of reasons. First, they offer a fund of information of a historical, biographical, and anecdotal nature. Furthermore, they are the first great landmark in Dante criticism, and they help us to measure the change in the intellectual climate that has already taken place; for much in Boccaccio's critical technique—his way of using etymologies and his recording of myths, for example—establishes a humanistic approach to Dante's great poem.[56] The *Esposizioni* also help us to understand Boccaccio by revealing, through Dante's text, Boccaccio's own sensibilities.

This is the last of Boccaccio's works, the effort that absorbed him until his death. What we know of his last days emerges from letters. In July 1374 Petrarch died, willing a fur blanket to his friend Boccaccio to warm him during his studies on long winter nights. Boccaccio mourns the death of his dear friend in a letter (*Epist.* XXIV) and a sonnet (CXXVI). But Boccaccio's own health, undermined by dropsy and scabies, continued to wane, and he passed his last months and weeks in serene study in Certaldo, where he died on December 21, 1375.

Chapter Six
Boccaccio and Posterity

Boccaccio's stature as a man of letters was apparent to his contemporaries even during his lifetime. Upon his death another famous narrator, Franco Sacchetti, expressed the bereavement of men of culture in rather dramatic terms:

Or è mancata ogni poesia
e vote or sono le case di Parnaso
po' che morte n'ha tolto ogni valore. . . .

(Now all poetry is gone, and the dwellings of
Parnassus are empty, since death has taken away
all virtue. . . .)

The significance of Boccaccio's work has of necessity varied with the tastes and attitudes of each subsequent age, and Boccaccio himself did much to establish the measure for the generation immediately succeeding him. Despite the interesting "hiatus" in which he took the time and trouble to recopy his great *Decameron,* he had spent the latter part of his life, along with Petrarch, in fostering interest in humanistic studies, namely study and scholarship applied to ancient works and a cultivation of erudition in Latin. Both men ostensibly scorned their works in Italian and the greatest, and only, tribute Petrarch could pay to Boccaccio's *Decameron* was to translate the story of Griselda into Latin.

As Coluccio Salutati indicates in the epitaph he wrote for Boccaccio, the century following the death of Boccaccio concentrated on his erudite works—the *De casibus, De mulieribus, De montibus,* and especially the *Genealogie.* This latter enjoyed immense popularity, and for two centuries it was the main source for knowledge of the gods.[1] After the invention of printing, between 1472 and 1532 it underwent eight printings in Latin alone. Nonetheless, the *Decameron* did become the

basis for narration in Italian (though some of the tales were translated
into Latin) and there was a proliferation of works based on stories told
within a frame. Toward the end of the fifteenth century in Italy there is
a revived interest in the use of Italian and throughout the sixteenth
century, as Petrarch is the model for poetry, so Boccaccio is the model
for prose. From here on the history of Boccaccio criticism is essentially
history of the *Decameron*. The *Decameron* is taken as the perfect fusion of
the Italian language with Latin style and Boccaccio becomes for scholars
of this period what Cicero had been for the humanists. Pietro Bembo
was the most ardent and prestigious advocate of the imitation of
Boccaccio's language as a canon of order and clarity, and while Castiglione in his *Courtier* presents the counterargument against exaggerated
servility to models, he too accepts the authority and excellence of
Boccaccio's language. There was also a flowering of the novella form on
the example of Boccaccio in the works of men such as Bandello,
Aretino, Il Lasca, and Giraldi Cinthio. Relatively little attention is
paid to the *Decameron* as an aesthetic whole, and only toward the end of
the century does the emphasis shift, with the Counter-Reformation, to
a consideration of the work in a moral context.

The story of the *Decameron* during the Counter-Reformation is one of
the more curious episodes in Boccaccio criticism, and can only be
described in broad outline here.[2] In 1559, the *Decameron* was put on the
Index, but in 1564 it was given a suspension conditional upon expurgation. In 1571 Pius V asked the deputies of the Accademia Fiorentina
under Vincenzo Borghini to revise and expurgate the *Decameron*. This
expurgation was completed in 1573. The linguistic authority of Boccaccio was too imposing to be ignored and it is indicative that much of
Borghini's discussion turns on Boccaccio's importance as a linguistic
model, even though he warns against the servile imitation advocated by
Bembo. The conditions of the expurgation imposed by the Inquisition
were solely ecclesiastic—there was to be no scandal on members or
aspects of the Church. No mean feat, it would seem, in the case of the
Decameron; but in many of the stories Borghini simply changed the
clergy to lay figures.

In 1580 a new correction was ordered and was carried out by
Leonardo Salviati. Though many of the changes wrought in this
edition, completed in 1582, may have reflected personal tastes and

pressures and not the official line of the Church, the 1582 expurgation was a new "moralized" *Decameron* which considerably changed the character of the work.[3]

The seventeenth and eighteenth centuries show a decline in the interest in the works of Boccaccio and the *Decameron* in particular. Despite the Accademia degli Incogniti, who joined together to write in the style of Boccaccio, his work takes on an antiquarian philological interest and seems to exhaust itself in academic discussions of grammar. This was particularly true with regard to the Accademia della Crusca and the publication of their dictionary in 1612. The assiduous effort of seventeenth-century poets to find new and surprising turns of language made them somewhat disdainful of the narrow confinements of Tuscan prose and the rules derived from its acknowledged master. For the eighteenth century, Boccaccio's work remained essentially a lesson in words and somewhat frivolous. But there was the beginning of a new interest in an historical perspective. More attention was paid to Boccaccio's sources, to his psychological characterization, and to his value as a painter of fourteenth-century society. There begins to develop the idea that the *Decameron* emerged from the darkness of the Middle Ages. This conception was furthered by the poet Ugo Foscolo, who saw the value of the *Decameron* in its poetic vitality and in its triumph of instinct and free thought against the oppression of the Church, and not in its over-Latinized language or in its morality.

The conception of the *Decameron* as something new and different is most remarkably expressed by the nineteenth-century critic Francesco DeSanctis, who calls the *Decameron* "not a revolution but a catastrophe"[4] and sees it as the subversion of the medieval system of values. In his view the *Decameron* brings the realm of nature and instinct into literature and is totally devoid of any moral seriousness. It ushers in the new society of the Renaissance. DeSanctis also paid more attention than most to Boccaccio's other works, setting the tone for the Positivist school, which devoted most of its attention to ferreting out Boccaccio's sources and collating biographical material.

Criticism in the twentieth century is more difficult to sum up briefly. Beginning with Benedetto Croce in Italy, who evaluates Boccaccio's prose as poetry that transcends the specific qualification of Medieval or Renaissance, there are many schools and critics all over the world who have made singular contributions. Boccaccio studies have flourished, producing valuable critical editions, more attention to minor works, new perspectives on his biography, and reevaluations of his work as both Medieval and Renaissance. The language and structure of the *Decameron* have been fertile territory for the semiologists, and recently the *Decameron* has been taken up by Russian formalists (Viktor Sklovskij, but more particularly Tzvetan Todorov) as a quintessential example of narrative patterns from which fundamental narrative formulas can be studied. By virtue of its multifarious interests and its technological advances, our age seems to be gleaning a most complete and diversified picture of the man and his works.

Boccaccio Abroad and as A Source

In contemplating Boccaccio's fame abroad, the first writer who comes to mind is Chaucer. Indeed, Chaucer's debt to Boccaccio and to Italy in general is considerable, though he may never have known the *Decameron* directly. He apparently knew the story of Griselda from Petrarch's Latin translation and not from the original. Nonetheless, he relied on Boccaccio's *Filostrato* for his *Troilus and Cressida,* on Boccaccio's *Teseida* for the *Knight's Tale,* on the *De casibus* for the Monk's Tale, and on the *De mulieribus* for the *Legend of Good Women.* In France the first work translated was the *De casibus,* translated about 1400 in a beautiful illuminated manuscript by Laurent de Premierfait—which later served Lydgate as his model for the *Fall of Princes* (1494). Also early in the fifteenth century came a translation of the *Decameron,* improved by Le Maçon in 1545, while ostensibly the first English translation of the whole *Decameron* came in 1620.[5]

As the father or definitive reviver of so many genres Boccaccio sired many offspring. His stories have inspired countless works,[6] and the history of the translations and adaptations of the individual stories would be far too long. The story of Ghismonda (*Dec.*IV,1) was translated into Latin by Bruni, made into a drama by Wilmot and a poem by Dryden. The story of Griselda (*Dec.* X,10) was translated into Latin by Petrarch, made into numerous operas, and used for a social drama for women's rights in Germany in the nineteenth century. Federico and his falcon (*Dec.* V,9) inspired a story by Lope de Vega and an opera by

Ruspiglioni. La Fontaine, Lessing, Keats, and many others all drew on Boccaccio's stories.

The organization of storytelling within a framework on Boccaccio's example inspired not only Italians, but works such as *Cent nouvelles nouvelles* and the *Heptameron* of Marguerite de Navarre. These collections in turn inspired Elizabethan dramatists, and thus the offspring become too indirect and too numerous to count. The *Corbaccio* became a prototype of misogynist literature inspiring the Archpriest of Hita, Dryden, de Musset, Longfellow, and others. From the *Ameto* and the *Ninfale fiesolano*, revivals of the pastoral romance, are derived Sannazaro's *Arcadia*, Cervantes's *Galatea*, Lope de Vega's *Arcadia*, d'Urfé's *Astrée*, Sidney's *Arcadia*, and many others. Boccaccio's epic romances, *Teseida* and *Filostrato*, influenced not only Chaucer but, via Pulci's *Morgante*, Ariosto's *Orlando Furioso* and Spenser's *Faerie Queen*. In this latter Spenser used a modified form of the *ottava rima*, used by Boccaccio in his epic romances and by Italian poets after him, which was revived in England by Byron. In painting, the *Decameron* inspired many works as well.[7] There is the story of Nastagio (*Dec.* V,8) represented by Botticelli on a cassone (Prado, Madrid), the Griselda story (*Dec.* X,10) on a cassone by Luca Signorelli (London, National Gallery) and the story of Cimone and Ifigenia (*Dec.* V,1) by Rubens (Kunsthistorisches Museum, Vienna), which are only a few of the most famous. And, to reiterate the truism that great works speak to every age, the *Decameron* was reconsidered in our day in a contemporary art form, the cinema, by Pier Paolo Pasolini, among others.[8]

It is not surprising that Boccaccio's works have been a source of inspiration in some manner for every century. Each age brings its own terms and its own experience. We can seek moral philosophy or philology, history or psychology; whatever we want we will find. And as we apply our sciences and rummage for our messages we will enjoy the additional pleasure of the hearty chuckle Boccaccio certainly intended us to have.

Notes and References

Chapter One

1. Angelo Solerti, *Le Vite di Dante, Petrarca e Boccaccio scritte fino al secolo decimosettimo* (Milan: Vallardi, 1904) pp. 675–76, translation mine.
2. Ibid., p. 676, translation mine.
3. Millard Meiss, *Painting in Florence and Siena After the Black Death* (Princeton, N.J., 1951; reprinted New York: Harper & Row, 1964), p. 10 n. 5. I am grateful to Marvin Becker for pointing out this note to me.
4. Cf. Vittore Branca, "Non Sconfessato il *Decameron,*" *La fiera letteraria* 40:49(1965):7, interprets this letter as a model of rhetoric and not a sincere rejection of the *Decameron.*
5. For the vicissitudes of the MS Hamilton 90, now conclusively proven an autograph of Boccaccio, see *Decameron,* facsimile autografo, ed. V. Branca (Firenze: Alinari, 1975), p. 15, for bibliography. Cf. also *Decameron: Edizione diplomatico–interpretativa dell' autografo Hamilton 90,* a cura di Charles S. Singleton (Baltimore: Johns Hopkins University Press, 1974).
6. The works on the history and cultural currents of this period are legion. The following are a few whose ideas are reflected in this discussion and that are particularly useful specifically for Boccaccio and the fourteenth century: Frederick Antal, *Florentine Painting and Its Social Background* (London, 1948); Marvin Becker, *Florence in Transition* (Baltimore, 1967); Gene Brucker, *Florentine Politics and Society* (Princeton, N.J., 1962); Romolo Caggese, *Roberto d'Angiò e suoi tempi* (Florence, 1921); Robert Davidsohn, *Geschicte von Florenz* (Berlin, 1896–1912), 8 vols.; Wallace K. Ferguson, *Europe in Transition* (Boston, 1962); Denys Hay, *The Italian Renaissance in its Historical Background* (Cambridge, England, 1961); Emile Léonard, *Les Angevins de Naples* (Paris, 1953); Millard Meiss, *Painting in Florence and Siena*; Ferdinand Schevill, *Medieval and Renaissance Florence* (New York, 1961); Charles Trinkaus, "Humanism," *Encyclopedia of World Art* (New York–London, 1963), pp. 702–43.
7. "In Rome, which was once the head of the world, just as today it is the tail" (*Dec.* V,3,4). See Bibliography for editions of Boccaccio's works. For quotations cited in this text an abbreviation of the title is used, followed by a roman numeral for the book or chapter number and an arabic numeral for the line. For the *Decameron* the roman numeral indicates the day and the arabic

numerals the story and line numbers. The translations are mine.
    8. Hans Baron, "Franciscan Poverty and Civic Wealth," *Speculum* 13 (1938):9.
    9. M. Meiss, *Painting in Florence and Siena*; M. Becker, *Florence in Transition*.
    10. For the importance of narration in the *Decameron* see, among others, Tzvetan Todorov, *Grammaire du Decameron* (Hague-Paris, 1969); Guido Almansi, *The Writer as Liar* (London, 1975); Alberto Moravia, *L'Uomo come fine* (Milan, 1964).
    11. V. Branca, *Boccaccio medievale* (Florence, 1956), p. 26.

Chapter Two

    1. The general outline of this biography is based on those of V. Branca, "Profilo," *Tutte le Opere*, Vol. 1, pp. 3–197; and Natalino Sapegno, "Giovanni Boccaccio," *Dizionario biografico degli italiani* (Rome, 1960–1967), pp. 838–56.
    2. Salvatore Battaglia, "Schemi lirici nell'arte di Boccaccio," *Archivium Romanicum* 19(1935):61–78; Giuseppe Billanovich, *Restauri boccacceschi* (Rome, 1946); V. Branca, *Boccaccio medievale, Ch. VII.*
    3. This reference is from a letter written by Petrarch to Boccaccio where Boccaccio is said to have called Dante his *primus studiorum dux et prima fax. Familiarum rerum libri,* XXI,15.
    4. V. Branca and P. G. Ricci, "L'incontro napoletano con Cino da Pistoia," *Studi sul Boccaccio* 5(1968):1–18.
    5. See *Genealogie,* XV,6, where he praises his mentors of this period. Another mentor was Andalò del Negro (*Gen.* XV,6), from whom Boccaccio learned astrology. Astrological references are particularly important in the *Filocolo* and the *Teseida*; see A. E. Quaglio, *Scienza e mito nell'arte di Boccaccio* (Padua, 1967), and Janet L. Smarr, "Boccaccio and the Stars: Astrology in the *Teseida,*" *Traditio* 35 (1979):303–32.
    6. The *Zibaldone magliabechiano* is a notebook where Boccaccio collected brief passages, annotations, translations, and the like. See Francesco Macrì-Leone, "Il Zibaldone boccaccesco della Magliabechiana, *"Giornale storico della letteratura italiana* 10(1887):39. An entry of interest is *De canaria,* in which he copied a Latin version of a report on the recently discovered Canary Islands sometime between 1342 and 1344. See Manlio Pastore-Stocchi, "Il *De canaria* boccaccesco," *Rinascimento* 10(1959):143–56; G. Padoan, "Petrarca, Boccaccio e la scoperta delle canarie," *Italia medievale e umanistica* 7(1964):263–67.

7. See Giuseppe Velli, "Sull'*Elegia di Costanza*," *Studi sul Boccaccio* 4(1967):241–54.

8. A. E. Quaglio, "Valerio Massimo e il *Filocolo*," *Cultura Neolatina* 20(1960):45–77; Maria Teresa Casella, "Il Valerio Massimo in volgare; dal Lancia al Boccaccio," *Italia medievale e umanistica* 6(1963):49–136.

9. S. Battaglia, "L'esempio medievale," *Filologia romanza* 6(1959): 45–82; "Dall' esempio alla novella," *Filologia romanza* 7(1960):43–85; V. Branca, *Boccaccio medievale,* Ch. VI; Erich Auerbach, *Memisis* (Princeton, N.J., 1953), Ch. 9.

10. V. Branca, *Tradizione delle opere di Giovanni Boccaccio* (Rome, 1958), pp. 287–306.

11. V. Branca, Intro. *Rime,* p. xxvi; *Boccaccio medievale,* Chs. III, VIII.

12. V. Branca, *Tradizione,* pp. 121–43, 144–98.

13. See R. Hollander, *Boccaccio's Two Venuses,* Ch. IV, for a discussion of the roles of the narrator.

14. V. Branca, *Caccia di Diana,* Intro., p. 5.

15. For this interpretation see Victoria Kirkham, "Numerology and Allegory in Boccaccio's *Caccia di Diana,*" *Traditio* 34 (1978):303–29; Robert Hollander, *Boccaccio's Two Venuses,* Ch. I.

16. See V. Branca, *Caccia di Diana,* notes, for a list of the echoes of Dante.

17. See Charles S. Singleton, *Essay on the Vita Nuova* (Cambridge, Mass.: Harvard University Press, 1958); V. Kirkham, "Numerology and Allegory."

18. V. Branca, *Caccia di Diana,* in the notes to Canto I identifies each of the women and her family.

19. Brooks Otis, *Virgil: A Study in Civilized Poetry* (Oxford: Oxford University Press, 1963), Ch. IV.

20. See J. L. Smarr, "Boccaccio and the Stars," for a discussion of the multiple identities of Venus.

21. R. Hollander, *Boccaccio's Two Venuses;* Joan M. Ferrante, *Woman as Image in Medieval Literature* (New York: Columbia University Press, 1975), passim.

22. The term "courtly love" was coined by Gaston Paris, "L'amour courtois," *Romania* 12 (1883):519. The interpretations of Andreas Capellanus's fundamental treatise, *De arte honesti amandi* (*De amore*) (ca. 1184–1186), range from viewing it as a straightforward exposition of the ideals of a society, to an ironic satire of lust in favor of Christian charity, to reflection of a consciously contrived game. The critics who have discussed the first point of view are numerous. An introductory bibliography can be found in Andreas

Capellanus, *The Art of Courtly Love,* trans. J. J. Parry, Intro., n. 3, p. 3. For the second point of view cf. D. W. Robertson, Jr., "The subject of the *De amore* of Andreas Capellanus," *Modern Philology* 50(1953):145–61, and *A Preface to Chaucer* (Princeton, N.J.: Princeton University Press, 1963). For the third view cf. W. T. H. Jackson, "The *De amore* of Andreas Capellanus and the Practice of Love at Court," *Romanic Review* 49 (1958):249.

23. Andreas Capellanus, *The Art,* trans. J. J. Parry, Bk. I, Ch. VI, dialogue 7, p. 100ff. W. T. H. Jackson, "The *De amore,*" points out that Andreas's definition of the love that is the subject of the treatise is Hugh of St. Victor's definition of *concupiscentia.*

24. The matter and tone of this work were apparently judged congenial to Boccaccio, for a fourteenth-century Tuscan translation was for a long time attributed to him. See Pio Rajna, "Il libro di Andrea Capellano in Italia nei secoli XIII a XIV," *Studi di filologia romanza* 13 (1890):206. It is the structure of a court of love that slowly evolves to the idyllic setting for storytelling in the *Decameron.*

25. C. S. Lewis, *Allegory of Love* (Oxford: Oxford University Press, 1936), Ch. I.

26. Andreas Capellanus, *The Art,* Bk. I, Ch. VI, dialogue 8, p. 112. It must also be remembered that Ovid offered a precedent for retraction in his *Remedia amoris.*

27. Among the most important of these critics were Vincenzo Crescini, *Contributo agli studi sul Boccaccio* (Turin: Loescher, 1887); Arnaldo Della Torre, *La Giovinezza di Giovanni Boccaccio* (Città di Castello: Lapi, 1905); Henri Hauvette, *Boccace* (Paris, 1914); Edward Hutton, *Giovanni Boccaccio* (London, 1909); Marcus Landau, *Giovanni Boccaccio* (Stuttgart: F.G. Cottafchen Buchhandlung 1877); Francesco Torraca, *Per la biografia di Giovanni Boccaccio* (Milan, Rome, Naples: Albrighi Segati, 1912).

28. See note 2 above.

29. Natalino Sapegno, *Diz. Biog.,* p. 843, maintains that the *cantare* of this story derived from the *Filocolo* and not vice versa. A more commonly held opinion is that both the *cantare* and the *Filocolo* derive from a French source. Cf. A. E. Quaglio, *Filocolo,* Intro., p. 48.

30. For the discussion of the title see Vincenzo Crescini, "Per il titolo del primo romanzo boccaccesco," *Miscellanea storica della Valdelsa* 21 (1913):49–54. E. H. Wilkins, *The Invention of the Sonnet and Other Studies in Italian Literature* (Rome: Edizioni di storia letteraria, Istituto grafico tiberino, 1959).

31. See Ernst Robert Curtius, *European Literature and the Latin Middle Ages* (New York, 1963), for a fundamental treatment of this and other *topoi*

common in Boccaccio's works that passed from classical into medieval literature.

32. A. E. Quaglio, *Filocolo,* Intro., p. 57.

33. S. Battaglia, "Schemi lirici," pp. 61–78.

34. Boccaccio echoes the wisdom of Dante concerning the importance of literature as a go-between, or learning to love by example. As the story of Gallehaut was a "Gallehaut" or go-between for Paolo and Francesca (*Inf.* V), so is Ovid for Florio and Biancifiore, and so, we surmise, should the *Decameron* be for the idle ladies. See R. Hollander, *Boccaccio's Two Venuses,* Ch. IV, for a discussion of Gallehaut.

35. For this discussion see Victoria Kirkham, "Reckoning with Boccaccio's *Questioni d'amore,*" *Modern Language Notes* 89 (Jan. 1974):47–59.

36. It is interesting to note that the source for this episode, Andreas Capellanus's *Art of Courtly Love,* bears much of the same ambiguity of Fiammetta's treatment. In Bk. I, Ch. VI, dialogue 8, for example, a lady of the nobility execrates love as a source of torment and an offence to God, and then proceeds to a discussion of love and her own loves.

37. The autonomy of this episode is also confirmed by the fact that it circulated separately. See A. E. Quaglio, *Filocolo,* IV, 18, n. 14.

38. For courts of love see Pio Rajna, *Le corti d'amore* (Milan: Hoepli, 1890); and for some of the meanings of the *locus amoenus* or the garden cf. E. R. Curtius, *European Literature,* Ch. 10; A. Bartlett Giamatti, *The Earthly Paradise and the Renaissance Epic* (Princeton, N.J.: Princeton University Press, 1966); D. W. Robertson, Jr., "The Doctrine of Charity in Medieval Literary Gardens," *Speculum* 26 (1951):24–49.

39. Raffaello Ramat, "Boccaccio 1340–44," *Belfagor* 19 (1964):17–30, 154–74, and "Indicazioni per una lettura del *Decameron,*" *Miscellanea Storica della Valdelsa* 69, Nos. 2 and 3 (1963):7–19, has emphasized the significance of the city in Boccaccio's works. Cf. also Marvin Becker, *Florence in Transition,* esp. Intro. and Ch. I, for the development of individual and communal goals. The *topos* of the geographic catalog, which possibly has roots in the vitality of mercantile expansion, also occurs first in this work. Filocolo's wanderings in the frame story, and Tarolfo's journey in the *Questions of Love* both offer long and detailed geographic descriptions. These are found again in the *Ameto,* and in the *Decameron* are turned into the comedy of Fra Cipolla's nonsensical journey. Geographical sites finally pass from a literary *topos* to the object of scholarly interest in Boccaccio's later works *De canaria* and *De montibus.*

40. The same image appears in his early poems, *Rime,* VI.

41. See Pio Rajna, "L'episodio delle *Quistioni d'amore* nel *Filocolo* di

Boccaccio," *Romania* 31(1902):28–81; V. Branca, *Dec.* X,4,n.1 and X,5,n.1, for further bibliography on sources.

42. Both stories mirror the pattern of the entire work in that they tell of the ultimate reconstruction of the marriage bond.

43. Cf. Pio Rajna, "L'episodio"; Raffaello Fornaciari, "Dal *Filocolo* al *Decameron*," *Miscellanea storica della Valdelsa* 21 (1913):196–201; Ciro Trabalza, *Studi sul Boccaccio,* p. 189ff.

44. V. Branca, *Filostrato,* Intro., pp. 3–13, decides for an anterior date for the *Filostrato* for reasons of the absence of the *senhal* of Fiammetta, more generic references to Fortune, the absence of the influence of Petrarch and the classics, and the greater presence of Dante, Stilnovo, and medieval romance techniques, along with relatively limited cultural scope and an uncertain prose style in the Proem in comparison to the *Filocolo*. P. G. Ricci, "Per la datazione del *Filostrato*," *Studi sul Boccaccio* 1(1963):333–48, adduces in addition the dedication of the *Filostrato* to Filomena-Giovanna, a mistress prior to Fiammetta (Fiammetta appears in all subsequent works from the *Filocolo* to the *Decameron*).

45. R. Hollander, *Boccaccio's Two Venuses,* Ch. II, claims that the *Filostrato* is a Christian work because it is a condemnation of concupiscence through an illustration of its dire consequences.

46. The similarities and differences of these two passages have been observed by V. Branca, *Filostrato,* II,80,n.46; R. Hollander, *Boccaccio's Two Venuses,* p. 50.

47. Charles Dahlberg, "Love and the *Roman de la Rose*," *Speculum* 44(1969):568–84, observes that the procedure of cupidinous love, from the eyes through all the five senses down to touch, is the exact opposite of the movement described by St. Bernard (*Sermo X, De diversis*) where beginning with touch one proceeds to the beatific vision.

48. Thomas A. Kirby, *Chaucer's Troilus: A Study in Courtly Love* (Gloucester, Mass: Peter Smith, 1958).

49. Boccaccio returns to the figure of the widow quite vehemently in two other instances. The longest story, and the nastiest trick, in the *Decameron* is dedicated to revenge upon a widow (*Dec.* VIII,7) and the entire *Corbaccio* is a diatribe against a widow.

50. Cf. D. W. Robertson, Jr., "The Doctrine of Charity," for the view that Andreas's garden is ironical.

51. See V. Branca, *Il cantare trecentesco e il Boccaccio del "Filostrato" e del "Teseida"* (Florence: Sansoni, 1936), and his notes to his edition of the *Filostrato, Tutte le Opere,* Vol. II.

52. Ovid is an important source for these tirades. Cf. V. Branca, *Filostrato,* VII,71–74.

53. Alberto Limentani, "Struttura e storia dell'ottava rima," *Lettere italiane* 13(1961):20–77.

54. A. Limentani, *Teseida,* Intro., p. 231. V. Branca, "Profilo," observes that Tuscan elements in the poem may indicate that the finishing touches and the glosses were written after Boccaccio's return to Florence.

55. See A. Limentani, *Teseida,* for a thorough indication in the notes of the elements that parallel and echo the *Thebaid.*

56. R. Hollander, *Boccaccio's Two Venuses,* Ch. II; V. Kirkham, " 'Chiuso parlare' in Boccaccio's *Teseida,* " forthcoming in a Festschrift volume for Charles S. Singleton under the tentative title *Studies in the Italian Trecento,* ed. Aldo S. Bernardo and Anthony Pellegrini; J. L. Smarr, "Boccaccio and the Stars."

57. J. L. Smarr, "The *Teseida,* Boccaccio's Allegorical Epic," NEMLA Italian Studies 1(1977):29–35.

58. The autograph of the *Teseida* is in the Biblioteca Laurenziana in Florence.

59. *Teseida,* I,38–39; II,1–2,1–5; cf. A. Limentani, "Struttura e storia."

Chapter Three

1. Gene Brucker, *Florentine Politics,* Ch. I; R. Ramat, "Boccaccio 1340–44."

2. See Charles S. Singleton, *Dante Studies,* Vol. I, *Commedia: Elements of Structure* (Cambridge, Mass.: Harvard University Press, 1954).

3. The *Arcadia* (1504) by Jacopo Sannazaro is generally considered the first pastoral romance. See Eduardo Saccone, "L'*Arcadia* di Jacopo Sannazaro: Storia e delineamento di una struttura," *Modern Language Notes* 84(Jan. 1969):46–97, for the *Arcadia* as a pastoral romance and its relation to earlier pastoral forms.

4. See A. B. Giamatti, *The Earthly Paradise*; D. W. Robertson, Jr., "The Doctrine of Charity," for some meanings of the garden. See also Marga Cottino-Jones, "The City/Country Conflict of the *Decameron,*" *Studi Sul Boccaccio* 8(1974):147–84.

5. R. Ramat, "Boccaccio 1340–44."

6. Francesco Sansovino, one of the first commentators of the *Ameto,* called it a *piccolo Decameron*—"a small *Decameron.*" *Ameto* edited by Francesco Sansovino (Venice, 1545).

7. V. Branca, Intro., *Amorosa Visione, Tutte le Opere,* Vol. III.

8. For example, Plato, Macrobius, Boethius, the Old and New Testaments and Gregory; cf. V. Branca, *Amorosa Visione,* p. 7.

9. V. Branca, *Amorosa Visione,* offers abundant echoes of Dante and other sources in his notes.

10. Branca (*Am. Vis.* XIV,vv. 23–33,note) observes that Boccaccio's less laudatory portrayal of King Robert in this work is evidence of his commitment to Florentine Guelfism and reflects Florentine resentment of King Robert. In the *Ameto* as well he referred to King Robert as Midas.

11. Praise of Giotto was common in writers of the fourteenth century. Dante praises him in *Purg.* XI, Petrarch in *Fam.* V, 17,6 and Boccaccio in *Dec.* VI,6 and *Gen.* XIV,6; cf. Branca, *Am. Vis.* IV, 16,n.

12. See J. L. Smarr, "Boccaccio and the Choice of Hercules," *Modern Language Notes* 92 (1977):46–52, for an interpretation of this episode as the central moral decision of the journey in the *Amorosa Visione.*

13. Cf. V. Branca, Intro., *Am. Vis.,* p. 8.

14. Two important articles on the *Fiammetta* to which my discussion is indebted are Cesare Segre, "Strutture e registri nella *Fiammetta,*" *Strumenti Critici* 6:18 (1972):133–62; Salvatore Battaglia, "Il Significato della *Fiammetta*" (1964), in his *Coscienza letteraria del medioevo* (Naples, 1965), pp. 659–68.

15. These echoes are carefully recorded in the notes by Maria Segre Consigli which accompany the Ageno edition reprinted in Cesare Segre, *Opere di Giovanni Boccaccio* (Milan, 1966).

16. C. Segre, "Strutture e registri," and Rodolfo Renier, *"La Vita Nuova" e la "Fiammetta"* (Turin: Loescher, 1879).

17. Guido DiPino, *La Polemica del Boccaccio* (Florence, 1953), traces Boccaccio's development in his early works through his increasingly subtle use of dialogue.

18. C. Segre, "Strutture e registri."

19. Pier Giorgio Ricci, "Dubbi gravi intorno al *Ninfale fiesolano,*" *Studi sul Boccaccio* 6(1971):109–24, for a confutation of this dating and the suggestion that the *Ninfale* belongs among Boccaccio's earliest works; but Ricci himself expresses doubts about the affirmation.

20. The use of *morta* transitively for "killed"; rhyme words like *tornoe* (*tornò*), *lascioe* (*lasciò*), *pregalle* (*la pregò*), *tene* (*te*), *boci* (*voci*), are vernacular peasant forms that Boccaccio will use again in similar contexts in the *Decameron.*

21. Armando Balduino, Intro., *Ninfale fiesolano, Tutte le opere,* Vol. III, p. 284.

Chapter Four

1. These translations have now been attributed to Boccaccio. See Giuseppe Billanovich, "Il Boccaccio e il Petrarca e le più antiche traduzioni

in italiano delle *Decadi* di Tito Livio," *Giornale storico della letteratura italiana* 130(1953):311–37; Maria Teresa Casella, "Il Volgarizzamento Liviano del Boccaccio," *Italia medievale e umanistica* 4(1961):77–129. For the early biographies see A. Solerti, *Le Vite,* p. 94.

  2. See Ferdinand Schevill, *Medieval and Renaissance Florence,* Vol.I, p. 239.

  3. Matteo Villani, *Cronica* (Florence: S. Coen, 1845), Bk.I, Ch. II.

  4. For the literary sources of Boccaccio's description of the plague and the relative bibliography see V. Branca, *Boccaccio medievale,* p. 301ff.

  5. See V. Branca, *Decameron,* p. 26, n. 5, for the tradition regarding the identification of the villas of the *Decameron.* Despite their apparent detail, the descriptions are considered literary exercises and not as correspondent to specific places. Cf. Edith Kern, "The Gardens in the *Decameron* Cornice," *PMLA* 66(1951):505–23.

  6. V. Branca, *Decameron,* p. 20, n. 3, views them as literary reminiscences or allusions to literary genres. Behind the number seven for the young ladies are the various meanings of the number seven common to medieval iconography: seven days, seven planets, seven virtues, seven liberal arts, etc. Cf. also Joan M. Ferrante, "Frame Characters of the *Decameron,*" *Romance Philology* 19 (1965):212, for a reading of the ten youths as symbolic of virtues.

  7. The stories for which sources have been identified are VII,9 from the *Comedia Lydiae* of Matthew of Vendôme; V,10 and VII,2 from the *Metamorphosis* of Apuleius; VII,4, VIII, 10, and X,8 from the *Disciplina clericalis* of Pietrus Alphonsus; IV,9 from the Provençal troubadour Guilhem de Cabestanh; V,8 and VII,10 from the *Speculum historiale* of Vincent of Beauvais, and even for these the possible sources are multiple. See V. Branca, notes to *Decameron,* for lists of sources.

  8. Boccaccio himself confirms that he has no specific models in his defense in the Introduction to the Fourth Day (39): ". . . as for . . . those who maintain that these things have not actually happened, I would be grateful should they produce the originals, wherefore, if they were discordant from what I wrote, I would declare their reprehension just and would attempt to correct myself; but until aught but words appears, I will leave them with their opinion, and keep my own, saying of them what they say of me." For popular narrative sources cf. Stith Thompson, *Motif Index of Folk Literature* (Helsinki: Academia scientiarum fennica, 1932), and more specifically, D. P. Rotunda, *Motif Index of the Italian Novella in Prose* (Bloomington: University of Indiana Press, 1942).

  9. The number of critical works on the *Decameron* is staggering. Some of the general modern works I have found useful are Mario Baratto, *Realtà e stile nel "Decameron"* (Vicenza, 1970); Salvatore Battaglia, *La Coscienza letteraria*

del Medio Evo; Vittore Branca, *Boccaccio medievale*; Giovanni Getto, *Vita di forme e forme di vita nel "Decameron"* (Turin, 1972); Giorgio Padoan, "Mondo aristocratico e mondo comunale nell'ideologia e nell'arte di Giovanni Boccaccio," *Studi sul Boccaccio* 2 (1964):81–216; Giuseppe Petronio, *Il "Decameron"* (Bari, 1935); Luigi Russo, *Letture critiche del "Decameron"* (Bari, 1956); Carlo Salinari, ed., Giovanni Boccaccio, *Decameron,* Introduzione (Bari, 1963); Natalino Sapegno, "Giovanni Boccaccio," in his *Il Trecento* (Milan, 1942); Cesare Segre, *Opere di Giovanni Boccaccio,* Introduzione (Milan, 1966). In dealing with the rich complexity of the *Decameron* the attempt will be to isolate themes around which to discuss some of the most well known stories. This grouping by no means exhausts their richness or infinite possibilities of interpretation, as an ample body of criticism attests. The story of Alibech (III, 10) for example, is a satire of the clergy; it is also a good illustration of Boccaccio's construction of a story around a metaphor (Baratto, *Realtà,* pp. 384–86). The story of Ghismonda (IV, 1) is a social commentary expounding democratic ideals over traditional hierarchies; it also exemplifies an Oedipal archetype (Almansi, *The Writer,* Ch. IV); and the examples could be multiplied for each of the hundred tales.

10. Some underlying moral messages have been discussed by the following: V. Branca, *Boccaccio medievale,* p. 101ff.; Joan M. Ferrante, "Frame Characters of the *Decameron*"; Victoria Kirkham, "Love's Labors Rewarded and Paradise Lost," paper read at annual meeting of American Boccaccio Association, San Francisco, Dec. 1975; Janet L. Smarr, "Symmetry and Balance in the *Decameron,*" *Medievalia* 2(1976):159–87.

11. The framework of the *Decameron* has received much critical attention. See V. Branca, *Decameron,* notes to Introduction, for bibliography. Important for my discussion is Charles S. Singleton, "On Meaning in the *Decameron,*" *Italica* 21 (1944):117; "Uses of the *Decameron,*" *Modern Language Notes* 79 (1964):71–76. See also Joy Potter, "Boccaccio as Illusionist: The Play of Frames in the *Decameron,*" *Humanities Association Review* 26,4(Fall, 1975):327–45.

12. G. Almansi, *The Writer,* Ch. I.

13. The expression is Branca's, *Boccaccio medievale,* Ch. V.

14. Cf. Roberto Lopez, *The Commercial Revolution* (New York: Prentice-Hall, 1971).

15. G. Almansi, *The Writer,* Ch. V; M. Baratto, *Realtà,* p. 101.

16. V. Branca, *Boccaccio medievale,* Ch. V.

17. Erich Auerbach, *Mimesis,* Ch. 9, presents one of the most basic analyses of Boccaccio's realism.

18. Though each story is placed in a real historical setting, the story does not usually derive from historical fact. See V. Branca, *Decameron,* notes to the stories for the identification of characters and narrative themes.

19. The contrast and combination of the old feudal world and the new mercantile society have been observed by many critics. Cf. M. Baratto, *Realtà,* Ch. I; G. Padoan, "Mondo aristocratico"; M. Becker, *Florence in Transition,* Ch. I.

20. M. Baratto, *Realtà,* Ch. II; G. Getto, *Vita di forme,* p. 11.

21. The Introduction to the Fourth Day has been variously interpreted, especially as a key to the meaning of the framework. Some maintain that the stories actually circulated, arousing criticism, hence the need to include a defense. Cf. V. Branca, "La prima diffusione del *Decameron,*" *Studi di filologia italiana* 8 (1950):29–143; while others (cf. C. S. Singleton, "On Meaning") maintain that the defense was included merely as a literary device to emphasize the author's position as established in the framework of the Introduction and the Conclusion. What is ultimately significant is that the author includes such a defense as part of his text. With regard to the pattern of truancy and recantation discussed in Chapter 2 above, it would appear that not only is Boccaccio not recanting, but he includes this defense to dramatize that fact.

22. Some of the same arguments recur in his defense of poetry in the *Genealogie.* It is interesting that while in the *Genealogie* he responds to these accusations with serious and scholarly consideration, here he uses the very significance of the *Decameron,* namely narrative art, as his best answer to such objections—he tells a story.

23. Jean de Meun, *The Romance of the Rose,* trans. Charles Dahlberg (Princeton, N.J.: Princeton University Press, 1971). Jean de Meun also observes the omnipotence of Nature in terms analogous to Boccaccio's: ". . . Horace says and well he knew what such words signified, 'Who against Nature to defend himself should seize a fork to thrust her forth would find she'd soon be back again.' . . . Each creature to its nature will return, nor can relinquish it for violence or force of covenant" (14019–24). For some useful discussions of the development of the concept of Nature see E. R. Curtius, *European Literature,* Ch. 6; R. H. Green, "Alan de Lille's *De planctu naturae,*" *Speculum* 31 (1956):649–74; George Economou, *The Goddess Natura in Medieval Literature* (Cambridge, Mass.: Harvard University Press, 1972). Economou observes that in the *Romance of the Rose,* Nature becomes not the minister of God, but a neutral force.

24. This punishment is to be found in Capellanus, *The Art,* Bk. I, Ch.

VI, dialogue 5, and is a traditional *topos,* stemming from mythology, to be found in Vincent of Beauvais, Passavanti, and other sources familiar to Boccaccio. Cf. V. Branca, *Decameron,* p. 502, n. 3, for the tradition.

25. Cf. Howard R. Patch, *The Goddess Fortuna in Medieval Literature* (Cambridge, Mass.: Harvard University Press, 1927): Vincenzo Cioffari, "The Conception of Fortune in the *Decameron*," *Italica* 17 (1940):129–37; "The Function of Fortune in Dante, Boccaccio and Machiavelli," *Italica* 24 (1947):1–13.

26. Cf. G. Getto, *Vita di forme,* who calls the "art of living" the primary message of the *Decameron.*

27. See G. Almansi, *The Writer,* Ch. I, for a discussion of Ciappelletto as a narrative artist. The story is also a good example of the *topos* of topsy turvy; cf. G. Getto,*Vita di forme,* Ch. II.

28. Even the framework offers a democratic modification of the traditional court of love from which it stems, for it is not up to a queen to hand down decisions, but rather it is a common enterprise among equals where the power is rotated.

29. Capellanus, *The Art,* Bk. I, Ch. XI.

30. Baratto points out (*Realtà,* pp. 23–48) that these moments do not ultimately subvert the social order. Chichibìo remains a cook, the groom remains a groom, and Cisti knows his place, but what is important is the momentary encounter that in forcing a social situation, concentrates on the ennoblement of the individual.

31. Boccaccio's source for this aphorism was probably Valerius Maximus (*Facta*VII,2). It was also to be found in contemporary works such as Paolo da Certaldo. Cf. V. Branca, *Decameron,* p. 516, n. 2.

32. See V. Branca, *Decameron,* p. 942, n. 6, for sources, and especially Thompson and Rotunda, H 461,S 62 and 400.

33. The observation was made by V. Branca, *Boccaccio medievale,* p. 140.

34. V. Branca, *Boccaccio medievale,* p. 101, views the *Decameron* as a kind of Christian ascent from Ciappelletto-Judas to Griselda-Mary.

35. The emerging importance of virtue as possible outside the Church was pointed out to me by Marvin Becker. See Marvin Becker, "Aspects of Lay Piety in Early Renaissance Florence," in *The Pursuit of Holiness in Late Medieval and Renaissance Religion,* ed. Charles Trinkaus and Heiko Oberman (Leiden: Borill, 1974), pp. 177–99. This idea is also presented in the *Divine Comedy* (e.g., *Inf.*XXVII, *Purg.* V, where salvation of the soul is independent of the ministrations of the Church).

36. Cf. Marga Cottino-Jones, "Fabula vs. Figura: Another Interpretation of the Griselda Story," *Italica* 50:1(1973):38–51, for an analysis of Griselda as a Christ figure.

37. Cf. Alberto Moravia, *L'uomo come fine*; M. Baratto, *Realtà,* Ch. IV; G. Getto, *Vita di forme,* pp. 3, 23.

38. M. Baratto, *Realtà,* Chs. 4–10.

39. M. Baratto, *Realtà,* p. 65, observes that rhetoric is the real protagonist of this story which is reminiscent of the early prose works, *Filocolo, Ameto, Fiammetta,* for that reason.

40. See G. DiPino, *La polemica del Boccaccio,* for a discussion of the importance of dialogue in Boccaccio's artistic development.

41. For example VII, 10, VIII, 8 for Sienese; VIII, 10 for Sicilian. Branca suggests that Boccaccio uses vernacular with a nuance of scorn for Venice and Siena, cities he did not like (*Decameron,* p. 374, n. 1).

42. M. T. Casella, "Il Volgarizzamento," pp. 77–129. See also Marga Cottino-Jones, *An Anatomy of Boccaccio's Style* (Naples, 1968) for Boccaccio's style in relation to medieval canons.

43. In English, if indeed any parallel can be drawn, the equivalent would probably be in placing the adjective after the noun as in "a garden full of *flowers gay."*

44. Giulio Herczeg, "Su Boccaccio e l'uso del gerundio," *Lingua nostra* 10 (1949):36–41.

45. E.g., "se io potuto avessi onestamente per altra parte menarvi" (*Dec.* Intro., 7): "if able I had been to lead you"; ". . . a coloro è massimamente richiesto li quali già hanno di conforto avuto mestiere" (*Dec.* Proem, 2): "it is all the more required of those who have of comfort had need"; ". . . in cotal consiglio seguire" (*Dec.* Intro., 70): "in such an opinion to follow."

46. Francesco De Sanctis, *Storia della letteratura italiana,* ed. M. T. Lanza (Milano: Feltrinelli, 1950), pp. 276, 379.

Chapter Five

1. Millard Meiss, *Painting in Florence and Siena*; Marvin Becker, *Florence in Transition,* Ch. I.

2. Giovanni Villani calls them "artisans and manual workers and simpletons"; *Cronica,* Bk. III, Ch. 43, quoted in Meiss, p. 64.

3. Millard Meiss, *Painting in Florence and Siena.* See also Giorgio Padoan, "Mondo Aristocratico," pp. 188–90.

4. See Vittore Branca, "Profilo," pp. 88–90; Ernest H. Wilkins, *The Making of the Canzoniere* (Rome: Edizioni di storia e letteratura, 1951), passim.

5. Giuseppe Billanovich, "Lo scrittoio del poeta," *Giornale storico della letteratura italiana* 123 (1946):1–52, attributes Petrarch's *Triumphs* to this

first meeting with Boccaccio in which he had occasion to read the latter's *Amorosa Visione.* V. Branca, "Profilo," p. 89, finds more, and more direct, derivations in the work of Petrarch: the *Triumphs* from the *Amorosa Visione,* the *De obedentia et fide uxoria* from the *Decameron* and the *Invective* from Bks. XIV and XV of the *Genealogie.*

6. *De lingua latina* of Varro, *Rhetorica ad Herennium* of pseudo-Cicero, *Annales* XI–XVI of Apuleius, and *Historiae* I–V of Tacitus. See V. Branca, "Profilo," p. 103.

7. V. Branca, on the contrary, assigns it to 1366 ("Profilo," p. 40). See also Giorgio Padoan, "Sulla datazione del *Corbaccio,*" *Lettere italiane* 15:1 (1963):1–27; "Ancora sulla datazione e sul titolo del *Corbaccio,*" *Lettere italiane* 15:2 (1963):199–201.

8. For a bibliography of the various evaluations of the significance of the *Corbaccio* and its position in the Boccaccio corpus see Tauno Nurmela, ed., *Corbaccio* (Helsinki: *Annales Academiae Scientiarum Fennicae,* 1968), pp. 16–21. This is the best edition of the *Corbaccio.* Since it was not accessible to me, quotations are from *Giovanni Boccaccio: Opere in versi, Corbaccio, Trattatello in laude di Dante, Prose latine, Epistole,* ed. Pier Giorgio Ricci (Milan: Ricciardi, 1965).

9. See Anthony K. Cassell, "The Crow of the Fable and the *Corbaccio,*" *Modern Language Notes* 85 (1970):83–91, for an important discussion of the title and its connection with the sumptuary laws of Florence. See also Marga Cottino-Jones, "The *Corbaccio*: Notes for a Mythical Perspective of Moral Alternatives," *Forum Italicum,* 4(1970):490–509.

10. Most of these critics take as significant the fact that the longest story in the *Decameron* is about a student's cruel revenge upon a widow who scorned him. Cf. Robert M. Durling, "A Long Day in the Sun" (*Dec.* VIII,7), article presented at the Fifteenth International Conference on Medieval Studies, Kalamazoo, Mich., May 1980, for some of the more complex meanings underlying this story. I am indebted to Victoria Kirkham for pointing this article out to me.

11. Anthony K. Cassell, "An Abandoned Canvas: Structural and Moral Conflict in the *Corbaccio,*" *Modern Language Notes* 89:1 (1974):60–70.

12. Boccaccio records the discovery of the Canary Islands in 1342–44 in his *Zibaldone magliabechiano.* See M. Pastore-Stocchi, "Il *De Canaria* boccaccesco," *Rinascimento* 10 (1959):143–56; G. Padoan, "Petrarca, Boccaccio e la scoperta delle Canarie," *Italia Medioevale e umanistica* 7 (1964):263–77.

13. Manlio Pastore-Stocchi, *Tradizione medioevale e gusto umanistico nel "De montibus"* (Padua: C.E.D.A.M., 1963), Ch. I.

14. See Manlio Pastore-Stocchi, *Tradizione medioevale,* for this discussion.

15. See Giovanni Boccaccio, *Opere in versi,* ed. Pier Giorgio Ricci, notes, p. 1278.

16. "Above all theories and minor motives which actuated Boccaccio is his conception of poetry as an agency of regeneration in the State. He saw about him an Italy deplorably given over to war, rapine, intrigue, greed, selfish ambition. Yet he saw her giving birth to men—notably Dante and Petrarch—as great as those who had glorified Rome. How, then, would her gifts be turned to her regeneration? By the moral and intellectual forces of poetry." C. Osgood, *Boccaccio on Poetry,* p. xliii.

17. *De casibus* in Giovanni Boccaccio, *Opere in versi,* ed. P. G. Ricci, Bk. I, p. 795.

18. Three editions of the Latin text, and twenty-eight translations between 1495 and 1602: fourteen in French, four in English, five in Italian, three in Spanish, two in German. See Attilio Hortis, *Studi sulle opere latine di Boccaccio* (Trieste: Dase, 1879); P. G. Ricci, Giovanni Boccaccio, *Opere in versi,* p. 1278.

19. See C. Osgood, *Boccaccio on Poetry,* p. xiii, for the dedication to Hugh in relation to the actual times of composition.

20. C. Osgood, *Boccaccio on Poetry,* Intro.

21. See C. Osgood, *Boccaccio on Poetry, Gen.* XV, 6, n. 9 for a discussion of Theodontius, about whom very little is known. Cf. also Jean Seznec, *The Survival of the Pagan Gods* (New York: Harper Torchbooks, 1961), p. 221.

22. Boccaccio is proud of his Greek (*Gen.* XV, 7) and these are said to be the first Greek quotations in a modern humanistic work. Cf. C. Osgood, XV, 7, n. 1; Oskar Hecker, *Boccaccio Funde* (Braunschweig: George Westermann), pp. 137–57.

23. See C. Osgood, *Boccaccio on Poetry,* p. xxvi and n. 32.

24. J. Seznec, *The Survival,* p. 224.

25. Quoted in Osgood, *Boccaccio on Poetry,* p. xviii.

26. Osgood, *Boccaccio on Poetry,* p. xvi.

27. Boccaccio discusses Plato (*Gen.* XIV, 19) and considers him a friend of poets. He did not know his works and could not believe Plato would banish poets from his Republic.

28. E. R. Curtius, *European Literature,* pp. 204–205; Etienne Gilson, "Poesie et Verité dans la *Genealogie* de Boccace," *Studi sul Boccaccio* 2 (1964):258–82.

29. Charles Trinkaus, *In Our Image and Likeness* (London, 1970), Vol. II, p. 688.

30. Boccaccio also says one should be well versed on Christianity before reading pagan poetry so as to be able properly to interpret the texts

(*Gen.* XV,9). But as Tateo points out in "Poesia e favola nella poetica di Giovanni Boccaccio," *Filologia Romanza* 5 (1958):267–342, Boccaccio's *theologia* is really more philosophy than Christian truth and he is ultimately secularizing poetry.

31. Quoted in C. Osgood, *Boccaccio on Poetry*, p. xix.

32. Ibid., p. xli.

33. Ibid., p. 48.

34. He also wrote a briefer biography of his other master, Petrarch.

35. V. Branca gives these dates, "Profilo," p. 108; P. G. Ricci, ed., *Trattatello*, Intro., pp. 424–27, says 1350–55. For bibliography on dating of revisions see P. G. Ricci, ed., *Trattatello*, p. 856. For an introduction to the influence of Dante on Boccaccio see Aldo Rossi, "Dante nella prospettiva del Boccaccio," *Studi Danteschi* 37 (1960):63–139; G. Padoan, *L'ultima opera di Giovanni Boccaccio* (Florence: Olschki, 1959); Pietro Mazzamuto, "Il Boccaccio biografo e critico di Dante," *Annali della facoltà del Magistero di Palermo* IV-VII (1963–66):29–66.

36. P. Mazzamuto, "Il Boccaccio biografo," p. 29.

37. The last request was made in 1864 and was also refused.

38. I owe this observation to Charles Singleton.

39. See P. G. Ricci, ed., G. B., *Opere in versi*, nota critica, p. 1275, for some indication of dates and bibliography. The dates are extremely doubtful and the order of composition is not necessarily the order in which Boccaccio organized the Eclogues. Cf. also A. Massera, *Opere Latine Minori*, nota critica, pp. 261–305.

40. Giuseppe Billanovich, *Petrarca letterato: Lo scrittoio del Petrarca* (Rome: Edizioni di Storia e Letteratura, 1947).

41. Guido Martellotti, "Dalla tenzone al carme bucolico," *Italia medioevale e umanistica*" 7 (1964):325–36.

42. See Giacomo Lidonnici, "Il significato storico e psicologico del *Buccolicum Carmen* e la sua cronologia," in *Il Buccolicum Carmen trascritto di su l'autografo Riccardiano* (Città di Castello: Lapi, 1914) p. 167ff. and notes for bibliography.

43. Lidonnici, "Il significato storico," p. 222ff.

44. See Agostino Pertusi, *Leonzio Pilato fra Petrarca e Boccaccio* (Venice: Istituto per la collab. culturale 1964).

45. V. Branca, "Profilo," p. 118.

46. Petrarch seems not to have answered Boccaccio's letter, nor any other letters sent from friends of the Florentine circle expressing dismay at Petrarch's decision. See E. H. Wilkins, *The Life of Petrarch* (Chicago: University of Chicago Press, 1961), Ch. XX.

47. Cf. note 5, Chapter 1 above for bibliography on the Hamilton 90 text.

48. Boccaccio ultimately left his library to the Augustinian monks of Santo Spirito but much of it was lost in a fire. See Antonia Mazza, "S. Spirito e la biblioteca di Boccaccio," *Italia medioevale e umanistica* 9 (1966):1–74.

49. Roberto Abbondanza, "Una lettera autografa del Boccaccio nell'archivio di Stato di Perugia," *Studi sul Boccaccio* 1 (1963):5–13. See G. Billanovich, *Petrarca letterato,* for dating of letters.

50. Boccaccio had left Naples in 1346 after the assassination of Andrew of Hungary, but was ready to return when Acciaiuoli, Queen Johann, and Luigi of Taranto had reestablished the Angevin reign.

51. See V. Branca, "Profilo," p. 127, and A. Foresti, "Il Boccaccio a Ravenna nell'inverno 1361–62," *Giornale Storico della letteratura italiana* 98 (1931) pp. 73–83; Aldo Massera, *Opere latine minori, Vita di San Pier Damiano.*

52. In *Ameto, Lettere, Il Corbaccio,* ed. Nicola Bruscoli (Bari: Laterza, 1940).

53. E. H. Wilkins, *The Making of the Canzoniere, passim.* Branca (see note 5, Chapter 1) believes this letter to be a literary *topos* and not self-deprecation.

54. See Charles S. Singleton, "Allegory," in *Commedia: Elements of Structure* (Cambridge, Mass.: Harvard University Press, 1954), pp. 1–17; Giorgio Padoan, "Introduzione," *Esposizioni,* in *Tutte le opere,* Vol. VI, p. xxxi; Robert Hollander, *Allegory in Dante's "Commedia"* (Princeton, N.J.: Princeton University Press, 1969) for an excellent discussion of medieval theories of allegory and Dante's allegory in particular. A few incisive pages on Boccaccio's *Esposizioni* establish Boccaccio's methods and theories with regard to Dante's poem (pp. 283–85).

55. Translations are from Dante Alighieri, *The Divine Comedy,* translated with commentary by Charles S. Singleton, Bollingen Series LXXX (Princeton, N.J.: Princeton University Press, 1970)

56. Giorgio Padoan, "Introduzione," *Esposizioni,* p. xxxi.

Chapter Six

1. J. Seznec, *The Survival,* p. 224.

2. Andrea Sorrentino, *La letteratura italiana e il Sant'Uffizio* (Naples: Perella, 1935), Ch. V.

3. Peter Brown, "Aims and Methods of the Second 'Rassettatura' of the *Decameron,*" *Studi seicenteschi* 8 (1967):3–40; "I Veri promotori della 'Rasset-

tatura' del *Decameron* nel 1582," *Giornale storico della letteratura italiana* 134 (1957):314–32.

4. Cf. Ch. 4, n. 46 above.

5. Cf. G. H. McWilliam, trans., *Decameron* (Harmondsworth: Penguin, 1972), Introduction for a good and concise history of translations of the *Decameron* in English.

6. Florence Nightingale Jones, *Boccaccio and His Imitators in German, English, French, Spanish and Italian Literature: The Decameron* (Chicago: University of Chicago Press, 1910); W. P. Friedrich, *Outline of Comparative Literature* (Chapel Hill: University of North Carolina Studies in Comp. Lit. II, 1954), pp. 66–74.

7. See V. Branca, "Le prime illustrazioni" in his volume *Boccaccio medievale*, pp. 315–23, for an introductory résumé of illustrations and some bibliographic indications.

8. Giovanni Grazzini, "Boccaccio sullo schermo," *Studi sul Boccaccio* 7 (1973):369–73.

Selected Bibliography

PRIMARY SOURCES

An excellent modern edition of the complete works of Giovanni Boccaccio is now in progress under the general editorship of Vittore Branca, *Tutte le opere di Giovanni Boccaccio*. Verona: Mondadori, 1964–. The volumes published to date will be listed separately under the appropriate headings below. The English translations listed are only the most recent.

1. Italian Works in Verse
Amorosa visione. Tutte le opere, Vol. III. Edited by Vittore Branca. Verona: Mondadori, 1974.
Caccia di Diana. Tutte le opere, Vol. I. Edited by Vittore Branca. Verona: Mondadori, 1967.
Filostrato. Tutte le opere, Vol. II. Edited by Vittore Branca. Verona: Mondadori, 1964.
Ninfale fiesolano. Tutte le opere, Vol. III. Edited by Armando Balduino. Verona: Mondadori, 1974.
Rime. Edited by Vittore Branca. Padua: Liviani, 1958; reprinted in *Opere di Giovanni Boccaccio.* Edited by Cesare Segre. Milan: Mursia, 1966.
Teseida. Tutte le opere, Vol. II. Edited by Alberto Limentani. Verona: Mondadori, 1964.

2. Italian Works in Prose
Comedia delle ninfe fiorentine (Ameto). Tutte le opere, Vol. II. Edited by Antonio Enzo Quaglio. Verona: Mondadori, 1964.
Corbaccio. Edited by Tauno Nurmela. Helsinki: *Annales Academiae Scientarium Fennicae,* Vol. CXLVI, 1968.
Decameron, Tutte le opere, Vol. IV. Edited by Vittore Branca. Verona: Mondadori, 1976.
Elegia di Madonna Fiammetta. Edited by Franca Ageno. Paris: Tallone, 1954. Reprinted in *Opere di Giovanni Boccaccio.* Edited by Cesare Segre. Milan: Mursia, 1966.
Esposizioni sopra la Comedia di Dante. Tutte le opere, Vol. VI. Edited by Giorgio Padoan. Verona: Mondadori, 1965.

Filocolo. Tutte le opere, Vol. I. Edited by Antonio Enzo Quaglio. Verona: Mondadori, 1967.
Trattatello in laude di Dante. Tutte le opere, Vol. III. Edited by Pier Giorgio Ricci. Verona: Mondadori, 1974.

3. Works in Latin

De casibus virorum illustrium. Facsimile reproduction of Paris edition of 1520; Introduction by Louis Brewer Hall. Gainesville, Fla.: Scholar's Facsimiles and Reprints, 1967.
De montibus. Venice: Vindelino da Spira, 1473.
De mulieribus claris. Tutte le opere, Vol. X. Edited by Vittorio Zaccaria. Verona: Mondadori, 1967.
Genealogie deorum gentilium. Edited by Vincenzo Romano. Bari: Laterza, 1951.
Opere latine minori: Epistole, Buccolicum carmen, Vita sanctissimi patri Petri Damiani eremite, De vita et moribus Francisci Petracchi, Carmine quae supersunt, Allegoria mitologica, Cenni intorno a Tito Livio. Edited by Aldo F. Massera. Bari: Laterza, 1938.
Zibaldone laurenziano. Facsimile. Florence: Olschki, 1915.
Zibaldone magliabechiano. Sala manoscritti, Biblioteca Nazionale, Florence, II,II,327.

4. Italian Works in Translation

Comedia delle ninfe fiorentine (Ameto). Translated by Judith P. Serafini-Sauli, unpublished dissertation, Johns Hopkins University, 1970.
Corbaccio. Translated by Anthony K. Cassell. Urbana: University of Illinois Press, 1975.
Decameron. Translated by G. H. McWilliam. Harmondsworth: Penguin, 1972.
Elegia di Madonna Fiammetta: Amorous Fiammetta. Translation revised by E. H. Hutton. London: Privately printed for Rarity Press, 1931.
Filocolo: Questioni d'amore. Translated by Victoria Kirkham, unpublished dissertation, Johns Hopkins University, 1971.
Filostrato. Translated by N. E. Griffin and A. B. Myrick. Philadelphia: University of Philadelphia Press, 1929.
Ninfale fiesolano. Translated by D. J. Donno. New York: Columbia University Press, 1960; Joseph Tusiani, Rutherford, New Jersey: Fairleigh Dickinson University Press, 1971.
Trattatello in laude di Dante: Life of Dante. Translated by P. H. Wicksteed. San Francisco: Printed by John Henry Nash for his friends, 1922.

5. Latin Works in Translation

De casibus: The Fates of Illustrious Men. Translated and abridged by Louis Brewer Hall. New York: Frederick Ungar, 1965.

De mulieribus: Concerning Famous Women. Translated by Guido A. Guarino. New Brunswick, N.J.: Rutgers University Press, 1963.

Genealogie deorum gentilium: Boccaccio on Poetry (Books XIV, XV). Translated by Charles Osgood. Princeton, N.J.: Princeton University Press, 1930.

SECONDARY SOURCES

Since a complete bibliography would run into hundreds of entries, the following is a reduced selection. It includes some general works on major currents in Boccaccio's time, some recent bibliographies, and some recent biographies. For the Boccaccio corpus I have listed only works that deal with more general aspects of Boccaccio's works or with more than one work. For the *Decameron* I have listed only some of the larger and more recent works devoted to this vast subject. The critical works are generally modern, since others can be found in histories of criticism, which are also listed below. An effort has been made to include as many English titles as possible.

Almansi, Guido. *The Writer as Liar.* London: Routledge Paul, 1975. An interesting analysis of certain stories and of the importance of narration in the *Decameron.*

Antal, Frederick. *Florentine Painting and its Social Background.* London: Kegan Paul, 1948. A discussion of developments in painting that illuminate and parallel trends in literature in Boccaccio's time.

Auerbach, Erich. *Mimesis.* Princeton, N.J.: Princeton University Press, 1953. The chapter on Boccaccio is still a fundamental discussion of realism in Boccaccio's art.

Bailet, Michel. *L'homme de verre.* Nice: Imprimerie universelle: for exclusive distribution by the Studio Bibliografico Antenore, Padua, 1972. A psychoanalytic approach to the *Decameron.*

Baratto, Mario. *Realtà e stile nel "Decameron."* Vicenza: Neri Pozza, 1970. A broad and profound analysis of patterns in the *Decameron,* with particular reference to literary style and genres.

Baron, Hans. "Franciscan Poverty and Civic Wealth as Factors in the Rise of Humanistic Thought." *Speculum* 13 (1938):1–37. An important study for the background of Boccaccio's thought.

Battaglia, Salvatore. *La Coscienza letteraria del medioevo*. Naples: Liguori, 1965. Essays on certain of Boccaccio's early works and on the *Decameron*, including some important earlier articles.

————. *Le Epoche della letteratura italiana*. Naples: Liguori, 1968. The chapter on Boccaccio is a general introduction to his major works.

————. "Schemi lirici nell'arte del Boccaccio." *Archivium Romanicum* 19 (1935):61–78. Traces the development of Boccaccio's work from the early works to the *Decameron*.

Becker, Marvin. *Florence in Transition*. Baltimore: Johns Hopkins University Press, 1967. An analysis of the historical and cultural currents in Boccaccio's Florence.

Billanovich, Giuseppe. *Restauri boccacceschi*. Rome: Istituto grafico tiberino, 1946. A pioneering reconstruction of the biography of Boccaccio with reference to literary forms in the early works.

Boccaccio, Giovanni. *Tutte le opere*. General editor, Vittore Branca. Vols. I, II, III, IV, VI, X, various editors. Verona: Mondadori, 1964–. Each volume contains one or more works and each work is accompanied by an excellent bibliography.

Branca, Vittore. *Boccaccio medievale*. Florence: Sansoni, 1970. Treats Boccaccio's position in literary, historical, and linguistic schemes; includes some articles printed previously.

————. *Boccaccio: The Man and His Work*. Translated by Richard Monges; cotranslator and editor, Dennis J. McAuliffe. New York: New York University Press, 1976. This contains, in translation, the important "Profilo biografico," found in Vol. I of *Tutte le opere*, and selected essays from the critical works of Branca, including some from *Boccaccio medievale*.

————. "Giovanni Boccaccio." In *Letteratura italiana: I Maggiori*. Milan: Marzorati, 1956. A general introduction to Boccaccio and his work, with bibliography.

————. *Linea d'una storia della critica al "Decameron."* Rome: Dante Alighieri, 1939. For a history of Boccaccio criticism.

Brucker, Gene. *Florentine Politics and Society, 1343–1378*. Princeton, N.J.: Princeton University Press, 1962. A study of the period of turmoil which embraces the major part of Boccaccio's life.

Caggese, Romolo. *Roberto d'Angiò e i suoi tempi*. Florence: Bemporad, 1921. A comprehensive study of Angevin Naples and the court of Robert of Anjou.

Curtius, Ernst Robert. *European Literature and the Latin Middle Ages*. New York: Harper & Row, 1963. A fundamental work, particularly useful for Boccaccio's sources and his role as a humanist.

Davidsohn, Robert. *Geschicte von Florenz*. Berlin: Mittler, 1896–1912. The most comprehensive history of medieval and early Renaissance Florence.

DiPino, Guido. *La Polemica del Boccaccio.* Florence: Vallecchi, 1953. A general review of Boccaccio's works in Italian.

Ferguson, Wallace K. *Europe in Transition.* Boston: Houghton Mifflin, 1972. A general introduction to Europe in Boccaccio's time.

Getto, Giovanni. *Vita di forme e forme di vita nel "Decameron."* 3rd edition. Turin: Petrini, 1972. A basic discussion of themes and literary patterns in the *Decameron.*

Hauvette, Henri. *Boccace.* Paris: Colin, 1914. Though somewhat superseded by modern criticism, it is a general introduction to all the works of Boccaccio.

Hay, Denys. *The Italian Renaissance in its Historical Background.* Cambridge: Cambridge University Press, 1961. A good general work with useful references to Boccaccio.

Hollander, Robert. *Boccaccio's Two Venuses.* New York: Columbia University Press, 1977. A provocative study of the moral significance of Boccaccio's minor works in Italian. The abundant notes contain an excellent bibliography.

Hutton, Edward. *Giovanni Boccaccio: A Biographical Study.* London: Lane, 1909. Though antequated in many aspects, it provides a general introduction, in English, to Boccaccio's works.

Léonard, Emile. *Les Angevins de Naples.* Paris: Presses Universitaires de France, 1953. For Angevin Naples and background to Boccaccio's early works.

Lepschy, Anna Laura. "Boccaccio Studies in English, 1945–69." *Studi sul Boccaccio* 6 (1971):211–29. An excellent bibliography for Boccaccio studies in English.

Meiss, Millard. *Painting in Florence and Siena After the Black Death.* Princeton, N.J.: Princeton University Press, 1951. A fundamental study of the art of the period, with a good chapter on Boccaccio.

Moravia, Alberto. *L'uomo come fine.* Milan: Bompiani, 1964. English translation: *Man as an End.* New York: Farrar, Strauss & Giroux, 1966. A good essay on Boccaccio's narrative art.

Osgood, Charles G. *Boccaccio on Poetry.* Indianapolis–New York: Bobbs Merrill, 1956. A translation of Books XIV and XV of Boccaccio's *Genealogie* with a good introduction.

Padoan, Giorgio. "Mondo aristocratico e mondo comunale nell'idealogia e nell'arte di Giovanni Boccaccio." *Studi sul Boccaccio* 2 (1964):81–216. A discussion of the reflections of social and political background in Boccaccio's works.

Petronio, Giuseppe. *Il Decameron.* Bari: Laterza, 1935. A good general introduction to the salient aspects of Boccaccio's art as found in the *Decameron*.

———. "Lineamenti della storia della critica boccaccesca." In *I Classici italiani nella storia della critica*. General editor, Walter Binni. Florence: La Nuova Italia, 1954, pp. 169–228. For the history of Boccaccio criticism.

Quaglio, Antonio Enzo. *Scienza e mito nel Boccaccio*. Padua: Liviana, 1967. Particularly important for the *Filocolo* and other early works.

Ramat, Raffaello. "Boccaccio 1340–1344." *Belfagor* 19 (1964):17–30, 154–74. On the tumultuous events of these years and their influence on Boccaccio.

Russo, Luigi. *Letture critiche del "Decameron."* Bari: Laterza, 1956. A general introduction to the *Decameron*.

Salinari, Carlo. Editor, Giovanni Boccaccio, *Decameron*. Bari: Laterza, 1963. A brief general introduction.

Sapegno, Natalino. "Giovanni Boccaccio." In *Dizionario biografico degli italiani*. Rome: Istituto della Enciclopedia italiana, 1960–1967, pp. 838–56. A concise but substantial biography.

———. *Il Trecento*. Milan: Vallardi, 1955. The chapter on Boccaccio is an important introduction to the entire Boccaccio corpus, followed by a concise but good bibliography.

Schevill, Ferdinand. *Medieval and Renaissance Florence*. New York: Harper & Row, 1963. A basic history of Florence.

Segre, Cesare, ed. *Opere di Giovanni Boccaccio*. Milan: Mursia, 1966. A brief but important introductory section.

Singleton, Charles S. "On Meaning in the *Decameron*." *Italica* 21(1944):117. On Boccaccio's position as a Renaissance writer.

———. "Uses of the *Decameron*." *Modern Language Notes* 79 (1964):71–76. On the literary and moral significance of the Introduction to the Fourth Day in the *Decameron*.

Studi sul Boccaccio. Edited by Vittore Branca. Vol. I (1963–). Volumes have come out almost every year. In addition to important articles, each volume contains an exhaustive bibliography of recent works on Boccaccio.

Todorov, Tzvetan. *Grammaire du "Decameron."* Hague-Paris: Mouton, 1969. A formalist analysis of narrative patterns in the *Decameron*.

Trinkaus, Charles. "Humanism." In *Encyclopedia of World Art*. New York–London: McGraw Hill, 1963, pp. 702–43.

———. *In Our Image and Likeness*. London: Constable, 1970. Both are important for Boccaccio and the development of humanism.

Index

"Abrotonia," *Ameto*, 32; pseudo-biography of Boccaccio, 18
Accademia degli Incogniti, 129
Accademia della Crusca, 129
Accademia Fiorentina, expurgation of *Decameron*, 128
Acciaiuoli, Andrea, *De mulieribus*, 104, 105
Acciaiuoli, Niccolò, 97, 98, 122; *Buccolicum Carmen*, 114, 115; friendship with Boccaccio, 8; letter to, 40, 121
Accursio, Mainardo, 58
"Adam and Eve," *De casibus*, 103
"Adonis and Venus," *De mulieribus*, 106
"Africo," *Ninfale fiesolano*, 54–57
"Agilulfo, King," *Decameron*, 78
"Alatiel," *Decameron*, language, 92, 93
Albanzani, Donato, 59; *Buccolicum Carmen*, 116
Alberico da Montecassino, Gregorian prose style, 89
Albizzi, Franceschino degli, 58, 59
"Alibech," *Decameron*, plot, 71
Alighieri, Dante, *see* Dante
Allegoria mitologica, 10
Allegory, *Ameto*, 41–42, 44, 45; *Amorosa Visione*, 48; Augustine,

St., 109; *Buccolicum Carmen*, 113; *Caccia di Diana*, 15–16; *De mulieribus*, 106; *Decameron*, 63n10; *Esposizioni*, 123–24, 125; *Filocolo*, 22–23; *Genealogie*, 107, 108, 110; Jerome, St., 109; Old Testament, 109; *Teseida*, 37; *Trattatello*, 113
"Ambruogia," *Decameron*, 67
Ameto, 41–46; "Abrotonia," 32; allegory in, 41–42, 44, 45; Angevin court, life in, 11; *ars dictandi* techniques, 91; *Buccolicum Carmen* compared, 114; *Caccia di Diana* compared, 41; catalog *topos*, 14; city *topos*, 24n39, 25, 43, 56–57, 101; courtly love, *Decameron*, compared, 82; Dante, influence on, 41; *De montibus* compared, 101; *Decameron* compared, 61, 82; dedication *topos*, 45; etymologies, 90; humor, 44–45; *locus amoenus topos*, 15, 42–43; narrative framework, 43–44; narrator, figure of, 14; *Ninfale fiesolano* compared, 56–57; nymphs, "brigata" in *Decameron* compared, 61; pastoral romances derived from, 131; plot, 41; sentence structure, 91–92; *terza rima*, 41

Amorosa Visione, 41, 45, 46–50; catalog *topos*, 14; *Corbaccio* compared, 100; Dante's influence on, 46, 47, 49; date of, 46; *donna angelicata*, 48; Fortune in, 48; *locus amoenus*, 48; love, sacred v. profane, 47–49, 50; mythology in, 48; narrative pattern, 50; narrator, figure of, 46–49; Petrarch, influence on, 97; plot, 46–49; sources of, 46; Stilnovo poetry, 47; structure of, 46; *terza rima*, 46; "vision" genre, 46; *Vita Nuova* compared, 49

Anaphora, *Decameron*, 91; *Fiammetta*, 91

Andalò del Negro, *Genealogie*, 107

"Andreuccio da Perugia," *Decameron*, 65; narrative techniques, 86

Andrew of Hungary, *Buccolicum Carmen*, 114

Anjou, House of, 3; *Buccolicum Carmen*, 114; court of, *see* Naples, Angevin court in

Apuleius, *Genealogie*, 107

Aquinas, St. Thomas, *Esposizioni*, 123

Arcadia, Lope de Vega, 131

Arcadia, Jacopo Sannazaro, 131

Arcadia, Sir Philip Sidney, 131

Archpriest of Hita, 131

Aretino, Pietro, novella form, 128

"Argenti, Filippo," *Decameron*, 66

Ariosto, Lodovico, *Orlando Furioso*, 131

Aristotle, translation of, 117

Arno River, *Ameto*, 41; *De montibus*, 102; *Decameron*, 79

Ars amatoria, Ovid, 22

ars dictandi, 4, 5; *Ameto*, 9; *Decameron*, 88–92; *Epistole*, 120; Hila-

rian style, 89; study by Boccaccio, 9

ars notaria, and *ars dictandi*, 89

Art of Courtly Love, Andreas Capellanus, 17n22, 24n36, 31–33, 70n24, 77

Astrée, Honore d'Urfé, 131

Augustine, St., defense of poetry, 107, 109, 119

Avarice, *Esposizioni*, 125

Avignon, Babylonian Captivity, 3, 115; diplomatic missions to, 3, 97, 114, 122

Babylonian Captivity, 3, 115

Baia, 11, 12, 53

"Balducci, Filippo," *Decameron*, 68, 69, 70

Bandello, Matteo, novella form, 128

Barbato da Sulmona, 98, 120

Bardi Company, 8, 40

Barlaam of Calabria, 10, 107

Barrili, Giovanni, 98

Battle of Poitiers, *De casibus*, 104

Beatrice, Dante and, *Trattatello*, 112, 113; *donna angelicata*, 18; "Fiammetta" compared, 51

Bembo, Pietro, 128

Benoit de Saint Maure, *Roman de Troie*, 29

Bernard Silvestris, 59

Bible, *see* Scripture

Binduccio dello Scelto, 29

Black Death, 5, 40, 59; aftermath of, 95, 96; described, *Decameron*, 60, 64, 95

Black Plague, *see* Black Death

Boccaccino, *see* Boccaccio di Chellino

Boccaccio di Chellino (father of Boccaccio), 1, 7, 8; *Amorosa Visione*,

47; death of, 59; financial failure, 40

Boccaccio, Giovanni, biographer's description, 1; biographical elements in works, 18–19, 99n10, 114, 115; birth of, 7, 119; children of, 115; death of, 126, 127; early poems, 12–13; education of, 7–9; epitaph, 1, 127; ill health, *Epistole,* 122; later poems, 12–13; literary vocation, 9; personal freedom, defense of, 117–18; physical appearance, 1; prose style, imitation of; 129; religious crisis, 119; self-evaluation, *Rime,* 12–13; tomb of, 1, 2n3; will of, 119

Boccaccius, *see* Boccaccio di Chellino

Boethius, 59, 123

Boniface VIII, Pope, 65

Borghini, Vincenzo, expurgation of *Decameron,* 128

Botticelli, Sandro, 131

"brigata," *Decameron,* described, 61–62; nymphs in *Ameto* compared, 61

Bruni, Leonardo, 130

Buccolicum Carmen (Eclogues), 59, 113–116; allegory in, 113; *Ameto* compared, 114; biographical elements, 114, 115; date, uncertainty, 113n39; described, 114–116; Petrarch in, 115; poetic sources, 113; poetry, value of, 116

Byron, George Gordon, 131

Caccia di Diana, 12, 14–16; allegory in, 15–16; *Ameto* compared, 41; catalog *topos* in, 14, 15; character portrayal, 34; Dante's influence on, 15; date of, 14; *Filocolo* compared, 21, 22, 34; *Filostrato* compared, 34; *locus amoenus topos,* 14–15; mythology and allegory, 15; narrative patterns, 14, 15, 50; narrator, figure of, 14–15; numerical structure in, 15; Ovid's influence on, 15

"Calandrino," *Decameron,* 66, 76

"Caleon," *Filocolo,* 23

Canon law, 4, 5, 9, 89

cantari, described, 19; *Filostrato,* 33–34; *Ninfale fiesolano,* 55, 57; ottava verse, relation to, 34; *Teseida,* 39

Capella, Martianus, *see* Martianus Capella

Capellanus, Andreas, *Art of Courtly Love,* 17n22, 24n36, 31–33, 70n24, 77

Carisendi family, 28

Casini, Bruno, 58, 59

Castiglione, Baldassare, *The Courtier,* 128

Catalog *topos, Ameto,* 14; *Amorosa Visione,* 14; *Caccia di Diana,* 14, 15; *De montibus,* 101, 102; in later works, 14; in *Teseida,* 14, 38

Catholicism, *Decameron,* 72; (*see also* Church)

Cavalcanti, Guido, 65–66, 68

Cavalcanti, Mainardo, letter to, 2, 7, 122

Cent nouvelles nouvelles, 131

"Ceres," *De mulieribus,* 106

Certaldo, birthplace of Boccaccio, 7; Boccaccio's retirement to, 96, 97, 104, 122; *Buccolicum Carmen,* 116; *Decameron,* 75, 93; *Filocolo,* 25; tomb in, 1

Cervantes, Miguel de, *Galatea,* 131

Charity (*Caritas*), *Ameto,* 41, 42; *Amorosa Visione,* 48. 49

Charles I of Anjou, 65, 104
Charles IV of Luxembourg, Emperor, 114
Chaucer, Geoffrey, Boccaccio's influence on, 130; *Canterbury Tales, Decameron* compared, 62, 83; *Filostrato,* 34, 130
Checco di Meletto Rossi, 59
"Chichibio," *Decameron,* 78
Church, Black Death, 95; *Buccolicum Carmen,* 115; satire of, *Decameron,* 70–76, 84; *Decameron,* expurgation of during Counter-Reformation, 128–29; v. Nature, 70–72
"Ciacco," *Decameron,* 66
"Ciappelletto," *Decameron,* 73, 74–75; narrative techniques, 85
Cicero, 89, 103
"Cimon," *Decameron,* 82, 131
Cino da Pistoia, 9, 68; canzone in *Filostrato,* 9, 31
Ciompi uprising, 5
Circe, *De mulieribus,* 106
"Cisti," *Decameron,* 78–89
City of God, St. Augustine, 109
City *topos, Ameto,* 24n39, 25, 43, 56–57, 101; *Decameron,* 24n39, 25; *Filocolo,* 24–25; *Ninfale fiesolano,* 25, 56–57
Civic humanism, *De casibus,* 102n16
Clergy, *see* Church
Comedia delle ninfe fiorentine, see Ameto
Convivio, Dante, allegory, 123
Corbaccio, 96, 98–101; *Amorosa Visione* compared, 100; Boccaccio's biography, 99n10; courtly love, 98; date of, 98; *Decameron* compared, 98, 99, 101; *donna angelicata,* 99; earlier works compared, 99, 101; *exemplum* tradition, 98, 99; love, sacred v. profane, 99, 100n11, 101; misogynism, 98–101, 113; misogynist literature influenced by, 131; narrator, figure of, 98, 99; plot, 98; realism in, 100; title, 98n9; "vision" genre, 98
Cornificia, *De mulieribus,* 107
Counter-Reformation, *Decameron,* effect on, 128–29
Court of love, *Filocolo, Questions of Love,* 25
Courtier, The, Baldassare Castiglione, 128
Courtly love, 17–18n22, 24n36; *Corbaccio,* 98; *Decameron,* 81, 82; *Fiammetta,* 51–52; *Filostrato,* 31–33
"Criseida and Troilus," *Filostrato,* 29–34
Croce, Benedetto, *Decameron,* criticism, 129
Cursus, De montibus, 101; described, 89; *Epistole,* 120; in Boccaccio's works, 90

Damian, Peter, biography of, 121; prose style, 89
Dante, *Amorosa Visione,* influence on, 46, 47, 49; Beatrice and *Trattatello,* 112, 113; biography of, *see Trattatello in laude di Dante;* *Buccolicum Carmen,* influence on, 114; *Caccia di Diana,* influence on, 14, 15; *Convivio,* allegory, 123; criticism, 6; daughter of, 96; *De vulgari eloquentia* and *Teseida,* 35; death of, 58, 112; *Decameron,* influence on, 59, 66, 68, 70; description of, *Trattatello,* 112; *Divine Comedy, see Divine Comedy,*

Dante; *Filocolo,* influence on, 21; *Filostrato,* echoes in, 30; importance for Boccaccio, 8, 9, 118; Isidorian prose style, 89; Italian language, *Trattatello,* 113; *Letter to Can Grande,* allegory, 123; love, sacred v. profane, 18; nationalism, 4; Petrarch's attitude toward, 118; praise of, 111–13; *(see also Trattatello in laude di Dante); Rime,* influence on, 13; *Vita Nuova,* 15, 41, 49, 51

Decades, Livy, translation by Boccaccio, 58–59n1, 90

De casibus virorum illustrium, 101, 102–104, 127; Battle of Poitiers, 104; Charles I of Anjou, 104; Chaucer's *Monk's Tale,* source of, 130; civic humanism, 102n16; date of, 102; *De mulieribus* compared, 104–105; *Decameron* compared, 103, 104; Duke of Athens, 103, 104; editions of, 103n18; *exemplum,* 103, 111; *exordium,* 102; Fortune in, 73, 103, 104; France, references to, 7; French translation, 130; historical figures in, 103–104; Jacopo, Master of Templars, 104; Lydgate's *Fall of Princes,* source of, 130; Old Testament, 103; Paolino Veneziano, 103; Paolo Diacono, 103; Petrarch, 103; realism, 104; structure of, 103, 104; "vision" genre, 103; *Zibaldone magliabechiano,* 103

de Meun, Jean, *Romance of the Rose,* 69n23, 72

De montibus, 101–102, 127; *Ameto* compared, 101; catalog *topos,* 101, 102; *cursus,* 101; *Decameron* compared, 101; described, 101–102;

exordium, 101, 102; *Filocolo* compared, 101; *Genealogie* compared, 102; mythology, 102

De mulieribus claris, 101, 104–107, 127; allegory, 106; Chaucer's *Legend of Good Women,* source of, 130; date, 104; *De casibus* compared, 104–105; *Decameron* compared, 105; dedication *topos,* 104–105; euhemerism in, 106; Fortune, 73; *Genealogie* compared, 106; love, sacred v. profane, 105; mythology, women in, 105; Nature, 105; Petrarch's work on famous men, 105

De Musset, Alfred, 131

De Navarre, Marguerite, *Heptameron,* 131

De Premierfait, Laurent, *De casibus,* translation, 130

De Sanctis, Francesco, *Decameron,* criticism, 94, 129

De Vega Carpio, Lope, *Arcadia,* 131; Federigo Story, 130

De vulgari eloquentia, Dante, *Teseida* and, 35

Decameron, 1, 2, 6, 58–94; *Ameto* compared, 61, 82; anaphora, 91; *ars dictandi,* 88–92; Black Death described, 60, 64, 95; Boccaccio's attitude toward, 122; "brigata" described, 61–62; *Buccolicum Carmen* compared, 115; catalog *topos,* 101; characters, identity of, 65n18, 66; Chaucer's *Canterbury Tales,* 62, 83; Church and clergy, satire of, 70–75, 84; city *topos,* 24n39, 25; classical rhetoric, 86, 88; colloquialisms, use of, 87–88; *Corbaccio* compared, 98, 99, 101; Counter-Reformation, effect on, 128–29; courtly love, 81–82; criticism, history of, 127–30; *cursus*, use in, 90; Dante's influence on, 59, 66, 68, 70; *De casibus* compared, 103–104; *De montibus* compared, 101; *De mulieribus* compared, 105; De Sanctis, criticism, 94, 129; dedication *topos*, 20; dialects, 87; dialogue, use in narrative techniques, 86–87; English translation, 130; etymology, 90; *exemplum* tradition, 11, 62, 85; expurgation of, 128–29; film, Pasolini, 131; *Filocolo* compared, 26–28; Florence, street names, 94; Fortune, 63, 67–85, 72n25, 104; Fourth Day, Introduction, 67–69; French translation, 130; Friuli, story locale, 97; "Ghismonda" story, 79–80, 130; Giotto, works of, realism, 4; "Griselda" story, *see* Griselda Story, *Decameron;* humor, 78–79; Italian language, use of 87–94; Italian prose, influence on, 127–28; licentiousness of, 68n22, 69, 122; *locus amoenus topos,* 15, 61; love, democracy of, 33; masterpiece of Boccaccio, 2; Naples, mercantile world, 8; narration, importance in, 73, 85–87; narrative framework, 63n11, 64, 67–68n21; narrative patterns, 65, 111; narrative techniques, 85–87; narrator, figure of, 15; "Nastagio degli Onesti," 32; Nature, 67–85; order of stories, 75, 84n34; paintings inspired by, 131; Petrarch, influence on, 97; poetry, defense of, 115; prosimet-

rum pattern, 59; *Questions of Love, Filocolo* compared, 26–28; realism, 62–67; recopying of, 118, 122, 127; repudiation of by Boccaccio, 2, 122; significance of, 94; story sources, 62ns7, 8; story themes, 61, 80; structure, 59, 61; title, 59; Venetians, depiction of, 72, 78, 87n41; virtue, Christian v. lay, 84–85

Dedication *topos, Ameto,* 45; *De mulieribus,* 104–105; *Decameron,* 20, 59–60, 64; *Fiammetta,* 20; *Filocolo,* 20; *Filostrato,* 20, 30; *Teseida,* 20

Democracy of love, Capellanus, Andreas, *Art of Courtly Love,* 32; *Decameron,* 33; *Filostrato,* 33; (*see also* Love theme)

Democracy of nature, *Decameron,* 77–80

Dialects, use of, *Decameron,* 87; *Epistole,* 120

Dialogue, use of, 52n17; *Decameron,* 86–87

Diana, *Caccia di Diana,* 14–16; *Ninfale fiesolano,* 54–57; *Teseida,* 37, 38

Diana's Hunt, *see Caccia di Diana*

"Dioneo," *Ameto,* 41; *Decameron,* 61, 64, 65, 71, 88

Dionigi da Borgo San Sepolcro, 10

Diplomatic missions, Avignon, 97, 114, 122; Petrarch, visit to, 97; Ravenna, 58; Rome, 122; Tyrol, 97

Disciplina clericalis, Pietrus Alphonsus, 80

Divine Comedy, The, Dante, 6; Boccaccio's commentary, 96; (*see also Esposizioni sopra la Comedia di*

Dante); interpretation, *Trattatello*, 112; Petrarch's view of, 118; public reading by Boccaccio, 13, 123

Donati, Gemma, Dante's marriage to, *Trattatello*, 113

Donna angelicata, 47; *Amorosa Visione*, 48; Beatrice, courtly love, 18; Beatrice, *Rime*, 13; *Corbaccio*, 99

Dreams, allegorical, *Filocolo*, 22–23

Dryden, John, 130, 131

Duke of Athens (Walter of Brienne), 40, 103, 104

Durazzo, Princes of, 97

D'Urfé, Honoré, 131

Eclogues, early, 59; *see Buccolicum Carmen*

Eclogues, Virgil, 16

Elegia di Costanza, 10

Elegia di Madonna Fiammetta, see Fiammetta

"Elissa," *Decameron*, 61, 62

"Emilia," *Decameron*, 61, 62; *Teseida*, 35–39

Epic genre, *Teseida*, 35–36

Epic romances, works derived from, 131

Epistole, 12, 120–22; Acciaiuoli, Niccolò, 40, 121; *ars dictandi*, 120; *Decameron*, licentiousness of, 122; *Esposizioni*, 122; *exemplum* tradition, 122; Fortune, 122; language of, 120; misogynism, 122; Petrarch-Boccaccio friendship, 97, 121; Petrarch's influence, 120–21; preservation of, 120; Zanobi da Strada, 121; Zanobi's laureation, 97

Esposizioni sopra la Comedia di Dante,

123–26; allegory, 124–25; *Epistole*, 122; etymology, 125; misogynism, 113, 125; poetry, defense of, 112, 125; significance of, 126

Etymology, *Ameto*, 90; *Decameron*, 90; *Esposizioni*, 125; "Fiammetta," 90; *Filocolo*, 90; *Genealogie*, 108; "Panfilo," 90; "poetry," *Genealogie*, 110

Euhemerism, *De mulieribus*, 106; *Genealogie*, 109–10

Euripides, translation of, 117

Europa, *De mulieribus*, 105

Eve, Adam and, *De casibus*, 103; life of, *De mulieribus*, 105

Exemplum tradition, 10–11; *Corbaccio*, 98, 99; *De casibus*, 103, 111; *Decameron*, 11, 62, 85; *Epistole*, 122; later works, 96; *Trattatello*, 111

Exordium, De casibus, 102; *De montibus*, 101, 102

Fabliaux, 11, 62, 71–72

Factorum et dictorum memorabilium, Valerius Maximus, 10

Faerie Queene, Edmund Spenser, 131

Fall of Princes, John Lydgate, source of, 130

Famous Men, Fates of, *see De casibus virorum illustrium*

Famous Women, Lives of, *see De mulieribus*

"Faunus," *Buccolicum Carmen*, 114

"Federigo degli Alberighi," *Decameron*, 66, 81–82, 130

"Fiammetta," 18; *Ameto*, 41; *Amorosa Visione*, 46, 48–49; *Decameron*, 61; etymology, 90; *Filocolo*, 23, 24, 25

Fiammetta (Elegia di Madonna Fiammetta), 41, 50–54; anaphora, 91; Angevin court, life in, 11; courtly love, 51–52; dedication *topos*, 20; dialogue, use of, 52n17; etymology, 90; love, sacred v. profane, 51; narrative patterns, 53; narrative realism, 54; narrator, figure of, 50; plot, 50–53; sources of, 51; *Vita Nuova*, Dante compared, 51

Fiction, poetic, defined, *Genealogie*, 110

Fiesole, *see Ninfale fiesolano*

"Filippo Balducci," *Decameron*, language and, 93

Filocolo, 12, 19–29; allegorical dreams, 22–23; Angevin court, life in, 11; *Caccia di Diana* compared, 21, 22, 34; catalog *topos*, 101; character portrayal, 34; city *topos*, 24–25; Dante, influence on, 21; date of, 29; *De montibus* compared, 101; dedication *topos*, 20; etymology, 90; *locus amoenus*, 21, 24; love, sacred v. profane, 21, 22, 23–24; metamorphoses, 21–22; mythology, 21; narrative framework, *Questions of Love*, 23, 24, 44; numerical patterns, 22n35; origins, 19; *ottava* verse, 35; Ovid's influence on, 21, 22; plot, 20; *Questions of Love, see Questions of Love, Filocolo;* title, 20

"Filomena," *Decameron*, 61; *Filostrato*, 30

Filostrato," *Decameron*, 61, 77

Filostrato, 12, 29–35; *Caccia di Diana* compared, 34; *cantari*, 33–34; character portrayal, 34; Chaucer's *Troilus and Cressida*, source of, 34, 130; Cino da Pistoia, canzone in, 9, 31; courtly love, 31–33; courtly poetry, 31;

Dante, echoes in, 30; date, 29n44; dedication topos, 20, 30; epic romances derived from, 131; language, 33–34; love, democracy of, 33; love, sacred v. profane, 29; narrator, figure of, 30; Nature, concept of, 31, 32; *Ninfale fiesolano* compared, 55; origins of, 29; *ottava* verse, 34–35; Ovid, *Ars amatoria* in, 32; Stilnovo poetry, 30–31

Florence, Bank failures in 14th century, 5; Black Death, *see* Black Death; Boccaccio's family residence, 7; Boccaccio's return to, 40; Dante's exile, *Trattatello*, 111, 112; diplomatic missions for, *see* Diplomatic missions; Duke of Athens, 40, 103, 104; families of, *Ameto*, 42; language of, *Decameron*, 87; literary circles, 97; mercantilism, *see* Florentine mercantilism; mythological history of, 43, 54, 56; street names, *Decameron*, 94; upheaval mid 14th century, 5, 40, 59, 95–96

Florentine mercantilism, *Decameron*, 65, 66; influence on arts and letters, 3–5; Naples, 3

Forlì, 59, 114

Fortune, theme of, 72–73; *Amorosa Visione*, 48; *De casibus*, 73, 103, 104; *De mulieribus*, 73; *Decameron*, 63, 67–85, 72n25, 104; democracy of, *Decameron*, 77n28; *Epistole*, 122

Foscolo, Ugo, *Decameron*, criticism, 129

"Fra Cipolla," *Decameron*, 75, 91; language, 93–94

Fra Martino da Signa, letter to, *Buccolicum Carmen*, 113, 120

Framework, *see* Narrative framework

France, merchant contacts with, *De casibus,* 7; Paris as birthplace, 7

Francesca da Rimini, 70; *Esposizioni,* 125

Francesco da Brossano, *Epistole,* 121

Franciscan Fraticelli, 5

"Frate Alberto," *Decameron,* 72

French literature, influence on Boccaccio, 11, 12

Friendship, theme of, *Decameron,* 80

Friuli, *Decameron,* story locale, 97

Fulgentius, *Genealogie,* 107

Galatea, Miguel de Cervantes, 131

"Galla," *Buccolicum Carmen,* 114

Gallehaut, 22n34

Genealogie decorum gentilium, 10, 101, 107–111; allegory, sources of, 107, 108, 110; *Buccolicum Carmen* compared, 115; date, 107; *De montibus* compared, 102; *De mulieribus* compared, 106; dedication, 107; etymology in, 108, 110; euhemerism, 109–10; fiction, poetic, defined, 110; Greek language, 108; Latin language, 108; mythology, sources of, 107–11; Petrarch, influence on, 97; poetry, defense of, 107, 109–11, 112, 115, 125; printings of, 127n1; structure, 107; *Trattatello* compared, origins of poetry, 112

Geographic catalog, *see* city *topos*

"Ghismonda" story, *Decameron,* 79–80; works based on, 130

Gian di Procida, 65

"Gianfigliazzi, Currado," *Decameron,* 78

Giotto, 95; *Amorosa Visione,* 47n11; *Decameron,* 4, 65; Santa Croce, Florence, 4; Scrovegni Chapel, Padua, 4; works of, realism, 4

Giovanni del Virgilio-Dante, correspondence, 114

Giovanni di Domenico Mazzuoli da Strada, 8

Giraldi Cinthio, novella form, 128

"Girolamo," *Decameron,* 77

"Gisippus," *Decameron,* 80–81; language, 88

"Gostanza," *Decameron,* 77

Greek classics, influence on Boccaccio's work, 10; study of, 6, 10; translation of, 116–17

Greek language, *Decameron* title, 59; *Genealogie,* 108

Greeks, poetry, origin of, 110

Gregorian prose style, 89

Gregory VIII, Pope, 89

"Griselda," *Decameron,* 65, 73, 75, 82–85, 83n32

"Griselda" story, *Decameron,* Chaucer, influence on, 130; Latin translation by Petrarch, 118–19, 127; works based on, 130

"Gualtieri," *Decameron,* 82–83

"Guccio," *Decameron,* 91, 93

Guelf terrorism, Florence, 121

Guido delle Colonne, *Historia troiana,* 29

"Guiscardo," *Decameron,* 79–80

"Gulfardo," *Decameron,* 67

Hebrews, poetry, origin of, 110

Heptameron, Marguerite de Navarre, 131

Hercules, *Amorosa Visione,* 48n12; *Genealogie,* 108

Hilarian prose style, 89

Historia Troiana, Guido delle Colonne, 29

Homer, *Genealogie,* 107; poetry-theology relationship, 109; translation of, 10, 116, 117

Hugues, King of Cyprus, *Genealogie*, 107
Humanism, ancient texts, 101; *De montibus*, 102; early examples, 5
Humor, *Ameto*, 44–45; *Decameron*, 76, 78–79; language, 92
Hunt of Diana, *see Caccia di Diana*

Idyllic garden, *topos* of, *see locus amoenus*
Il Lasca, novella form, 128
Innocent VI, Pope, diplomatic missions to, 97, 119
Ipsiphyle, *De mulieribus*, 105
Isidore of Seville, 89; etymologies, *Esposizioni*, 110, 125; *Genealogie*, 107; prose style, 89, 90
Italian language, *Ameto*, syntax in, 91–92; Boccaccio's style, development, 59; *Buccolicum Carmen*, 115; colloquialisms, *Decameron*, 87–88; *Decameron*, use in, 63, 87–94, 128; dialects, use of, 87, 120; emergence of, 3–4; humor and, 92; *Ninfale fiesolano*, 56n20; Petrarch-Boccaccio relationship, 97n5, 117–18; popular language, *Filostrato*, 33–34; syntax, 91; *Trattatello*, 112, 113
Italian literature, *Decameron's* influence on, 127–28; notaries' influence on, 3
Italian nationalism, 4
Italy, 14th century, reflection in Boccaccio's works, 2–5

Jacopo, Master of Templars, *De casibus*, 104
Jerome, St., allegory, 109; *Genealogie*, 107; poetry, 119
Johanna, Queen of Naples, 122; *De mulieribus*, 105

John of Garland, *Poetria*, 89
Jove, *De mulieribus*, 105, 106; *Genealogie*, 108

Keats, John, 131
Kingdom of Naples, 3; *see also* Naples, Angevin Court in
Knight's Tale, Chaucer, 62, 83

Lactantius, *Genealogie*, 107, 108; poetry, 119
La Fontaine, Jean de, 131
Latin classics, revival of, 127
Latin language, relation to emerging Italian, 3–4; *Genealogie*, 108; v. Italian, Petrarch-Boccaccio disagreement, 117–18
Latin literature, praise of, *De mulieribus*, 106–107; translations, effect on Italian prose, 90
Latin works by Boccaccio, 1, 101; eclogues, 59, 113
"Lauretta," *Decameron*, 61
Law, relation to Italian language, 3–4
Le Maçon, translation of *Decameron*, 130
Lectura Dantis, 13; commencement, 123
Legend of Good Women, Chaucer, 130
Leontius Pilatus, *Genealogie*, 108; Greek translation, 116–17
Lessing, Gotthold E., 131
Letters of Boccaccio, *see Epistole*
Letter of Consolation to Pino de' Rossi, 95, 121–22; Fortune, 73
Letter to Can Grande, Dante, allegory, 123
Lewis, C. S., "truancy" theory, 17
Library of Boccaccio, 2; offered to Petrarch, 119

Literature, classical, study of, 97, 101, 127

Livy, (Titus Livius) *Decades,* translation by Boccaccio, 58–59n1, 90; *De mulieribus,* 105

Locus amoenus topos, 11; *Ameto,* 15, 42–43; *Amorosa Visione,* 48; *Art of Courtly Love,* Andreas Capellanus, 31, 32; *Caccia di Diana,* 14–15; *Decameron,* 15, 61; *Filocolo,* 21, 24; *Ninfale fiesolano,* 15; *Teseida,* 38

Longfellow, Henry W., 131

Love, court of, *Filocolo, Questions of Love,* 25

Love, sacred v. profane, *Amorosa Visione,* 47–49, 50; *Corbaccio,* 99, 100n11, 101; Dante, 18; *De mulieribus,* 105; *Fiammetta,* 51; *Filocolo,* 21, 22, 23–24; *Filostrato,* 29; *Ninfale fiesolano,* 57; Stilnovo poetry, 18; *Teseida,* 37–38; (*see also* Love theme)

Love theme, 16, 96; autobiographical references in works, 18; *Corbaccio,* 98–101; courtly love, *see* Courtly love; democracy of love, 32, 33; duality of Venus, *Teseida,* 17; kinds of love, 23–24; money v. love, 66–67, 81–82; Ovid, 16; profane love, 70n24, 125 (*see also* Love, sacred v. profane); religion of love, 22; sacred v. profane love, *see* Love, sacred v. profane; youth and love, *Decameron,* 31–32, 70

Lydgate, John, *Fall of Princes,* 130

Macrobius, *Genealogie,* 107

"Madam Beritola," *Decameron,* 65

Margherita dei Mardoli (stepmother), 7; death of, 59

Maria dei Conti d'Aquino, 18, 19

"Marriage of Emilia," *see Teseida*

Mars, house of, *Teseida,* 37; and Venus, *De mulieribus,* 106

Martianus Capella, 59; *Genealogie,* 107

"Martuccio," *Decameron,* 77

"Masetto da Lamporecchio," *Decameron,* 77; language, 93; plot, 73–74

Megulia Dotata, *De mulieribus,* 105–106

"Mensola," 55–57

Mercantilism, Church and, 95–96; realism and, *Decameron,* 64–67; lay morality, *Decameron,* 84; (*see also* Florentine mercantilism)

"Messer Ansaldo," *Decameron,* 66

Metamorphoses, in *Caccia di Diana,* 15; *Filocolo,* 21–22

Minerva, *De mulieribus,* 106

Minyans, wives of, *De mulieribus,* 105

Misogynism, *Corbaccio,* 98–101, 113; *Epistole,* 122; *Esposizioni,* 113, 125; *Trattatello,* 113

Money, v. love, theme, *Decameron,* 66–67, 81–82; *Teseida* 67

Monk's Tale, Chaucer, source of, 130

"Monna Belcolore," *Decameron,* language of, 88

"Monna Giovanna," *Decameron,* 66, 81–82

Montecassino, library, Boccaccio's visit to, 98

Morgante, Il, Luigi Pulci, 131

Mother of Boccaccio, 7

Mugnone river, Florence, 41, 55, 56, 76

Muses, *Decameron,* and *Corbaccio* compared, 101; dedication, *Filostrato,* 30; inspiration by, *Decameron,* 68

Mussato, Albertino, *Genealogie*, 107; poetry, defense of, 110

Mythology, allegory and *Caccia di Diana*, 15; *Amorosa Visione*, 48; *De montibus*, 102; *De mulieribus*, 105, 106; *Filocolo*, 21; *Genealogie*, 107–11; *Ninfale fiesolano*, 55; poetry, relation to, *Genealogie*, 109; St. Augustine, 109; Scripture, 109; *Teseida*, 38; Varro, 109; women in, *De mulieribus*, 105

Naples, Angevin Court in, 3; Boccaccio's early years in, 8–12; Boccaccio's return to, 40, 97, 98, 116; *Buccolicum Carmen*, 114, 115, 116; cultural ambience, 5; *Epistole*, 122; political situation 1355, 97–98; Royal library, 9–10; work in, Boccaccino, 8

Narrative framework, *Ameto*, 43–44; *Decameron*, 63n11, 64, 67–68n21; *Filocolo*, 23, 24, 44 (*see also* Narrative pattern; Narration)

Narrative pattern, *Amorosa Visione*, 50; *Caccia di Diana*, 14, 15, 50; *Decameron*, 65, 111; *Fiammetta*, 53; other works inspired by, 131; *Rime*, 13; *Teseida*, 50; (*see also* Narrative framework; Narration)

Narrative realism, *Fiammetta*, 54; (*see also* Realism)

Narrative techniques, *Decameron*, 85–87; (*see also* Narrative framework; Narrative pattern; Narration)

Narration, change in, 96; *Esposizioni*, 125; *Filocolo* and *Decameron* compared, 28; *ottava* verse scheme, development, 35; preeminence in Boccaccio's works, 6;

significance, *Decameron*, 73, 85–87; *Trattatello*, 111; (*see also* Narrative framework; Narrative pattern; Narrator, figure of)

Narrator, figure of, 18; *Ameto*, 14; *Amorosa Visione*, 46–49; *Caccia di Diana*, 14–15; *Corbaccio*, 98, 99; *Decameron*, 15; *Fiammetta*, 50; *Filostrato*, 30

"Nastagio degli Onesti," *Decameron*, 32, 131

"Natural reason," theory, *Decameron*, 60–61, 67, 70

Nature, *De mulieribus*, 105; *Decameron*, 63, 67–85; democracy of, *Decameron*, 77–80; *Filostrato*, 31, 32; *Romance of the Rose*, de Meun, 69n23; v. Church, 70–72

"Neifile," *Decameron*, 61

Nelli, Francesco, *Epistole*, 12, 122

Ninfale fiesolano, 41, 54–57; *Ameto* compared, 56–57; *cantari*, 55, 57; city *topos*, 25, 56–57; date, 54n19; *Filostrato* compared, 55; language, 56n20; *locus amoenus topos*, 15; love, sacred v. profane, 57; mythology in, 55; pastoral genre, 56; pastoral romances derived from, 131; plot, 54–55

Novella form, *Decameron*, inspiration for, 128

Numerical patterns, *Caccia di Diana*, 15; *Filocolo*, 22n35

"Nymphs of Fiesole," *see Ninfale fiesolano*

Old Testament, *see* Scripture

"Olympia," *Buccolicum Carmen*, 115

Ordelaffi, Francesco, 59; *Buccolicum Carmen*, 114

Orlando Furioso, Lodovico Ariosto, 131

Ostasio da Polenta, court of, 58
Ottava verse, as epic stanza, 6; development by Boccaccio, 35; English revival, 131; *Filocolo*, 35; *Filostrato*, 34–35; narration, development of, 35; Spenser's *Faerie Queene*, 131; *Teseida*, 38
Ovid, *Ars Amatoria*, *Filostrato*, 32; *Caccia di Diana*, influence on, 15; *De mulieribus*, 105; *Filocolo*, influence on, 21, 22; *Genealogie*, 107; *Heroides*, influence on *Fiammetta*, 51; love, theme of, 16; *Metamorphoses*, influence on Boccaccio's works, 10

"Paganino Monaco," *Decameron*, 67
Painting, *Decameron* stories, representation of, 131; realism, 14th century Florence, 4
"Palemone," *Buccolicum Carmen*, 114
"Pamphylus," *Buccolicum Carmen*, 114; (*see also* "Panfilo")
"Pampinea," 18, 60, 61, 62, 64, 78; *Buccolicum Carmen*, 114; *Decameron*, 67, 70
"Pandarus," *Filostrato*, 29–34
"Panfilo," *Decameron*, 61, 76; etymology, 90; *Fiammetta*, 50, 52, 53
Paolino Veneziano, *De casibus*, 103
Paolo da Perugia, 9–10; *Genealogie*, 107–108
Paolo Diacono, *De casibus*, 103
Papacy, Avignon, transfer to, 3
Pasolini, Pier Paolo, *Decameron* film, 131
"Pasquino and Simona," *Decameron*, 65; language, 93
Pastoral genre, *Ninfale fiesolano*, 56

Pastoral poetry, classical, *Buccolicum Carmen*, 113
Pastoral romance, 6; *Ameto*, 42, 131; *Ninfale fiesolano*, influence of, 131
Pastoral theme, 96
Peasants, courtly love, 33
Perseus, myth, *Genealogie*, 108
Peruzzi Company, 40
"Peter, King of Aragon," *Decameron*, 77
Petrarch, Francesco, 59; *Amorosa Visione*'s influence on, 97; ancient texts, study of, 97; biography of, by Boccaccio, 58; birthdate, 7; birthplace, *De montibus*, 102; Boccaccio's friendship with, 97, 116–19, 121; Boccaccio's visit to, 97; *Buccolicum Carmen*, 115; *Canzoniere*, 122; Dante, attitude toward, 118; *De casibus* theme, 103; death of, 126; *Decameron*'s influence on, 97; diplomatic mission to, 122; Eclogues, model for, 113; *Epistole*, influence on, 120–21; famous men, lives of, 105; *Genealogie*, 97, 107; Greek translation, encouragement, 116–17; Griselda story, *Decameron*, translation, 83, 118–19, 127; humanism, 5, 101; Italian verse, relation to Boccaccio, 97; nationalism and, 4; personal freedom v. dependency on patrons, 117–18; poetry, defense of, 110, 125; *Rime* of Boccaccio, influence on, 12; "school" of friends, 96–97; visit to Florence, 96
Petroni, Pietro, 119
Pietrus Alphonsus, *Disciplina clericalis*, 80
Pilatus, Leontius, *see* Leontius Pilatus

Pino de' Rossi, exile of, *Epistole*, 121

Pius V, Pope, expurgation of *Decameron*, 128

Plato, *Genealogie*, 107; poetry, value of, 109

Poetry, as vocation of Boccaccio, 6; defense of, *see* Poetry, defense of; definitions, *Genealogie*, 110; detractors described, *Genealogie*, 110; myth, relation to, 109; origins of, 110, 112; "poetic fiction," defined, *Genealogie*, 110; purpose of, *Genealogie*, 110–11; theology, relation to, 109, 110; value of, 98, 100, 101, 102, 103, 104, 105, 107n20, 109, 111, 115, 116, 119; word "poetry," etymology, 110, 112

Poetry, defense of, *Buccolicum Carmen*, 115; *Esposizioni*, 112, 125; *Genealogie*, 109–11, 112, 115, 125 (*see also* Poetry)

Poets laureate, Petrarch and Zanobi, 97

Poitiers, Battle of, *De casibus*, 104

Polo, Marco, *De montibus*, 102

Popolo grasso, 40

Popolo minuto, 5, 40

Poverty, theme of, 121–22; *Epistole*, 121; Franciscans, 5

Prisci poetae, 109

Profane love, etymology, *Esposizioni*, 125; punishment, *Decameron*, 70n24; v. sacred love, *see* Love, sacred v. profane

Prosimetrum pattern, *Ameto*, 41; *Decameron*, 59

Psychological novel, *Fiammetta*, 50, 53–54

Pucci, Antonio, 58; *sirventese* and *Caccia di Diana*, 14

Pulci, Luigi, *Il Morgante*, 131

Pyramus and Thisbe, *De mulieribus*, 105

Questions of Love, *Filocolo*, 22–23, 25–26; court of love, 25; *Decameron* compared, 26–28; love, sacred v. profane, 23–24; narration, framework for, 24, 44

Rabanus, *Genealogie*, 107, 108

Ravenna, Dante, death of, 112; diplomatic mission to, 58, 96

Realism, Corbaccio, 100; *De casibus*, 104; *Decameron*, 62–67; mercantilism and, 64–67; narrative, *Fiammetta*, 54; *Trattatello*, 113

Religion of love, 22; (*see also* Love theme)

Religion, Boccaccio's attitude toward, 2

Rhetoric, classical, *Decameron*, 86, 88

Rhetorica ad Herennium, 89

"Riccardo di Chinzica", *Decameron*, 67, 71

Rime, 12–13, 59; Dante, influence on, 13; *donna angelicata*, 13; narrative patterns in, 13; Petrarch's influence on, 12; significance in body of works, 13

Robert of Anjou, King of Naples, 3, 40; *Amorosa Visione*, 47n10, *De casibus*, 104; death of, 5

Roman de Troie, Benoit de Saint Maure, 29

Romance of the Rose, de Meun, Nature in, 69n23; clergy in, 72

Rome, diplomatic mission to, 122; Jubilee in, Petrarch, 96, 97; removal of Papacy from, 3

Rubens, Peter Paul, "Cimon" story, representation, 131
Ruspiglioni, "Federigo" story, opera based on, 130, 131
Russian Formalism, criticism of *Decameron*, 130
"Rustico," *Decameron*, 71

Sacchetti, Franco, 58; death of Boccaccio, 127
"Salabaetto," *Decameron*, 65, 88
Salutati, Coluccio, 1; *De montibus*, 101; epitaph for Boccaccio, 127
"Salvestra," *Decameron*, 77
Salviati, Leonardo, *Decameron*, expurgation, 128
"Samson," *De casibus*, 103
San Giovanni ("church"), 76
Sannazaro, Jacopo, *Arcadia*, 131
Santa Maria Novella, Church of, 60
Sarcasm, *Corbaccio*, 98–101
Satire, of Church and clergy, *Decameron*, 70–75, 84
Scripture, 102; allegory, Old Testament, 109; *De casibus*, Old Testament, 103; mythology, 109; poetry in, *Esposizioni*, 125
Semiramis, *De mulieribus*, 106
Sennuccio del Bene, 58, 59
Servius, *Genealogie*, 107; *Esposizioni*, 123
Shakespeare, William, Pandarus, depiction of, 34
Sidney, Sir Philip, *Arcadia*, 131
Signorelli, Luca, "Griselda" story, representation, 131
Silvestris, Bernard *see* Bernard Silvestris
"Simona and Pasquino," *Decameron*, 65, 66; language and, 93

Sirventese, Dante and Pucci, influence on *Caccia di Diana*, 14
Sister Beatrice, daughter of Dante, 96
Sklovskij, Viktor, 130
Social order, democracy in, *Decameron*, 78–80, 79n30
Spenser, Edmund, *Faerie Queene*, 131
"Spina, Geri," *Decameron*, plot, 78–79
Statius, *Genealogie*, 107; *Thebaid* and *Teseida*, 36
Stilnovo poetry, 12, 13, 58; *Amorosa Visione*, 47; *Filostrato*, 30–31; love, sacred v. profane, 18; study of, 8; *Teseida*, 36–37
Studio in Florence, Leontius Pilatus, 116, 117; Petrarch, offer of chair to, 97, 117
Studio in Naples, 9

Tacitus, *De mulieribus*, 105
Tenzone, avoidance of, *Buccolicum Carmen*, 113–14
Terza rima, *Amorosa Visione*, 46
Teseida, 12, 35–39; allegory in, 37; *cantari* techniques in, 39; catalog *topos*, 14, 38; Chaucer's *Knight's Tale*, source of, 130; date of, 35; dedication *topos*, 20; Diana in, 37, 38; epic genre, 36–37; epic romances derived from, 131; *locus amoenus* in, 38; love, sacred v. profane, 37–38; love v. money theme, 67; Mars, House of, 37; mythology, 38; narrative pattern, 50; *ottava* verse, 38; plot, 36; sources of, 35–36; Statius' *Thebaid* and, 36; Stilnovo poetry, 36–37; structure of, 35; Venus, duality of, 17, 37–38

Terza rima, *Ameto*, 41; *Amorosa Visione*, 46
Theocritus, *Buccolicum Carmen*, 113
Theodontius, *Genealogie*, 107–108
Theologia poetica, 109n30, 119
Theology, relation to poetry, 109, 110
"Titus," *Decameron*, 80–81; language, 88
Todorov, Tzvetan, 130
Translations by Boccaccio, Livy, *Decades*, 58–59n1, 90; Greek classics, 116–17; Homer, 10, 116–17
Translations of *Decameron*, 130
Trattatello in laude di Dante, 111–13; Beatrice and Dante, 112, 113; Dante, description of, 112; Dante's exile from Florence, 111, 112; date, 111n35; etymology, "poetry," 112; *exemplum* tradition, 111; *Genealogie* compared, origins of poetry, 112; Italian language and Dante, 113; misogynism in, 113; narration, 111; realism in, 113; versions of, 111–13
"Triumph," *Amorosa Visione*, 50; *De casibus*, 103
"Troilus," *Ameto*, 43
"Troilus and Criseida," *Filostrato*, 29–34
Troilus and Cressida, Chaucer, *Filostrato* as source of, 130
"Truancy" theory, 17
Tullian prose style, 89
Tuscan allegorical literature, 5; *Amorosa Visione*, 46
Tuscan poetry, influence on Boccaccio, 40, 43
Tyrol, mission to, 97

Valerius Maximus, *De mulieribus*, 105; influence of, 10
Varro, mythology, 109
Venetians, depiction in *Decameron*, 72, 78, 87n41
Venus, *Ameto*, 41, 42; *Caccia di Diana*, 14–16; *De mulieribus*, 105, 106; dual identity, *Teseida*, 17, 37–38; *Fiammetta*, 53; *Genealogie*, 108; *Ninfale fiesolano*, 56, 57
Villa, *Decameron*, 61n5
Villani, Filippo, 1
Villani, Giovanni, 58, 59
Violante, Boccaccio's daughter, *Buccolicum Carmen*, 115; letter to Petrarch, 115
Virgil, *Buccolicum Carmen*, 113, 114; *Eclogues*, 16; *Fiammetta*, influence in, 51; *Genealogie*, 107
Virtue, Christian v. lay, in *Decameron*, 84–85
Visconti court, Milan, 117
"Vision" genre of poetry, *Amorosa Visione*, 46; *Corbaccio*, 98; *De casibus*, 103
Vita Nuova, Dante, *Ameto*, influence on, 41; *Amorosa Visione* compared, 49; *Caccia di Diana*, influence on, 15; *Fiammetta* compared, 51
Vulcan, and Venus, *De mulieribus*, 106

Walter of Brienne (Duke of Athens), 40, 103, 104
Wilmot, Robert, "Ghismonda story," dramatization, 130
Women, *De mulieribus*, 104–107; intelligence of, *De mulieribus*, 107; persecution of, Griselda story, 83n32

Youth, and love, theme, *Decameron*, 31–32, 70

Zanobi da Strada, 8; Boccaccio's visit with, 98; *Epistole,* 121; poet laureate, 97
Zibaldone Laurenziano, 10
Zibaldone Magliabechiano, 9, 103

DATE DUE

DEMCO 38-297